Wakefield Press

On a Clare Day

Burt Surmon was born and bred in King's Bloody Cross, of the good old days, to a well-travelled father who exposed him early on to food, wine, music, art and different cultures. He thinks this might be the reason he ended up in the Clare Valley with Jeni to develop a vineyard and open a cellar door–art gallery, attracting visitors from all over the world.

A vine change story

Wakefield
Press

Wakefield Press
16 Rose Street
Mile End
South Australia 5031
www.wakefieldpress.com.au

First published 2017
Reprinted 2017

Cover designed by Liz Nicholson, designBITE
Edited by Julia Beaven, Wakefield Press
Typeset by Michael Deves, Wakefield Press

National Library of Australia Cataloguing-in-Publication entry

Creator:	Surmon, Burt, author.
Title:	On a Clare day: a vine change story / Burt Surmon.
ISBN:	978 1 74305 481 9 (paperback).
Subjects:	Burt Surmon, 1932- .
	Vineyards – South Australia – Clare Valley – Anecdotes.
	Wineries – South Australia – Clare Valley.
	Cooking (Wine).
	Clare Valley (S.A.).

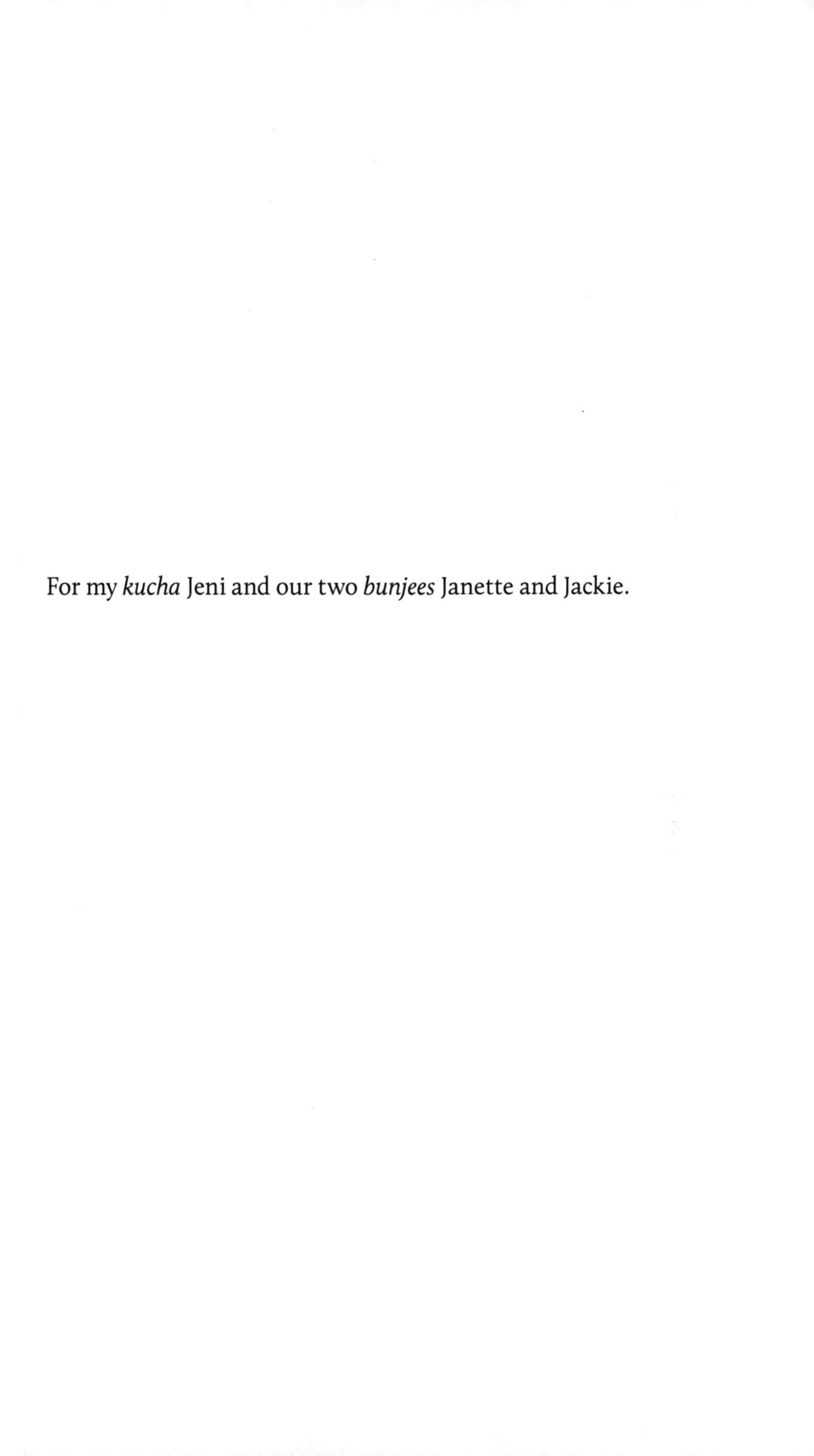

For my *kucha* Jeni and our two *bunjees* Janette and Jackie.

Author's Note

This story is an account of events on a hill in the Clare Valley of South Australia, set against the background of this beautiful small wine region – its vineyards, wineries and food culture. I very much hope that the people whose establishments are mentioned accept my apologies for taking artistic liberties in writing about them. This is not an historic account, rather a simple interpretation of events based on a true story. Minor characters are composite figures and along with some stories are figments of the author's imagination.

The book is best described as an impressionistic memoir rather than autobiography, but as Ernest Hemmingway once said: 'The book's the book. It's not life.' But let Kabat-Zim have the last word. He says that writing partially true stories creates difficulties because 'there is always the lingering sense that we are not entirely who we think we are'.

Nomenclature

Over the last decade or so Australia has by international agreement dropped the use of European wine names, such as 'Champagne', for Australian wines. When this book refers to Sherry and Port, technically we are referring to Spanish Sherry and Portuguese Port. The terms now for the Australian equivalents are 'apera' for Sherry, and descriptors such as 'tawny', or 'fortified/dessert/sweet red wine' for Port. The Australian wines can be substituted in recipes when necessary. As 'brandy' is a generic term, it applies to brandy from any provenance.

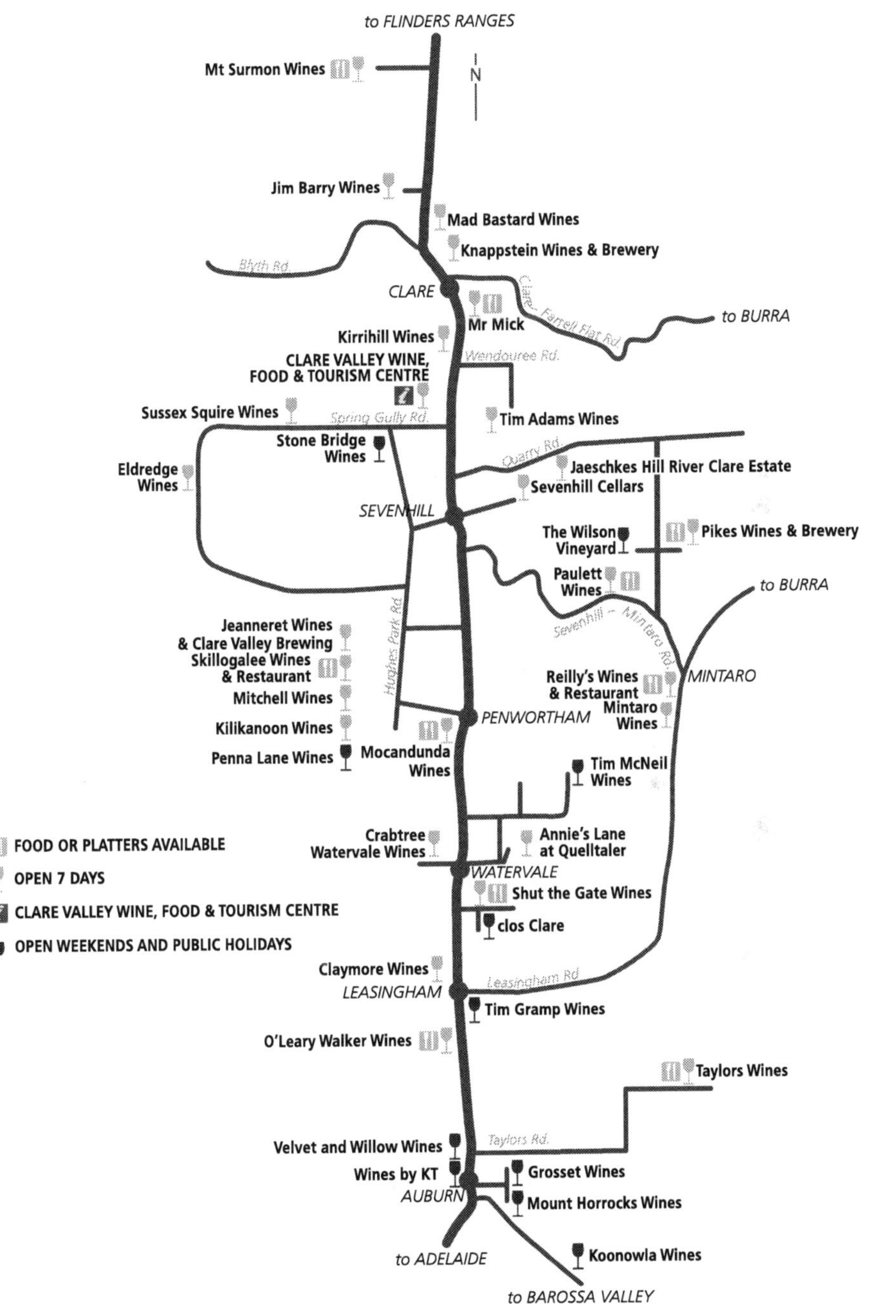

Clare Valley Wineries

Map courtesy of Clare Valley Winemakers, © 2017

1

It started with a call from the agent. A property that might interest us was coming up for sale.

'It's actually on the side of a hill, in the northern part of Clare Valley,' the agent said. 'I could meet you Saturday morning at the racecourse at ten. It's not far from there.'

My response was half-hearted. We were starting to think we should broaden our search from the Clare Valley to McLaren Vale, for instance. But Jeni and I really loved the Clare Valley, its beauty and romance and the sense that it is still fresh and untouched. Located in the Mid North of South Australia, long famous for its merino sheep studs and broad-acre grain cropping, especially malting barley, Clare is also wine country. The vineyards, wineries and tourism industry are all labour intensive, resulting in the Clare township being a growth centre, in stark contrast to surrounding towns and villages, which are in decline. Even as a growth centre, however, Clare has its own ways and special charm and lights up with major annual events such as 'A Day on the Green', 'Shakespeare in the Vines' and of course 'Clare Valley Gourmet Weekend'.

Stanley Flat where the racecourse is located is the northern entrance to the The Valley. The vineyards here along Main North Road are very old, planted with grapevines used for the fortified wines so popular last century. The vines had been planted here to take advantage of the deep alluvial soils that collected winter rains and held them for the vines to access in dry summers.

Over the past six months Jeni and I had looked at many very different vineyards in The Valley, including a couple in the Skilly Hills that we decided against as that ridgeline had been severely fire-ravaged some years before. In any case, the agent who took us there was much more interested in his mobile phone than in talking to us about properties.

So, here we were, up again for the weekend. We climbed into the agent's smart four-wheel drive with its 'roo bars and spotlights. He drove down the gravel road for a way, then turned north onto a rutted track, climbing through a eucalypt scrub and on, up, to the top of the hill.

We rounded a huge ancient gum and, there, an extraordinary, almighty panorama burst upon us. The vista was breathtaking, exhilarating – we were incredulous at the scene before us, like a dream unfolding, a paradise giving of its emotional and sensual bounty. Could it be ours for the asking? Would this hill allow us to unearth its wondrous possibilities? *Bacchus amat colles* popped into my head. If Bacchus loved the hills, would he love this one, unconditionally? I did – it was love at first sight – which made it twice; first Jeni and now this.

We drove down the steep slope of the hill, skirted the outer perimeter, crossed a dry winter creek and then drove back up the slope to the flat top of this 400-metre hill where we stopped. As we got out of the car, I was overwhelmed by a rush of excitement that took my breath away – this is our future, I thought.

'Just stunning,' Jeni said looking about her, awestruck.

The bottom of the valley was immediately in front of us and, to the north, range after range all the way to the Flinders. We were surrounded – soft hills, higher ridges, vast expanses of broadacre farmland, remnant tree lines, rocky outcrops, a few creek beds, dams and a natural, almighty beauty which seduced us on the spot.

'We'll take it,' I said, to an astonished agent. 'How much is it? Do you think we could grow grapes here?'

'Our hill,' said Jeni, 'how wonderful.'

'Are you serious? The owner hasn't really listed it yet but he was thinking around a hundred and twenty thousand which, I must say, isn't cheap for broadacre land. But it's a smaller block so that would push up the price because people from the city are looking for hobby farms.'

'Right, we'll offer a hundred and ten with a three-month settlement.'

'You want me to submit that? Right, and I'll ask my mate Vince about growing grapes here. He's the vineyard boss for one of the large wineries.'

~ * ~

The agent drove us back to our car. We sat in it for a few minutes without saying a word. I was thinking about my impulsive behaviour and not having consulted Jeni before putting in the offer. Jeni wasn't saying anything.

'Have I done the wrong thing?' I asked. 'We haven't signed anything so I can withdraw the offer if you think I've been hasty.'

'Don't be ridiculous, Burtie. I adore it. It's certainly a wild dream, but I can see us making our future here. Let's go somewhere for a bite and a bottle to talk it over.'

'What about that pub at Sevenhill? Let's see if there is something interesting on the menu.'

The Sevenhill pub takes its name, as does the surrounding

area, from the nearby Jesuit Seminary and winery not far along a side road. Snuggled by the roadside, with smoke curling from its venerable chimney, surrounded by vines and a scattering of houses, the Sevenhill pub is an unpretentiously welcoming sight to travellers moving along the Main North Road.

The long narrow front bar has a large fireplace at one end into which one or other of the local blokes feeds logs as the need arises. They tend to regard this space at the fireplace end of the bar as more or less their domain. But strangers are greeted pleasantly and newcomers to the valley are given a genial, rowdy welcome. In the football season, players and supporters from local teams crowd into the warmth after a game and, in summer, cricketers in their soiled green whites thread through the bar with hot afternoon thirsts.

The Sevenhill's somewhat small front bar is a place where you can easily converse with the locals – there is no canned music, no pokies and the volume of the flat-screen TV is turned up only after some unspoken consensus among the drinkers – like Black Caviar winning again, or the Crows or Port footballers smashing a Victorian team. We encountered the winter version of this marvellous hubbub, as we ducked through the low doorway, still buzzing with the excitement of our sudden, amazing offer.

'Look,' said Jeni pointing to the specials board, 'there's vongole on rice cooked with fish stock. Let's have that.'

'Excellent, I'll look in the fridge for a white.'

We're in Riesling country, 'The Heart of Australia's Riesling', as the Clare Valley Winemakers tagline reads. The choice was plentiful, including two Rieslings from Watervale, one of the succession of small villages on the road through the Clare Valley between Auburn at the southern end and Clare township to the north. The Rieslings produced in this area, interestingly, have a fruity flavour with a dry, acid spine that carries the pallet to a long finish. I selected a Kilikanoon Mort's Block Watervale Riesling.

The vongole – to Italians, but called pipis or cockles by Australians – were tender and succulent. What a wonderful match for the citric edge of the Riesling.

Vongole

Ingredients for 2 servings

1 kg vongole (otherwise known as pipis or cockles)
olive oil
garlic, chopped
a glass of dry Riesling or Viognier
spring onions, chopped
chopped parsley for garnish
steamed rice or crusty bread

Put the oil in a pan and heat until hot. Gently add the vongole and heat until they open. Add the garlic, spring onions and wine and simmer for a few minutes to reduce the liquid. Serve into warmed bowls and dress with parsley. Sop the juices with the bread. Drink the remaining wine.

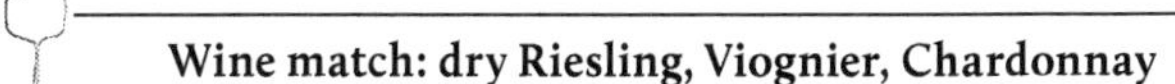

Wine match: dry Riesling, Viognier, Chardonnay

'I loved your impetuosity this morning, Burtie,' Jeni said. 'I gave you a nod of approval when we got out of the car on top of the hill. I really hope the offer is accepted. Our Hill, just think of it. How fantastic. We'll build our life there and leave all the old rubbish behind us.'

'That's if our offer is accepted and then we'll only have three months to sort out our stuff,' I said. 'Do you think we should have another bottle? It's excellent, and we could get to the caravan park on the back track.'

But we didn't, driving instead along the back track to Kilikanoon's cellar door to buy a couple of bottles of Mort's Block and then on to Mitchell Wines to taste and buy two of their excellent Rieslings. In the process we picked up some interesting information from the people at these cellar doors. I was interested in how wine from one grape variety, such as Riesling, could vary so much from one winemaker to another.

'*Terroir*,' the young man at the cellar door told us. He went on to say it's a French word and difficult to pronounce, but it sums things up nicely. It means the micro-environment in which the vines grow. He told us there's a big difference in the Rieslings as you move from the south to the north of the valley. In the south the soil is shaley, often on a limestone bedrock. Here the wines are flinty with lean citrus characters and an acid spine. As you move north, the wines become fruitier but still have that dry acid spine. By the time you get to Stanley Flat, the wines have a much bigger mouth feel and tropical fruit flavours. Even there you'll find that the wines made from fruit from the bottom of the valley differ from those grown on the hillsides.

'Well, I'll be buggered,' I said as we drove off. 'We've certainly got a lot to learn if we're to become vignerons.'

Over the past months we had talked to every agent in the Clare Valley and inspected every vineyard for sale without finding anything we thought would suit us. Maybe we didn't really know what we wanted. One block we considered, in an attempt to refine our thinking, consisted of about four hectares of Mataro and five of Pedro Ximines, and listed for $100,000. I knew these varieties were used for making fortified wines but this segment of the market was in decline. Would there still be a demand for these grapes, I wondered.

'No,' said one agent, 'Chardonnay, Shiraz and Cab Sav are the go today.' But this was Riesling country, I thought, why not plant Riesling?

~ * ~

It's funny sometimes how things seem to sort themselves out. For some reason one agent had persisted with us. He hung around and would ring us when he came across a property he thought might be of interest. So we had made many trips to Clare to inspect them, and he had phoned so often that Jeni had dubbed him 'Velcro'. In time he suggested we look at broadacres rather than vineyards.

Jeni was enthusiastic. 'Let's do it,' she said. 'Start from scratch, and have it just as we want it.'

'Maybe you're right – even though we know nothing about how to develop a vineyard or grow grapes.'

It was an interesting point. So far we'd only picked up snippets of information from agents, cellar-door staff and blokes in the pubs who worked in the vineyards, but now it was time to research our idea more carefully.

'Tourists, are you?' said one young bloke in the front bar of the Watervale pub. 'Where're you from?'

'Adelaide – Seacliff actually, and I reckon you'd be a vineyard worker by the look of your boots.'

'Yep, I work in the vineyard where we grow one of the world's best Rieslings.' He sounded pretty relaxed. 'Come to our cellar door and taste it for yourself. I'll guarantee it's the best.'

The small cellar doors were excellent places for acquiring information – it might be from the winemaker or maybe a cellar door hand, or someone who worked in the vineyard – who seemed to take a personal interest in helping you. They offered their thoughts on wine styles and food matches and could also talk intelligently and interestingly about the vine blocks, types of trellising, the quality of irrigation water and then give their views, sometimes conflicting, on where the best soils for grapes were to be found in the valley. We loved it and could not get enough of it.

~ * ~

Velcro submitted our offer and rang a week later to say the owner had been so surprised to receive such an early bid that he thought it better to advertise the sale to canvass wider interest. That took the puff out of our sails for a couple of weeks, but we were mollified when he rang to say that if we were available next Saturday morning Vince would show us how to take soil samples for analysis by the Department of Agriculture.

Vince arrived with an auger, a shovel and some small plastic containers. We dug a series of random holes across an area where he thought we should develop a block. I drew a mud map in my little book of the relative location of the holes and allotted numbers to map and containers. Vince instructed us where to take the samples and who to talk to in the department. The results showed that the soil profiles in this area were quite different from the black cracking clay of the valley bottom.

A month later we heard that our offer would be accepted with a two-month settlement. Just like that.

Subsequently we came to know Velcro rather well. He, too, was developing a vineyard, and we came across him at field days and growers' gatherings. He had quit the large agency in Adelaide because he was taken off sales and put in charge of the firm's rental properties, which he said was a soul-destroying job.

As it turned out the property was on his boss's list, so the boss would draw up the contract and collect the commission. We wondered why Velcro had spent so much of his time to seal the deal with us.

The boss – who was short with that jauntiness and push so characteristic of short men – now took over negotiations. When we met to sign the contract, he told us that a Possessory Title of 2.5 hectares ran with the main Torrens Title. He said that in the 1850s the owner had given his daughter these hectares and registered them in her name. At some stage her name had disappeared from the records in the Titles Office and so the 2.5 hectares were deemed to be of unknown ownership and attached to the original property as a Possessory Title. There are many such pieces of land in the Mid North, one of which adjoins our property on its northeast fenceline. This piece of land had been set aside long ago for use as an overnight holding area for herds of sheep and cattle and their drovers moving down to Adelaide from the northern pastoral country.

By definition a Possessory Title is one of unknown ownership, otherwise it would be called a Torrens Title. But the boss told us, in confidence, that the vendor had spent much time and money in legal fees in an effort to gain the full Torrens Title. These efforts had become bogged down in bureaucratic detail, but he did say that the owner would be willing to let us have the accumulated paperwork and ownership of the Possessory Title for only ten thousand. 'It's a bargain price, to keep the two titles together,' he said.

In the past I had completed a real estate sales agent's course and knew that nobody legally owns land under a Possessory Title and therefore can't legally sell it. 'You know, of course,' I said casually, 'to sell land you don't own is to commit fraud.'

'Don't you call us fraudsters' came his sharp response.

'What I said was that to enact such a deal would be to commit fraud. I won't have anything to do with that.'

There was no further talk of the vendor wanting to sell the Possessory Title.

~ * ~

From the moment we had driven up the rutted track and rounded the mighty, ancient gum, I knew this would be a special place for us. After many fraught years of searching, Jeni and I had found each other, and now, at last, we had found the ironstone rock on which to build our future together.

Although the view from the top of The Hill – as we came to call it – was stupendous, The Hill was more of a monticule than a grand mountain, but as our bedrock it offered its eroded materials as soil in which to plant our dreams. It was our virgin block of marble to fashion, nurture, destroy even, if we abused it.

We would be only the latest occupiers, however, or perhaps just the next in line to make use of its possibilities, or to be tamed by its moods and requirements. Henry James wrote in his diary when first he saw Rome, 'At last, for the first time, I live.' That's what I felt about the possibilities of life on The Hill.

For decades the soils of The Hill had been used to grow grains and for stock agistment on the stubble. There were a couple of small stock dams and a wobbly, rusted barbed-wire fence dividing the 36 hectares into four paddocks.

There were no ancient villas awaiting restoration, or thousand-year-old Etruscan burial caves, but I would guess that hundreds of Aboriginal families had wandered its surface and camped near the creeks for tens of thousands of years. Later, as we worked our vine rows and trudged the hillside, I found a number of stones that were carefully shaped to fit palm and fingers – clearly fashioned for pounding and scraping.

The Hill was used by the local pony club as a cross-country course and recently had hosted an international event. Jumps and obstacles were everywhere – through tree clumps, across boundary fences and spanning dry creek banks and water hazards at the stock dams.

Materials to build these features were spread across the hillside where surplus items had been abandoned – wooden railway sleepers, long bamboo canes cut from local creeks, large tree trunks, pine posts, steel piping and rusted sheets of galvanised iron.

The owner should have cleared this rubbish before settlement or the pony club would forfeit their use. Maybe they would like to retrieve the useful bits. Velcro gave me the name of the club president, and I left many messages on his answering machine, without response. We started asking about him in the pubs and a message got through to him at last. He rang to ask if I'd been looking for him. I asked if he ever monitored his answering machine.

'Nah, that's no good, tape's worn out. What d'yer want?'

I told him I'd just bought the property used by his pony club and wanted to know if he'd like to take the jumps and obstacle materials for use elsewhere.

'Jeez, I didn't even know it was for sale – only completed that course the other day. The old bastard, fancy not telling us he was going to sell.'

'If you want the gear,' I said, 'you'll have to get it off before settlement, over the next couple of weeks.'

'Took us a long time to get that stuff together and to build that course. Don't s'pose we could continue to use it? Don't hold events very often.'

'Trouble is I'm going to plant a vineyard, and I wouldn't want a rider falling in a rip and suing me for negligence,' I said.

I arranged for the agent to delay settlement for two weeks. Much of the gear was moved, but a lot of rubbish was left behind, and it took us a number of months before we cleared it all to the local dump. We were to find many nests of newly hatched brown snakes and their mothers under the iron sheets.

I rang Vince to discuss the results of the soil samples.

'The results look good for grapes,' he said. 'You're in luck. I'll give you the name of a consultant who'll get an investment proposal together for you. When you're ready, I'd like to talk to you about a contract for your fruit.'

I didn't believe in luck, but I did like the sound of an investment proposal and a contract. My lifelong view had been that, to make things happen, you have to put a plan together, trust your instincts, back yourself, and just do it.

This was the middle of the nineties, with the Australian wine industry expanding its capacity in order to meet burgeoning demand for its products in the UK and later in the US. We didn't know it at the time but another Australian wine industry boom was taking off.

So here we were, all ready to go. Are all economic adventures predicated on a romantic faith in yourself and your partner, I wondered. We were establishing a new partnership, the one to see us through to the end, and the superannuation investment to finance it; this was thrilling, so full of promise. We were flying as we had never flown before, blasting off into our very own orbit.

The Hill, our sticking place, would cast its influence on our field of endeavour, a field about which we knew nothing. Essentially, we were city people. When Jeni had turned sixteen, living in Murray Bridge, a country town in South Australia, her mother sold her pushbike, bought her city clothes and a suitcase and packed her off to a job in the Department of Lands which her father had lined up for her.

I was born and bred in 'King's Bloody Cross' surrounded by highrise and people from many parts of the world. It was then known as Sydney's Golden Mile, maybe because it was the locale for a couple of well-known madams and illicit trades. We knew nothing about farming and tractors or even how to run our own business, for that matter. Should such naïveté and faith in yourself be admired or scoffed at?

The Hill would be our rock, the iron-rock base of our future life. For the first time we had a solid base on which to build. For the first time we would control our financial future. Our story had begun, and just as slow cooking is cooking with love, taking your time and being interested in what you're doing, so this story will unfold, not dictated by recipe, but by the addition of ingredient on ingredient to achieve a fulsome, satisfying result. Only in fiction does the story end, in real life it never really does, especially in The Valley with so much warmth and unending surprises.

We were soul mates living our dreams. Little did we realise as we left the city to plant a vineyard and build our house on The Hill that we'd become millionaires several times over – for a few years anyway. In the process, however, we were putting ourselves under extraordinary pressure, allowing only two months to work through a very long agenda.

The finance for our new venture would come from two sources. We had just converted a large house on a superb block at Seacliff with spectacular views of Gulf St Vincent into a modern Mediterranean villa that blended beautifully with its seaside position. We hoped to sell it for half a million. I resigned from my job, negotiating a package that included seventeen years' long service leave, two years' annual holidays and whatever else my employers were gracious enough to grant me. Certainly there was nothing to be had from 387 days of unused sick leave.

Altogether we'd have about $700,000 to develop the first stage of the vineyard and build a new house. I wouldn't have an income but I would have the time to concentrate on closing down the Seacliff job and to start on planning the vineyard while Jeni pursued her business career.

So, off to The Valley again to have to talk with Vince about a fruit contract and how that would work, locate the consultant to draw up the vineyard investment plan and, of course, find somewhere to store our furniture and the building gear I'd bought in Adelaide for our new home along with somewhere to live. But most of all we would have to stay calm, positive and on course over the coming two months.

~ * ~

Travelling north we left behind the stress and confusion of the suburbs, merging into open rolling country. To the west the wintry sky was showing a magnificent display of huge, fluffy white thunderheads, rouged and smeared with pink and peach and silver rays, all soft and romantic and very dramatic.

'Look at the great sunset, Jeni, it's the colours of those peace roses I picked for you the other day. It's a Lloyd Rees sky, all smudgy and soft and full of brilliant light.' I was off on a flight of fancy. 'I love his landscapes, especially the skies. Years ago I was tempted to buy one of his huge canvases, but I decided to put the money into my mortgage account instead. It was so large I wouldn't have had anywhere to hang it anyway.'

Jeni had booked us into a B & B for our weekend stay, a few kilometres from The Hill. 'It's the closest I could find,' she said, 'but I wonder what we're in for – the lady promised a candlelit breakfast.' Other guests at the breakfast included two young men from America and the mother of one of them. Our host informed us that eggs were not available as her sister had borrowed them. This was a quaint encounter.

For dinner that night I had booked a table at Crawley's in Leasingham. The old villa was now serving as a homely, inviting restaurant. Jeni ordered a rack of Jamestown lamb, which had been chargrilled and served with an intensely flavoured red wine jus. You don't often find venison on menus in South Australia, especially in the Clare Valley, but my cut was from a wild kill that an enterprising local hunter had brought to the restaurant kitchen door. Deer had been introduced in the early days of the South Australian settlement for sport and food and still roam the Skilly Hills and further north into the grazing country. The local farmers consider them a pest, especially the grape growers, but the hunters of gourmet prey think the venison delicious.

Venison with quince

Ingredients for 6 servings

a piece of venison 1.5–2 kg
1 cup Port wine
½ cup red wine vinegar
2 tbs olive oil
salt and pepper
10 juniper berries, crushed
grated nutmeg
3 tbs self-raising flour
several fatty pork ribs or sliced bacon
onions and garlic, sliced
3 bay leaves
10 sprigs each of thyme and coriander
2 quinces peeled, cored and quartered

Marinate the pork in the Port, vinegar and olive oil for a day or two. Remove the marinaded meat and roll it in the flour and spices. This is easily done using a large plastic bag.

Place the venison in an oven dish and layer the pork on the top. Add the onion, garlic, fresh herbs and pour in the marinade. Seal the dish with alfoil. Cook slowly in a low oven for 3 hours.

Add the quince slices and cook for another 30 minutes.

It is easy to overcook venison, which will dry it, hence the fatty pork, so check to see if it requires further time before adding the quinces.

Wine match: Nero d'Avola, Montepulciano, Mataro, Cabernet Sauvignon

I rang Vince to get the name and contact details of the consultant he had mentioned, a couple of times, leaving messages, but to no avail. I wondered if his message tape was also on the blink. Without expert advice we were in trouble. We had gathered a lot of anecdotal information, only some of which seemed to hang together and a good deal of which was contradictory, especially about the cost of the big items. What would trellising and irrigation cost, how many posts and droppers would be needed, what length of wire and how many vines? And who were the local suppliers and contractors we would need to make all this happen? So many questions.

Also, we had to find someone to design our house and build it. We decided to look at a few rental properties and to ask the agents about local builders and architects. We soon discovered that vacant accommodation was scarce, rents were expensive in this growth centre and there was only one architect.

Later, over a cup of coffee, we considered how far we'd got – which was not far, we concluded.

'It's Saturday so we can't do much more today,' Jeni said. 'Let's do some wine tasting.'

What a delight it is to explore the lovely little cellar doors of The Valley, some hidden down narrow bush tracks with the winemaker or a vineyard worker to talk about all aspects of growing and making the wines. After visiting three small wineries we decided to give our palates a break.

'Now what?' I said.

'What about a drive? This country is so beautiful and soulful,' Jeni said. 'My mother was born in Balaklava and I was born in the Maitland Hospital, and in a little cemetery somewhere around here are some of Mum's ancestors, which we'll have to find one day.'

'Well, believe it or not, my mother's ancestors are buried in the Moonta Cemetery. It's only an hour's drive to the coast from here, and Maitland isn't much further. Let's do a mystery history tour.'

'And I'll be able to show you the hospital and the house I lived in before we moved to Murray Bridge.'

At Moonta Cemetery we walked up and down the rows, reading names and inscriptions and at last we came upon an impressive marble monument about three metres high with just two names on it – James Trezona 1830–1902 and Sally Trezona 1835–1911. They had been enticed from Cornwell to Moonta by the copper mining boom. Judging from the opulence of the marble monument, James was probably very satisfied with the move. But perhaps Sally was less pleased, for my mother's father was the only one of eight children to survive the dysentery epidemics – caused by poor sewerage and the lack of clean drinkable water – that plagued the settlement in its early years. His siblings are interred here with hundreds of other children in small, unmarked graves.

After exploring the cemetery, we came upon a small café-cum-deli at Moonta Bay. Here we found good old-fashioned Australian hamburgers with 'the lot'. The diminutive woman who served us had an intriguing accent – obviously English, but I couldn't quite place the soft burr.

'Newcastle-upon-Tyne,' she said.

I was delighted and told her I went to the university there for a time.

'Well would you believe,' she said looking me in the eye. 'What a small world, I worked in the admin section there.'

Turkey burger

Ingredients for 4 servings

500 g turkey mince
1 onion, chopped
1 garlic clove, crushed
2 eggs, beaten
1 can corn kernels, drained
200 g frozen green peas
250 g fresh white breadcrumbs
fresh thyme
grated nutmeg
salt and pepper
self-raising flour in a bowl
125 g polenta
olive oil for frying
4 burger buns, sliced through and toasted

Place all of these ingredients except the flour, polenta, oil and burger buns in a bowl and combine with your hands. Divide into four parts and flatten into patties. Dip the patties into the flour and then into the polenta. Coat well to give a brown crusty finish.
Heat the oil in a pan and gently fry the patties until cooked and brown. Drain on kitchen paper and place on the bun bottoms.
Add what pleases you: sliced lettuce, tomato, beetroot, fried egg, bacon, cranberry sauce or mayo.

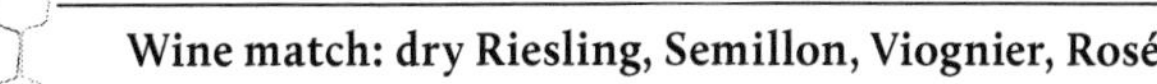

Wine match: dry Riesling, Semillon, Viognier, Rosé

Returning to Clare we passed the Sevenhill pub and just had to call in for a draught Guinness or two, and to warm ourselves by the fire. These kindly pints seemed to have a liberating effect on us and we began to dream, to imagine.

'Burtie, order another and I'll tell you my brilliant insight about how we go about things,' Jeni said.

So I ordered and while we waited Jeni told me her plan. 'I think we'll need a shed for the vineyard as a workshop, something like that, so first we get one built. Then we move our furniture and building supplies into one half of the shed and set up camp in the other while the house is designed, approved and built. Most of all we'll need a solar shower, a portaloo and a water tank – just think of it as up-market camping without the canvas. How's that for planning?'

'Brilliant! Thank God for a country girl. My turn – let me tell you my ideas.'

I asked the bartender for a pen and paper on which I drew a long rectangle, putting in east and west markers and then dividing the rectangle into rooms. Two variables dictated the design. To make the most of the views and to take advantage of the summer and winter sun, proper orientation was a must. The other was where to put a very large glass-topped dining table we had acquired from Jeni's cousin Nicholas who had fashioned it for feasting and revelry. It measured 2.8 by 1.5 metres and easily seated twelve. The top consisted of two very thick pieces of shop window glass laminated together and weighing a tonne. It sat on four elaborately moulded concrete pillars and was a bugger to move, taking six strong blokes to lift the glass. It became a central place in our story as the scene of memorable celebrations.

~ * ~

Back in Seacliff I found a draughtsman working in nearby Brighton to turn my mud map into building code for lodgement with the Clare Council. Next we would need to find a builder, so back to Clare we went, again on a Friday afternoon hoping to be able to talk with the right people on the Saturday morning. I packed a couple of bottles of Champagne, handmade chocolates, some Rio Royal coffee grounds and a few cryptics and suggested to Jeni she book us into a snug cabin at the caravan park, without a candlelit breakfast.

Lloyd Rees was absent this time, replaced by ominous black clouds scudding in on a decidedly cold blast from the northwest. Velcro had given us the names of a couple of builders, an older one who had been around forever and a recently arrived younger man. We discussed the house plan, the building materials and an approximate price with them both. The older man's quote was significantly higher than the younger man's, but even that was about double what we wanted to spend.

We were more concerned to put our assets into the vineyard than into a posh house. We had a long way to go with our planned development and really had no idea how far our piggy bank would stretch.

'Well, maybe we could get one of those transportables in the interim,' Jeni said, 'and build the dream house later after we get a cash flow going from the grapes. That way we would have time to find a builder whose ideas and price we like. After all, once we submit plans to council it'll be months before they make their way through the system and then it will take months to build the house. Maybe a transportable would be easier and quicker.'

We went to a firm in Clare that built sheds. We discussed the options and finally ordered a corrugated-iron structure with a concrete floor with double doors at one end and a 'front' door at the other. The southern section was to be left open as a parking area for the ute and a place nearby for the rainwater tank. We agreed on a finishing date and paid the required fifty per cent deposit. We were told that we'd have to go to a different bloke to order the tank, and to talk to ETSA about supplying electricity.

~ * ~

For our first night I had booked dinner at the Brice Hill restaurant, an easy walk from the caravan park and overlooking vineyards on the southern entrance to the Clare township. Brice Hill had been given a favourable review in a food and wine magazine I had read, describing its food as 'an Australian take on traditional French and Italian dishes'.

We arrived to find guests clustered around a circular wood fire in the middle of the restaurant. We joined them and conversation flowed easily with the help of a bottle of Tim Adams Riesling, a young fresh wine with lime flavours and a lovely dry palate.

Simon, our host, emerged from the kitchen to chat about the menu and to suggest wine matches for each course.

'It's a nice personal touch, to greet us before the meal,' I said.

'I think it counts. I'll be out again after the meal to see how things went.'

Riesling saw us through our chargrilled calamari entrée and then onto a Jeanneret Wines Cabernet Sauvignon to accompany Jeni's favoured lamb crown roast and my fillet steak, all pink and juicy. We chose the Cabernet rather than a Shiraz because we prefer its complexity and thought it would also match the next three-cheese selection.

I reminded Jeni about the Jeanneret vineyard and winery at Penwortham. On a visit to the winery, we had come upon the winemaker, Ben Jeanneret, trying to eliminate blackberry bushes in the new block he had recently planted.

'They're very bloody difficult to move,' I had said to a sweating, bare-chested Ben.

'Just makes me more determined to get rid of the bastards,' he'd said as he ushered us into his cellar door. Graciously, he explained his approach to winemaking as he took us through a wine tasting.

I was telling Jeni that the fruit for Ben's Cabernet Sauvignon was hand harvested from old bush vines and that Philip White, a respected Australian wine critic, had commented on the elegance of his wines. At this point Simon strolled over to our table. 'I see you've finished your meal with cheese rather than sweets.'

I said my father had told me that in France it was customary to have cheese with red wine before sweets; that my palate becomes confused when I drink red with mains, then sweet white with sweets and then move back to drinking red wine with cheese.

'I guess he'd never tried Sauternes with cheese then,' he quipped. 'Each to his own.'

~ * ~

Next morning, on the off chance, I phoned the consultant recommended by Vince.

'G'day, AK here,' came a loud voice.

I explained what we were after and arranged to meet at his place in Leasingham at ten that morning. 'Look for my gate sign on the main road,' he said.

We discussed vineyard layout, materials required, which varieties to plant in our first stage and how to look after them.

'First of all, don't plant Riesling,' he said, as he poured us coffee. 'Most people choosing white wine today are drinking Chardonnay.'

'But this is Riesling country.'

'Maybe, but you won't be able to sell your grapes. There's too many here already. Plant Cab Sav and Shiraz, which are the most popular red wines,' AK said, 'and both varieties suit The Valley's various microclimates. I know your land so I'll go up there and have a look – eight hectares as a first stage, you say? I'll sketch out an area for three blocks and then draw up a computer spreadsheet with the materials required, when and who to get them from, what they'll cost and your expected income over seven years. Seven years will bring you to break-even. But first you'll have to get the rows surveyed and ripped, and that'll take time. There are so many vineyards being developed, you'll have to get in the queue. And for all that work I'll charge you four thousand dollars.'

'Right, but we'll definitely need follow-up support. We know nothing about farming.'

'You'll soon learn. Tell you what, I'll charge you three thousand up front and then ask a monthly fee for a couple of years to keep my eye on things.'

Chatting over coffee he explained that only some of the Clare Valley's winemakers produced Riesling, which they labelled Rhine Riesling to distinguish their quality wines from cask 'Riesling' of lower quality made from various white grapes of doubtful provenance with just a drop of Riesling grapes for flavour.

~ * ~

After settlement we went to The Hill to camp most weekends. Our excursions were basic. We dug out my old tent, a double sleeping bag and a few cooking utensils and set off like a couple of kids on their first country adventure. We selected a flatter site on the hillside in the scrub for our tent and used field rocks to fashion a fireplace.

While I was preparing a hot breakfast one Saturday morning, the blokes from the shed company arrived to peg out the shed site. They weren't pleased to see our camp fire in the scrub area.

'This is the fire ban season, you know. You'd best put it out before it gets away. You shouldn't have lit it.' It turned out they were members of the local CFS and were being cautious.

Jeni discovered a large dead tree that had been felled recently with most of its limbs sawn off. Was someone stealing our wood? A couple of weeks later we found a mob of calves grazing near the small stock dam. We guessed these must belong to one of our neighbours, so we went to the pub to make inquiries and, once we had some leads, used the local phone book to find numbers. We didn't want to start a blue with our neighbours but at least they could have asked before moving the calves in. After a few calls I located the owner and firmly suggested he remove his stock.

'Now, hang on a sec, don't be so hasty, I'm preparing for the agricultural show and I can't move them till after that. So if you don't mind I'd like to leave them there a littler longer.'

We were on a steep learning curve with our country cousins. Subsequently, we were told the neighbour had cut the timber when he knew the property had been sold and then had cleaned out the three small stock dams of yabbies, transferring them into his own.

~ * ~

The Shed Man greeted us warmly when we popped in to ask about progress.

'What seems to be your problem?'

'You've signed a contract to build our shed and taken our deposit. The promised starting date has been and gone – that's your problem.'

'No, no, mate, that's no problem. We've got this contract to erect a very large piggery and that's taking precedence. It'll be finished in a few weeks and then we'll start on yours, okay?'

'Well, what say you return our deposit and we'll go elsewhere.'

'We can't do that, you've signed a contract.'

'True, and so have you, and it specifies a finishing date which, from what you say, you have no intention of meeting. So the options are that you start this Monday or return our deposit. Failing either, I'm off to Consumer Affairs and the Ombudsman and probably the local rag.'

'I can see you're the friendly type, mate. You new blokes are all the same. Tell you what I'll do, I'll get a subcontractor to lay the slab Monday. The concrete will take a couple of weeks to cure and then we'll start on the shed.'

Excellent, I thought, I've got things moving. But Jeni was silent as we drove off, a sure sign she wasn't happy.

'Why did you have to have a confrontation?' she said. 'I don't like the tone of voice you use to get your way. Why be so hard on him?'

'We seem to be fair game for the locals.'

'Country people are laidback. You need to go with the flow instead of going around upsetting people.'

'You're right, Jeni, we want to leave all that city pressure stuff behind, so let's go to the pub for a couple of beers.'

~ * ~

The shed was now complete except for electricity. ETSA could bring a run from a ruin on the eastern side of the property at a cost of $11,050 if I signed a contract before the end of June. The cost would blow out after that because world demand for copper was pushing the price sky high. Turned out the longer the run, the more copper required in the cable.

'Then why not bring the supply from the cottage a few hundred metres to the south of us instead of across country from the Main North Road. That'd be about a third of the distance.'

'No, we couldn't do that. We'd have to take out a couple of gums and that would get the greens howling,' he said. 'We're a favourite target when it comes to trees.'

The irony was that many of the trees were dying because of mistletoe, which another green group didn't want removed claiming it was part of the natural bush. What about the fire risk presented by the dead trees, I thought, and what about the trees themselves?

~ * ~

Moving into the shed was a hectic blur. We had a garage sale at Seacliff to offload our antique furniture and many farewells and resulting hangovers, but at one of these Jeni's boss suggested we talk to his mate about building the house. The mate was a licensed builder and had done a good job on the boss's extensions. We talked with him a few days later, discussed the plan, starting time and the cost – which came in about where I wanted it. We were making progress at last, I thought.

There were to be many dealings with council people and engineers about soil reports and footings and sewage disposal from the septic. At the same time I was trying to come to grips with developments in the vineyard. The plan was easy to understand on paper, but its implementation was far from simple, with the need to lock into a timetable the many contractors and their heavy equipment.

Coming to an understanding of how the many pieces of the puzzle fitted was one thing. Endeavouring to mesh the arrival of materials with that of the contractors – to peg the rows, rip them, excavate trenches, install the irrigation system, knock in hundreds of wooden posts and steels for the trellising wires, and eventually source and plant the vines – on time, in the correct sequence and without becoming enraged at the off-handedness of some people, required much of Jeni's calming care and many visits to the pub for comic relief.

The hardest bloke to pin down – the surveyor we had engaged to peg out the vine rows – revealed himself as the pony club president with the non-functioning answering machine. I think I sparked some life into him by offering to buy a new tape for his machine, but instead he installed one himself a few days later.

It soon became clear that liquidity was the key to success. Irrigation was needed to keep the vines happy during the long dry summers, especially when the spring rainfall didn't arrive. I remembered reading historian Geoffrey Blainey's sobering reminder that 'a drought can die slowly', so, for our household supply, we had more than the usual number of tanks put in place. And cash flow liquidity was needed to keep the bank manager happy. The first payment for the grapes would not be made until the second year after planting and then we wouldn't receive the full payment until six months after the fruit was delivered. In the meantime we had to cover the costs of running the vineyard for two years including harvesting and pruning costs.

We engaged a water engineer to advise us where to drill a bore into the shattered rock aquifer at a cost of several hundred dollars. Dig near the large rocky outcrop in the southeast corner of the property, was the answer. I was later told by the veteran driller that any twit would have dug near a rocky outcrop as that was the obvious place to sink a bore.

The well was drilled to a depth of 90 metres at a cost of several thousand dollars, resulting in a flow of 11,500 litres an hour. This was good but not sufficient for the total area of vineyard eventually to be planted, and the water was rather salty. Word got around that a woman with a wire coathanger was having great success in divining water sources. She had found a huge supply of unsalted water for the Pike's vineyard in Polish Hill River further down the valley. Would you believe though, across the road from Pike's, on the Annie's Lane blocks, there was not even one tug on her coathanger.

She walked all over our property and I walked with her with my own wire coathanger and certainly felt the pull of an underground force in several places. We dug where she suggested, again to 90 metres, resulting in a flow of 3500 litres an hour of somewhat salty water.

To deal with the salt we were advised to push out a very large dam, to use the fresh winter rain runoff to water the vines at the beginning of the season and so flush out the salt from the vine roots from the last season. We contracted S.C. Heinrich & Co. (whose tag line advised 'We Move the Earth') to build the dam but they advised us not to start until the soil had had a good winter soaking; working dry earth risked future cracking in the dam wall. This sage advice quelled my eagerness to get started.

~ * ~

Rain it certainly did, that first year, and I came to know a different, but not obvious, aspect of The Hill when driving around the property and finding myself in difficulties. The ute would take over from me and waltz over the surface as I came across seepage vents. Many times the front wheels disappeared to the axle in what looked like innocent puddles. In this way I learned to locate the spots where underground drainage broke through the surface.

We had been referred to a surveyor in the Department of Environment to talk about the size of the dam. He offered to design it and suggested we put in drainage banks across the property to bring surface run-off to the dam. Given the long-term annual average rainfall for Clare of 630 millilitres and the size of our property, 36 hectares, he calculated that we would need a dam holding 5.2 megalitres.

He defined a survey starting point near the northeast corner of the property and from this mark defined gradients for the drainage banks from the highest points of the southern and the western boundaries to harvest the run-off to bring to the dam on the northern boundary. The day we helped him put in the survey pegs for banks and dam was bizarre. A very cold southwesterly from the Antarctic kept a constant blow, which froze us to the bone despite all the gear we were wearing.

We started early in the morning but didn't finish until mid afternoon when we hot-footed it back to the shed for a heart starter, but all I could find was a half-empty bottle of Stone's Mac Full Strength Green Ginger Wine, which really didn't do the trick, even in mugs of scalding hot coffee.

~ * ~

Malcolm Heinrich called in to advise us it was time to start work on the dam. Stan and his son Robbie arrived with two bulldozers, a huge front-end loader and a grader. Stan was a gentle man and a natural with a bulldozer. His left hip had been badly injured and he walked with a decided lean and limp, but once behind the controls of his large machines he waltzed the mighty things like a dancer. Robbie likewise drove his beast with great panache as if he and his machine had become part of a gigantic mechanised ballet. I marvelled at their skills as they moved tonnes of damp rich red clay to form a giant hole and deposited it to form the dam wall.

During this process a neighbour's sheep strayed into the dam works and became bogged in the sloppy clay. I was endeavouring to free her when a rep from a wine company came to talk about a contract.

'I'm buggered if I can shift her,' I said.

'No worries, here,' he said as he bent over and tucked his arms under her belly and lifted her easily to dry land. His beautifully ironed moleskins and blue-checked shirt were now a muddy red, which didn't seem to worry him in the least.

The dam filled to brimming a few months after its construction was finished, and one night, during a tropical downpour that had moved in from Queensland, it could have overflowed the dam wall and breached it because the spillway was choked with large Salvation Jane that had not been cleared when the headlands were slashed. I immediately rang the Heinrichs who dashed over from their nearby house to make a channel through the main drainage bank to divert the flow into the neighbour's dam.

In downpours I often watched the runoff swirling and gurgling along the drainage banks on its way to the dam and I always kept my eye on the spillway to check it is clear of weeds.

~ * ~

Some people set out to develop immunity from convention as they step outside the norm with an idiosyncratic take on what and how to do things. Many talk about their passion, others demonstrate theirs by taking action. We met Drew and Doreen, idealists and doers, at the Sevenhill pub one night when we'd gone there to sit by the fire. They did most of the talking over a couple of beers and later a leisurely meal and a bottle of Grenache, telling us about their romantic holiday in Tuscany soon after they met. They were taken by the beauty of the rural landscape dotted with hilltop villages, castles and churches and by the wide variety of simple peasant food that was everywhere abundant. When they first visited Clare Valley it reminded them so much of their Tuscan idyll they were prompted to make the move from Adelaide to grow olives – about which they had known nothing when they set out. We seemed to have met some like-minded people.

The olive industry – growing trees, making oil and selling olive products – had been a thriving concern in South Australia more or less since the foundation of the colony. Despite their Anglo–German culinary traditions, early South Australian settlers planted olives and pressed oil with such great enthusiasm as to be pre-eminent in Australia for olives and olive oil. The initial burst of success of the early olive industry then waned for a long time until a recovery started in the mid 1990s.

I had worked for a number of years with the noted gerontologist, the late Dr Michael Burr, and he was now a good friend of ours. As a serious sideline to his professional life, he had become fascinated by this puzzle at the heart of colonial South Australia's successful flirtation with the olive: why a settler group with no obvious Mediterranean background took to olive production. Michael planted olive trees at his property in the Beetaloo Valley in South Australia's Mid North and began studying the olive's history in the state. In his quest for background information he travelled through Spain, Italy, Greece, Turkey and France. This firsthand experience, a growing store of knowledge and a willingness to share what he had learnt resulted in Michael becoming a crucial figure in olive production in his home state and beyond.

When Michael urged us to consider olive growing in planning our Clare Valley adventure, the least we could do was to listen and look. We accepted an invitation to his eyrie in the hills at Beetaloo Valley, about ninety minutes drive north of Clare. The property consisted of a rugged, jagged hill with an old schoolhouse on the top. Michael was in the process of converting this relic into habitable quarters with some very idiosyncratic features.

We clambered around his hill looking at olive varieties while Michael discussed their differing features. We inspected vats of maturing olives growing the most amazing fungus which, he assured us, was not harmful. He had begun a collection of aberrations in the olive tree's expression, searching for them all over South Australia and showed us odd examples – branches with a leaf growing from the trip of another leaf, an olive fruit growing out of the tip of a leaf and leaves of widely different shapes.

Preserved olives

Ingredients

olives – just as many as you have gathered

cooking salt

vinegar

olive oil

Soak the olives in water in a bucket, or laundry sink, for 2 to 3 weeks, changing the water daily until they have lost the bitterness.
Prepare brine with 120 g of salt per litre of water, then make a solution of 1 part vinegar to 3 parts brine.
Pickle the olives in the brine/vinegar. Cover the pickle with 10 mm of olive oil and leave the olives for another 2–3 months, when they should be ready to eat.

We weren't won over by Michael's urging though. Jeni and I had picked olives from the wild trees that grew at Seacliff near our house and from large trees at a nearby friend's property. If you've ever tried to pick olives by hand you may well have concluded, as we did, that you would need an army of extended family members working for nothing to manage the grove and to pick and process the fruit to keep costs sustainable. And then of course you would have to market them. After we had established ourselves on The Hill, Michael would visit us on his way to and from Beetaloo Valley for a stretch, refreshments and a chat, especially about what we were missing by not getting into olives.

Looking at the economics of olive growing and the return on investment, we decided there would not be enough in it for us, especially with break-even coming after about twelve years hard labour. But Drew and Doreen were so keen about the potential of olives and the health benefits of its oil they dedicated themselves wholeheartedly to their tree change on 12 hectares at Armagh, which lies a little to the northwest of the Clare township and a kilometre or so from our vineyard. They spent a great deal of time renovating their old farmhouse, pushing over a derelict outhouse and using the bricks to build a new shed for processing the olives.

Development of an olive growing business requires patient money. This really is a long-term investment for your kids and grandchildren. Drew and Doreen kept at it, ploughing in money for groundsheets and electric wands to take the strain out of picking. Production costs were high making it difficult to compete with imported products but locally produced olive oil was fresh, with a deeply more-ish flavour and a great point of difference from the imported olive oils.

Over the years, however, Drew came to see that wine grapes were bringing in a much better return so he grubbed out half of the olive grove and planted Shiraz grapes, enabling them to join the wine boom. The large shed they had restored for processing olives now also became their cellar door, for oil, olives and wine.

Doreen was a great champion of the health benefits of olive oil and generously took samples of their produce when they were invited to meals with friends and when they dined in restaurants and pubs. We were invited to view their newly renovated house and to share a bottle of Wendouree Cabernet Malbec, a wondrous treat.

We had first visited the Wendouree Winery before we moved to the Clare Valley – in the days when Mr Birks owned it. The cellar door then consisted of a table and two large glass-fronted dressers in a tin shed – one housed the bottles for tasting and the other the tasting glasses.

Mr Birks served everyone in strict order of arrival. He would ask what you wanted to try, retrieve the bottles, put them on the table, open the other dresser, take out the glasses and pour the wine. You could spend as much time as you wanted talking about the wines, asking questions about the vineyard and wine-making techniques and he would give you his full attention. There was to be no hurry, and people who tried to rush the process or push themselves forward were suitably ignored. Having made your decision, without hurry, he would pack your purchase, process the payment, put the bottles away on the dresser, wash the glasses, wipe them, store them once again in the second dresser and close its large doors. Only then would he greet the next customer and start proceedings all over again.

The vines from which the Wendouree wines are made were planted in 1892 by Alfred Percy Birks and today the dry-grown grapes produce about 50 tonnes of fruit a year from about 11.5 hectares. The grapes are handpicked at around 13.5° Baumé (13.5 °Be), a reading of the sugar level in the grapes, and fermented in open slate fermenters.

Today the property is owned by Tony and Lita Brady and the wine produced, according to the distinguished Australian wine critic James Halliday, is 'a cult legend of Australian wines'. James Pettigrew, the owner of Wickman's Fine Wine Auctions, tells how he decanted and consumed a bottle of Wendouree red over three days by which time he noted that the tannins had smoothed out 'fresh, pure, monumental, sublime'. Perhaps this explains why demand for these wines far exceeds supply and why Wendouree Wines has legendary status.

The only way to buy the wines directly from the winery is to get on Wendouree's active mailing list and the only way to get on that is to get on the waiting list, and even then purchases are limited to six bottles a vintage. Drew had been on the mailing list for years so in offering to share a bottle with us he was offering us something very special.

Drew was the inventive cook in this house using his beloved solid fuel oven, a notable feature of the kitchen, along with a long, old wooden table. The former formal dining area of the kitchen was now overtaken by sofas and an overly large, flat TV screen broadcasting a must-see footy clash. To match the Wendouree Cabernet Malbec, Drew had slow roasted a leg of saltbush mutton with home-grown, freshly picked broad beans, pods and all, and wild artichokes that had been stir-fried for a few minutes in black butter, stuffed with breadcrumbs and garlic and then simmered for a lengthy time. What a delightful combination of flavours, and a splendid match for this big and well-structured wine.

Saltbush mutton

Ingredients for 8 servings

leg of saltbush mutton
150 mL water
50 mL olive oil
baby potatoes, unpeeled
baby onions, peeled
12 cloves garlic, peeled
10 baby tomatoes
several sprigs of oregano
several sprigs of mint
4 preserved lemon quarters
1 tsp turmeric

Remove excess fat from the leg. Brown the leg in the oil in the bottom of a large lidded saucepan. Add all of the other ingredients. Simmer gently for about 3 hours, turning occasionally until the meat is starting to fall from the bone.

The ingredients will cook in their own juices but check occasionally and add a little more water if required.

Cut thickish slices of meat. Place the leg and the slices in a deep serving dish and pour the other ingredients over the slices. Allow guests to serve themselves.

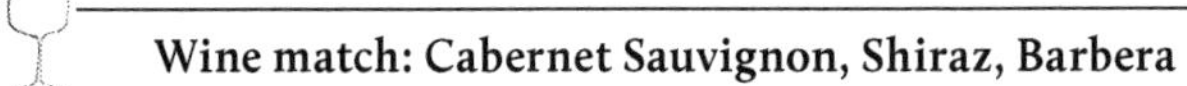

Wine match: Cabernet Sauvignon, Shiraz, Barbera

I had never really understood Wendouree wines, but this time the palate was a revelation. Drew had decanted the wine twenty-four hours earlier, giving it lots of time to breathe.

'The experts say it's important to let a good wine breathe for one hour for every year of age,' he said, 'but these big beauties need a much longer time to really open up.'

'What bloody romantics we are, Drew,' I said. 'You two spend a couple of weeks in Tuscany and fall in love with the idea of growing olives and we fall in love with the romance of growing grapes after two weeks in the Clare Valley.'

He laughed. 'The real estate people call it lifestyle, which is code for working our arses off like peasants but really loving it.'

It was Drew who introduced us to Brooks Lookout. Floyd Brooks owned a large area of land on top of and down the escarpment west of Armagh. Each year the colours of the local winning football team would be painted on the blades of his windmill and his water tank on the road to Blyth. We thought it was a grand gesture to the community when he offered some of this land to be developed for a lookout.

The vista from this vantage point is stupendous – going for kilometres to the Barunga Ranges in the west, on which dozens of wind turbines turn their lazy geared-down blades, all the way south to the Adelaide Plains, and across the Gulf on a clear day to Ardrossan. As evening falls, breathtaking sunsets give way to the lights of small towns and villages along the coast that twinkle their welcome and, there, far to the south, are the lights of Adelaide reflected in the sky.

Nearby, on the plain below us, Drew pointed out the property of Ian Roberts, a environmentalist who revegetated his 16-hectare Blyth property with indigenous flowering shrubs and trees and is said to be bent on revegetating the Blyth Plains. He also was a noted local footballer. Obviously a man of many talents he converted an old stone church into an art gallery and studio – Medika Gallery. Opposite his gallery he refurbished the inside of the former Masonic Hall into a modern boutique cinema. Ian's talents go further than restoring old buildings though. He is a talented painter of detailed images of birds, flowers and eucalypts.

He was also one of the movers behind Brooks Lookout. He rounded up the resources to plant hardy indigenous groundcovers and shrubs, identified with name tags along the path to the lookout, replete with a picnic shed and seats. At the edge of the lookout a cairn was erected on which was placed a large bronze plate with distance markers to local and overseas locations. At the time it was put in it was not properly secured; possibly because someone thought its weight would be enough to deter thieves. The thieves thought otherwise, however, and nicked off with it.

Having heard about this theft we offered Ian a dozen bottles of wine for his cinema patrons to raise funds for a replacement. The few hundred dollars raised, however, were insufficient to finish the job so I persuaded Drew to contribute a dozen Shiraz for another raffle. This time the bronze plate was firmly cemented into place.

Drew and I rounded up a group of friends to celebrate the occasion at dusk. Drew ordered fifty dozen Cowell oysters – grown in Franklin Harbour on the Eyre Peninsula – arranging delivery by overnight coach as it passed through Lochiel, a half hour's drive to the west of Armagh, at 3 am. We all chipped in for our dozen or two, and each brought a plate of food along to enjoy with some very fine Clare Rieslings.

3

We had each other and we had The Hill; we had the shed to live in and planting the vineyard was about to begin. But we were not complete, not yet. Living at Seacliff after Jeni and I had first got together, we were taking our constitutional one morning on the beach and in a passion-filled moment I stopped Jeni, turned her to face me and blurted out, 'Jeni, I want to have a couple of kids with you. I'd just love you to be the mother of my children.'

'Don't be fucking ridiculous,' she answered immediately, 'we'd still be paying for them to go to university when we're old age pensioners.'

'Come on, Jen, this is really important.'

'And so is keeping our sanity. We'll get a couple of dogs – they're so much more loving and loyal than kids. Just look at these two.'

Coming towards us was a young woman with a couple of magnificent-looking animals. They were on leads behaving themselves, but the woman looked unhappy. We just had to stop and have a talk, especially to the dogs. Although only medium sized, they were regal with elegant snouts, large triangular ears and beautiful red-tanned coats.

'What breed are they?' Jeni asked the miserable-looking owner.

'Red kelpies – cost me a packet because they're stud males from a good line, but they get the quivers a lot, seem to be nervous, have so much energy. They're working dogs – probably best for the country.'

We walked on. 'I reckon they're magnificent – bloody beautiful,' I said looking back.

'That's what we'll get, Burtie, a couple of kelpies – they'll be our children.'

~ * ~

We didn't have a laundry in the shed, so we would go to the Clare laundromat. On a Saturday afternoon, while others were playing or watching footy or cricket, we'd have the laundry to ourselves, reading the weekend papers while the machines clattered and spun. One Saturday I was reading the local paper and there it was.

'Jeni, listen to this, "Two red kelpies, working dogs, vaccinated – a hundred each." I reckon our two offspring might have arrived.'

'What's the number?' Jeni said as she fumbled to find the mobile in her moleskins and to dial the number. 'It's the Ashby merino stud about an hour's drive to the north, near Bundaleer somewhere. I said we'd be coming now.'

Jeni and I are usually hopeless navigators, but this time for some reason we found the large front gates to the property without trouble. Jeni told me these were the last of an eight-puppy litter. There, in a makeshift mesh cage with a couple of sheets of corrugated iron for the roof, were two tiny jumping, barking bundles of red, who won our hearts immediately. It appeared the feeling was mutual given the enthusiastic reception they gave us.

'This one's the runt of the litter,' said the breeder. 'She popped out twenty-four hours after we thought it was all over. They say runts are the brightest ones in the litter.'

'We'll take them – what about a hundred and fifty for the two?'

'Done, let's shake on it,' she said.

'What's the mother's name?' Jeni asked.

'Jac – she's getting old, but she's such a great working dog we just wanted one last litter from her.'

The drive back to The Hill was slowed by dense driving rain. In the cabin of the small Brumbie ute, the heat from the four of us fogged up the windows until moisture ran down the inside of the windscreen making it hard to see. I opened my window just enough for the cold wind to freeze my face but also to stop the moisture build-up inside. Jeni happily cuddled the two very subdued bundles on a towel on her lap. She told me that when puppies leave their mother for good they vomit, which these two duly did. Jeni was ready for it.

'Burtie, what are we going to call them? I'd like their names to start with 'J', just like their mother's.'

We tossed a few names about and came up with 'Janette' for the larger puppy and 'Jackie' for the runt; when we called them, their ears pricked up at the sounds.

I had a strong view that as these were working dogs their abilities should not be corrupted by treating them like children or feeding them chocolate. They should live outside, not inside as pets.

'I'm sure you're right,' said Jeni.

I was stunned. I had expected a protest from she who is nutty about dogs. I lined a large laundry basket with thick underlay and put a blanket on top. 'There, look at that, all soft and warm – much better than a mesh cage in a paddock.'

I took the basket outside and put it under the table in the carport. Rain was still dumping down and a cold wind persisted. Later, as I was uncorking a bottle, there was a flash of lightning followed by huge thunderous rumbling right overhead. The almighty thunderclap frightened the hell out of us.

'Christ, I hope they haven't bolted. Dogs don't like thunder, do they?' I hurried outside and there they were, huddled together. A trickle of water was doubling back underneath from the table top and dripping into the basket. I picked them up, basket and all, and took them inside.

'It's bloody cold out there and I wouldn't want them to run off into this storm. They can stay inside for tonight, but *only* for tonight.'

'That'll be good, Burtie.'

They clambered out from the basket for a sniff around and then with a great struggle scrambled onto the sofa where I was sitting, settled in with a sigh, ears erect and eyes everywhere. What bliss. Our little family on The Hill was now complete, ready for the big adventure.

Next morning, low thick black clouds moved slowly across the valley and up to the eastern ridge top. Rain was still bucketing down with water running through the chocolate-brown soil of the vineyard rows. Vines snuggled in for their winter sojourn awaiting pruning. By contrast surrounding fields were emerald green with winter crops. Then, the rain stopped, the temperature dropped, a hush spread around and light snowflakes drifted down.

'No wonder it's so bloody cold. We won't be able to work outside.'

'Good,' Jeni said. 'We need to toast our feet in front of that open fire at the pub, and a plate of something substantial and some good company. The kelpies can stay in the ute – I'll take a blanket for them.'

Working dogs in a ute, yes, but in the cabin, under a blanket?

I asked the barman if it was too early for a draft Guinness.

'Never too early in winter, mate. Two pints?'

The menu was short and simple, a couple of hearty soups, four mains and two puds. The soup would have been sufficient by itself, richly thick with cannellini and borlotti beans cooked slowly with smoked ham hocks, onions, tomatoes and herbs, thickened with lentils and served with battard halves toasted on a chasseur with olive oil.

Ham hock and bean soup

Ingredients for 6 servings

500 g cannellini and/or white or borlotti or black eye, or red kidney beans
1 ham hock
100 g brown lentils
1 large onion, chopped
3 large cloves of garlic, chopped
2 outer celery sticks, chopped
4 sage leaves
thyme sprigs
mint sprigs
50 mL red wine vinegar
pepper
nutmeg, freshly grated
allspice
ground cumin
slices of ciabatta loaf cut into small cubes for croutons
olive oil
chopped parsley

Soak the beans overnight. Drain and save the water.
Place the hock and the vinegar in the bean water, add more if necessary to cover. Boil/simmer until the meat is falling from the bone. Keep your eye on the level of liquid and add more if necessary. Remove the meat from the water; save the water. Remove the meat from the bone.

In a frying pan fry the onion, garlic, celery, herbs and spices until browned.

Place these in the meat water along with meat and the lentils and cook gently until the lentils are soft. Allow to cool and then vitamise, adjusting with salt if necessary.

Heat the oil in the frying pan or a chasseur and brown the bread cubes until crisp.

Pour the hot soup into warmed bowls, add the croutons and dress with parsley.

Wine match: Cabernet Sauvignon, Merlot, Verdelho, Rosé

But we were here to indulge. I selected a bottle of Kilikanoon Grenache to match our main course, which was Jamestown saltbush mutton shanks with wild artichoke, baby beets and preserved lemon – what a blow-out.

Grenache was once the most widely grown red grape in Australia until overtaken by Cabernet Sauvignon in the 1970s which, in turn, was displaced by Shiraz. Kevin Mitchell, the winemaker at Kilikanoon Wines, had tracked down small, local blocks of old Grenache vines and lovingly crafted the fruit into superb wines with a distinctive palate, which Jeni likened to a mouthful of peace roses. The Kilikanoon winery is on Main North Road just south of Leasingham but the cellar door is on Penna Lane Road, off Hughes Park Road, a little to the west of Penwortham.

After lunch, I ordered a couple of Guinness cleansers – really as an excuse to stay by the fire. As we contemplated our draughts, we watched the snow hit the road and melt. A bloke wandered over for a chat.

'I hear you bought the pony club property. Going to build up there?'

'We just love the vista from the top of the hill.'

'We don't build on tops of hills round here, too much wind, too open – best to snug down at the bottom away from the westerlies.'

Next morning, as Jeni was outside filling the kettle, the kelpies – irresistible, energetic and commanding with their look-at-me barks – tumbled and groaned in playful wrestling. They had settled in and bonded with us and The Hill and made their contribution to the running of the property right from the beginning, hunting mice in grass tufts and chasing hares and rabbits. The older hares were too fast and clever for them, but their leverets, hiding against clumps, could not disguise their scent. Janette would clamp onto the small animals while Jackie would tear off limbs into sizeable portions for gnawing. After such a feast they wouldn't eat for a couple of days.

Foxes and wedgetailed eagles also contributed to limiting the pest population, and visiting kangaroos added romance. They would move from the scrub next door down to a stock dam in the morning and graze their way back up The Hill during the day. We also had a pair of raptors lurking overhead, and some swallows took up residence under the carport.

~ * ~

Vineyards were popping up throughout The Valley. Many of them were small, only two to five hectares, but the large wineries were also expanding their holdings. In a first for Clare, and everywhere else for that matter, a real estate agent and his accountant friend came up with the idea of a 'community title' ownership. They lobbied the Government for the *South Australian Strata Titles Act* to be amended to allow for investment by many people in a large vineyard company. Individual investors would own a percentage of the property commensurate with their investment, not a specific area of its land. They would share in the costs of developing and running the vineyard and in profits distributed as dividends, if any. In this way, city professionals planning tax commitments could participate in and support the Australian wine boom.

The Federal Government encouraged this investment in vineyards by amending tax rules from the standardised twenty-five-year term over which to depreciate an asset to a ten-year term. This was very good news for us because it would help to fast track payback time so we could bring forward further development of our vineyard. The community title concept took off around Australia but, ten years later, it resulted in a sea of surplus wine causing the industry to crash.

The boom, whilst it lasted, was also good news for the many small contractors in the valley offering services required to develop and manage the vineyards. This meant that young vines, trellis materials and irrigation equipment were hard to come by, resulting in delays to well-laid plans. I applied the 'squeaky door' principle in dealing with recalcitrant suppliers but, remembering Jeni's advice, moderated my 'tone of voice' and tried to use gentle diplomacy and discussion instead.

The next few months were a hectic time working as we did from dawn to dusk seven days a week on physical tasks in the vineyard helping to get the pegged-out blocks ready for planting and then administrative work in the evening, trying to co-ordinate the delivery of materials and contractors to install these, whilst managing the accounts, all of which required dedicated attention to detail.

Jeni had set up quarters in the shed with gusto. Most of it was taken up with our furniture and building materials, which were screened off with portable clothes hangers and our four-fold Chinese screen with all its gold and carved imagery, which Jeni had positioned behind the king-sized bed. In front of the bed was a sofa with a stunning piece of African tapestry thrown over it. Forget the cultural mishmash, it was comfortable and colourful and looked great.

In the corner near the front door, she set up a kitchen table for the electrical cooking equipment. Outside, she put the barbecue and the sink under the carport, where the ute was supposed to be parked, along with outdoor tables and seats to make up an outdoor eating area. In no time, we became so inventive with menus and recipes that we didn't rely too much on the barbecue.

Jeni loved my French and Italian peasant cooking and added her specialties from Asia and the Middle East. She was a dab hand at these cuisines, and I matched her offerings with good wines, both Clare Valley and imported, emerging varieties.

Chicken wings in mother stock

Ingredients for 4 servings as entrée or finger food

12 large chicken wings

325 mL cold water

325 mL dark soy sauce

60 mL Chinese wine

5 cm piece ginger chopped

1 clove garlic

3 star anise

50 g palm or brown sugar

Place everything into a saucepan large enough so the wings are well covered and simmer for 20 minutes.

Remove the wings, allow to cool and disjoint into 3 pieces.

The stock can be frozen and reused, adding ingredients as necessary to replace lost flavour and to develop as mother stock.

Wine match: dry Riesling, Viognier, Pinot Gris, Vermentino

The only thing missing, Jeni said, was an old bathtub outside with a fire under it for long hot soaks after a cold day's hard slog. And cold it was, the coldest for years. Blokes in the pub reported burst water pipes in the ceilings of old houses flooding rooms below. We were so cold we piled all the blankets we owned onto the bed along with the double swag, donned thermals under our pyjamas and wore beanies and gloves and still cuddled together for warmth. Condensation from the unlined roof splattered onto unsuspecting cheeks during the night.

I became adept at moving quickly between Jeni doffing her working clothes and donning her thermals to entice her into action; the kelpies responded to the carry-on and laughter with encouraging barks.

Full-body washing depended on a burst of sunshine to heat the solar shower. This plastic bladder is a very efficient means of heating water, requiring only a short break in the clouds to get the water to a sufficient temperature. The biochem toilet boasted a moulded throne with a chemical chamber underneath, which Jeni emptied weekly into a hole I had dug. Later I planted native shrubs on top of the deposits; none of which survived.

Jeni likened our domestic set-up to up-market camping. 'At least we're not under canvas,' she said.

After a few days of really heavy rain the surface of the sloping ground just down from the shed was slippery enough already and who was to know an innocent-looking puddle would turn out to be a surface seepage vent where underground water seeped to the surface. That morning, as we stood watching, two long-loaders arrived with hundreds of wooden pine posts and strainers. The middle wheels of the leading freighter sank, nearly tipping the load from the tray.

The drive unit of the second freighter was uncoupled and with chains attached to the front of the stricken unit futile attempts were made to shift it. Then its load was taken off; try again, but to no avail. The next day the drivers borrowed a neighbour's tractor to support the drive unit; not a budge. Then they went to Heinrichs to borrow a dozer. All three units slowly eased the lorry out of its quagmire.

The posts and strainers had been unloaded nowhere near where they were required. They were left for the trellising contractor to move into place, which slowed his progress considerably.

We joined the contractor's team to plant the vine cuttings, which was especially thrilling. Jeni was allotted the task of driving the tractor. She said this was easy; having pressed the tortoise button that geared down the sped to a couple of kilometres an hour all she had to do was to steer whilst she listened to the women's session on the radio.

Moving along the mid row the tractor pulled a long sled on which was a tank of water with pump, another bloke and myself sat at the back, one each side, clutching a bundle of rooted cuttings. A third bloke standing on the sled deftly worked a hose from one side to the other drilling water holes at regular intervals into which we poked a cutting. Two other blokes walked behind the sled tamping down soil around each one.

The giant was starting to take shape. We marvelled at the skill of the workmen as they installed the trellising in each block. The vine rows had been pegged at three-metre intervals, each starting and ending with a strainer, and between these were six-metre-wide panels consisting of a wooden post, a six-metre space then a steel post with a series of slots to hold wires. Within each panel three vines were spaced at two-metre intervals. Then wires were run from strainer to strainer; the first about 40 centimetres above the ground to carry the irrigation polypipe, one about a metre above the ground – the cordon wire on which the vines were trained up to and then along – with each wire slotted into the steel posts. Two more wires were then run along the ground, one on either side of the posts; these are the lifting wires, which, as the canopy of the vines grow, are lifted to keep the canopy in an upright position, to control the amount of sunlight filtering through the leaves onto the grape bunches that would grow just above the cordon wire. There were hundreds of posts and kilometres of wires to each block.

Another skilled operation was the installation of the irrigation infrastructure. Trenches were dug by a small machine along one side of each block into which kilometres of PVC submains were laid with polypipe risers plugged into them at intervals next to each strainer. Irrigation polypiping was attached to the risers and strung along the wire near to the ground. Solenoids, mechanisms to control the on-off function of the irrigation, were glued in at regular intervals to divide the block into irrigation segments, with electrical wires running from the submains back to a computer controlling the pumping and filter systems in the pump house.

We were the dogs' bodies unloading and fetching things, digging and filling in, along with loading the rubbish left by the pony club people to take to the dump. At the end of each day, needless to say, we were wrecks, but our euphoria kept us going as did the love and company of the kelpies.

The very expensive irrigation system would be used in the early years to get the young plants off to a good start; subsequently it would come into play only for supplementary watering if spring and summer rains were inadequate. By early October installation of the infrastructure was completed and it was time for testing the whole system for problems. Winter rains had resulted in the subsoil being nicely saturated but the surface soil had shed its moisture in the sunny, dry early weeks of spring. I was anxious to get water onto the roots of the vines before they had time to dry out.

Inauguration of the irrigation system revealed a complete balls-up with the polypipe. The price quoted for materials and installation for the eight hectares from the only local supplier was $80,000, way above AK's budget estimate. After much discussion, the supplier suggested using a South Australian dripper tube instead of the imported one. Right, we'd be patriotic, we decided, make a choice that would help keep jobs in South Australia and incidentally benefit us – the South Australian dripper line was $10,000 cheaper than the imported model.

But the local product turned out to be rubbish, all 27 kilometres of it. It consisted of polyurethane tubing with external drippers inserted as the tube passed through a machine – at least that was the theory. A huge number of drippers, however, were missing, with only a dent in the tube to show where they should have been. In other instances a hole had been punched, but the dripper was missing, or it had been inserted at an angle allowing water under pressure to gush out. Wherever water escaped from these missed connections, weeds grew in abundance.

The manufacturer denied any responsibility for these faults, first saying the water pressure was too high – in which case where were the blown-out drippers? – and then that the level of iron in the water was the cause of the troubles. The local retailer denied responsibility saying he was the meat in the sandwich and would not take up the argument with the manufacturer. I had paid a $10,000 deposit, but refused to pay any more until the problem was fixed. Talk about tone of voice.

At this stage Jeni was reading *Peel Me a Lotus*, Charmian Clift's book about life in a Greek village on Hydra, which wasn't going so well for Charmian. I also read it and was struck by Clift's comment that her life was balanced so precariously between laughter and tears that she had to hang on to stop herself toppling into hysteria. I thought I knew what she was talking about and so did Jeni.

'Burtie, I'm buggered if I'm going to become an emotional wreck over this,' Jeni said. 'Forget the anger and rage. Let's concentrate on laughter and accepting that sometimes you can't have the good bits without some pain.'

The stand-off went on for eighteen months and was only resolved one morning when, to our great surprise, a team arrived and started removing the tubing. It was replaced by the imported Israeli product – the one on which we were first quoted. This worked like a charm. I don't know who paid for the changeover, but after testing of the entire system was completed I paid the balance owing.

The immediate outcome of the polypipe fiasco was the abundant growth of weeds. We bought a couple of hoes and started hoeing, which wasn't too hard when the soil was moist but as the sun dried out the surface during October and November we made short work of the metal hoes and bought many more. We would finish the end of a hot day feeling like zombies.

~ * ~

Christmas was coming and the rural supply companies mailed out invitations for barbecues and drinks. Jeni thought it nice of them to include us and said we should go to them all, to meet locals, some of whom surely would also be establishing vineyards.

At the Elder's party a couple wandered over to introduce themselves. 'I'm Mike McIntyre and this is my missus, Liz,' Mike said. 'We're from the northern pastoral country, retired down here onto a small block of dry-grown Shiraz. Don't know anything about growing wine grapes, but it can't be much different from lemons and roses, which I grew up north. But we do know something about drinking the product,' he said with a huge smile.

Good, we should be able to build on this common ground, I thought. Liz quickly took over, jumping from one subject to the next and we soon discovered she was a keen talker. She and Mike had lived an isolated life, managing a cattle station and I guess Liz was grateful to have people to talk to, especially women. Mike was a typical tall, slim country bloke, friendly and effusive but on his guard for any sign of one-upmanship or putdown.

Sausages, rissoles and onions sizzled on a huge hotplate with lamb chops and beef steaks. A long table was lined with large plastic containers of tomato sauce and bundles of white, sliced bread: two huge eskies overflowed with beer cans piled on ice.

Jeni, enjoying a chop, opined that her preserved lemons would go very nicely with the lamb. 'Well,' said Liz, 'with all the lemons our old trees produce I'd love to have the recipe. I could make jars of preserved lemons to sell at one of the charities I belong to.'

Preserved lemons

Ingredients

½ cup coarse rock salt
5 lemons, quartered
5 bay leaves
1 tbs black peppercorns
lemon juice to fill
3 tbs extra-virgin olive oil

You will need a 1-litre (4-cup) screw or clip-top airtight jar.

Sterilise the jar and place 1 tbs salt in the bottom. Place the lemons in a bowl with the remaining salt and rub all of the salt firmly into the lemon quarters.

Pack the lemons into the jar with the rind facing out, adding the bay leaves and peppercorns as you go. Press the ingredients down firmly to pack them in. Add enough lemon juice to the jar to cover the fruit. Top with olive oil to seal, then seal with the lid. Allow the jar to stand in a cool, dark place for a month before using the preserved fruit.

To use the preserved lemons, scrape away the flesh and pith, rinse and finely chop the rind and add to your favourite savoury recipe.

Mike eyed all of the offerings. 'What more could a man need for a good session? You could get nicely mellow on all of this.' He looked around for someone to challenge him.

'Don't even think about it,' Liz said, 'you've got lots of things to do in the morning.'

'Ease up, Liz, it's Christmas remember, time to be merry.'

Liz was stocky and square cut, perhaps from a lifetime of eating fruit cake and the small cupcakes for which, she told Jeni, she was famous.

Trying to come to Mike's rescue, I told him about the viticulture course we had just enrolled in. 'It will help you come to grips with how to grow Shiraz, as well as welding, calibrating spray equipment and which chemicals to use for what.'

'Look, mate, I've been driving a tractor and welding every bloody thing within cooee for the past forty years. You'll never get me into a classroom again, had too much of that as a kid.'

'Right, I'll let you know how we go,' I responded, rather lamely.

Another couple wandered over to join Mike and Liz. Mike shouted that he was pleased to see them again.

In a whisper, Jeni asked me if I thought Mike might be deaf.

'That's his back paddock voice,' I said. 'He's used to shouting over the din of a mob of cattle.'

We were introduced as vignerons to Jack and Deidre Castlereagh. They and their forebears had been growing grain and Merinos in the district for decades. Jack told me he wasn't keen to see broadacres turned into vineyards. 'The trouble with grape growers and winemakers is they want to encourage tourism to get people into the cellar doors,' he said. 'Then B & B operators set up to service the tourists who come to visit the wineries. Next, the operators want the council to provide public toilets and visitor information centres. Then the council puts up our rates to pay for the new infrastructure. I've got a few broadacres up there to the north, so I end up paying a huge amount for facilities I don't use and for bureaucrats to sit in large council offices thinking up petty regulations to control how tourists park their vehicles and where to sit – more regulation, more costs.'

'Fair enough,' Jeni said, 'but don't the tourists contribute to the local economy?'

'Don't listen to Jack,' Deidre said, 'he'd be lost without the wineries given the amount of wine he drinks. Besides, our son has 80 hectares of vines.'

Driving back to the shed along the back road, I said to Jeni that we'd better keep our views to ourselves until we knew more about Clare and its people. 'Just listen and learn and not tell the old hands how to do things.'

'I guess you're right. We came here because we fell in love with the place and its old-fashioned feel. I think we should ask the McIntyres for lunch. We might be able to get a friendship going there.'

Clare is a small Australian township providing rural services for farmers, wineries and vineyards and we loved its atmosphere stemming from the rich mixture of Irish, Scottish, Silesian and English ancestry. Clare and its neighbouring towns and villages have networks of community support and voluntary groups that are quietly organised when necessary. Acknowledging ourselves as blow-ins and finding contentment in the social tranquillity of the area, we felt our way cautiously as we sussed out the network of customs and practices and soon began to feel at home in the setting of Australian scrub ridgelines, soft rounded hills and peaceful landscape.

Most country kids nowadays move to the cities to find opportunities and employment, but a counter movement is also taking place, with city professionals and others moving to rural areas to develop hobby farms or rural retreats or to help save the environment. Ironically, however, the modern, tertiary-educated farmers know that bad farming practices will ruin their farms and their future. They really know how to tend the environment of their holdings so that they can pass them on to their grandchildren.

Many people like us find an egalitarian ethos in the front bars of the hotels in The Valley, of which there are six all up. The pub near the northern bridge in Clare township is the Taminga, named after a variety of wine grape bred by A.J. Antcliff specifically for Australian conditions. It is said to 'produce white wine of fair quality over a wide variety of sites'. I have never come across a bottle of it.

The Taminga is our nearest pub, the one we most frequent and enjoy. Happenings, appearing as disasters on the front page of the local rag, are treated with laughter by the bar crowd in this pub with an attitude of 'we're all here, so what's the problem'. In all of these front bars you'll find a great bunch of women and blokes, all very welcoming of strangers and all willing to help with information about anything you want to know, especially the growing of grapes and the making of wine.

Egalitarianism also pervades the sports fields and the myriad organisations where people of like interests gather to socialise and do good deeds. Such groups seem to have flourished as church attendance has diminished. On the surface, the main community fracture seems to be the historic north–south divide based on footy club allegiance fostered by some of the old codgers.

We joined the social club at the Taminga as a way of meeting new people and providing light relief. The social club would have occasional excursions but more often would run a Saturday lunch and socialising afternoon. Sport, local gossip and piss-taking were the main topics.

One bloke we met at the social club in the middle of January turned out to be our neighbour and it was through him that we came to learn a lot about sheep.

'I'm Fred, Fredrick Farrington Fawcett actually,' he said, thrusting out his hand.

'Glad to know you, Fred. This is Jeni. Like a beer?'

'No thanks, gotta get home for tea, but I'll call up tomorrow, something to talk about.'

Sure enough he arrived at drinks time. 'Glass of Riesling, Fred?'

'Nah, I'm a beer man. Got a heavy?'

Fred was stocky, squat and broad in the shoulders from years of country grind, and rather quiet and intense. He had an odd gait, a stiff-legged, jerky sort of walk, with short arms swinging. 'I wanted to ask you about agisting sheep on your property – on the land you're not using for vines,' he said.

'No, Fred,' Jeni cut in quickly, 'we're going to run our own sheep.' Jeni and I had already talked about running sheep to control weed growth on those areas not under vines. The alternative was to have them slashed, but we decided it would be a pity to waste the stock food potential.

Later Jeni told me that while Fred had been introducing himself to me in the pub she had been talking to Rob Broughton, a stock agent. 'He said there's no money in agistment, and it would be much better to run our own small flock. Six-year-old ewes make great mothers, according to Rob, and most will drop twins. He'd like to take us to the next Jamestown sale.'

This was very exciting. We'd never been to Jamestown – let alone a sheep sale. Rob led us around the pens pointing to differences in age, and quality he thought commensurate with the likely price. We came to a pen holding sixty six-year-old ewes, which Rob thought was about the number we needed, but he wasn't happy about the price.

He tracked down the owner for a chat and agreed to the price when a ram was thrown in for nothing. A ram for nothing? It was apparent why the ram was a freebie. In place of two shapely twisting horns, a horny mass protruded from the centre of his head.

'Now before you say anything, let me say I agree he looks odd, but I'll guarantee he'll do his job,' Rob said. 'Let me assure you that horny mess on top won't stop his other horn from doing its job. He's well hung.'

We called him Prince Albert because of his wonky crown and the other ram Victor. Both of them did their job admirably and all the ewes dropped lambs, most of them having twins.

Suddenly we were sheep owners with delivery expected in a few days, which didn't leave much time to get the fencing up around the vineyard blocks. I rang Mike McIntyre to see if he knew a fencer.

'No worries, I've strung and strained hundreds of kilometres of fencing wire in my day. I'll come around tomorrow – won't take long. You can pay me a hundred a day. If you've got an account at Elders I'll collect wire, droppers and stabilisers and posts on the way.'

And so we learnt about sighting a fenceline, corner assemblies, how many wires to string, and where to put the barbwire. We loved coming out of the shed each morning to watch the sheep grazing, and we trained the kelpies to leave them be.

When lambing time arrived, one old girl tried so hard during birthing that she extruded her uterus which, in my ignorance, I mistook for afterbirth. Thinking I was helping her, I tried to remove it until I realised my mistake. She lay there eyeing me coolly, not uttering a sound, completely unable to help herself. I knew that if I left her, a fox would move in overnight.

I walked back to the shed to collect the ute, and Jeni to help me load the sheep to take her to the vet.

'Don't know much about sheep, do you?' he said. 'Anyone else would have thrown her into the creek for the foxes. I'll give her a shot and dump her into the incinerator.'

'Right, thanks – how much do I owe you?'

'Nah, forget it. Put it down to experience.'

~ * ~

The thing to do on Australia Day is to go to Pioneer Park by eight in the morning to get one of the bench seats for the eight-thirty breakfast start. The event is paid for by the council and cooked by members of the local service clubs. There are generous servings of toast, fried eggs, crispy bacon, sausages, and tomatoes. You help yourself to tomato sauce from the large plastic bottle and drink fizz and/or orange juice. Many people bring their own additional supply of local sparkling Riesling.

The food queues are long, the park packed with people scattered under the gums. The buzz of gossip competes loudly with the noise coming from the Ennovy Band, which anyone can join. The band was the result of a donation by Stan Heinrich to some local musicians in memory of his late wife. The mayor struts around in his bling, kids annoy everyone by racing through the crowded areas, patriotic flags and tinsel flutter, speeches are made but not listened to, and citizenship is conferred on new arrivals. Teens are glued to their smartphones determined not to be part of this reality.

One Australia Day we watched on as a young mother, pushing a pram and with three kids in tow, was admonished by the eldest, a six-year-old girl, saying, 'Mum, you look so uncoordinated, those colours just don't go.'

To cement our acquaintance with the McIntyres and the Castlereaghs we invited them to share lunch with us later that day. As we were the Surmons living on the mount we billed it as a 'biblical lunch'. Deidre arrived with a gift jar of anchovies and a loaf of crusty bread. She was onto our pun.

To accompany drinks under the carport Jeni had warmed black olives with fresh herbs in a little olive oil to serve with Retsina. Whilst we thought we could come close to foods from that time we were buggered as to where to buy any authentic wines, even if we knew what they were. Retsina was all we could come up with and it met a mixed reception but I thought it matched well with the bigness of the olive flavours.

For entrée we skinned and boned a smoked rainbow trout to make a spread.

I had read that aged white wines were the go in ancient times so an older Vermentino was the offering.

Smoked rainbow trout and ricotta spread

Ingredients for 4 servings as hors d'oeuvre

1 smoked rainbow trout skinned and boned

1 small tub of ricotta cheese

a nob of soft butter

1 tsp lemon juice and zest of 1 lemon

thin slices of lemon

fresh thyme sprigs

slices of ciabatta bread for bruschetta

2 tsp olive oil

With a fork blend all of the ingredients, except the bread, to a lumpish mash.

Heat the oil in a chasseur or frying pan and brown the bread.

Spread the mash thickly on the ciabatta. Place a lemon slice on top.

Wine match: Vermentino, Rosé, or as an aperitive, Viognier, crisp cold sparkling wine

Mains consisted of mutton leg very slowly cooked with barley, onions, garlic, stock and half a bottle of Sherry served with English spinach leaves as the nearest equivalent to wild field greens. I dragged out an old Cabernet Sauvignon to match the bold flavours of the meat.

Cheeses were skipped for a dessert platter of goat's curd semi-squashed, with Leatherwood honey drizzled along it, with pieces of honeycomb and cracked, roasted almonds, all served with pieces of crusty bread. With this I served one of those almost black, sweet Spanish Sherries, which have been coloured with arrope grape concentrate.

What a blast and in such a rustic setting.

4

Heeding the advice of the bloke in the pub, we chose a position for the house site halfway down The Hill, close to the shed. We planned on living in the shed for about six months by which time we thought we should have an understanding of how the wind patterns impacted across The Hill. We had observed that over a few days the prevailing wind would start in the southwest to bring in 'weather', as the locals called rain, work around to the southeast and then drop off, emerge again in the northeast travel to the northwest and so back to the southwest to end the sequence.

But our best rain came from the northwest, all the way down from Broome in Western Australia. Further south in the valley the best rain came up from the southwest, and there is even a point about two kilometres to the south of us, at McRae Wood Road, where the rain from the south ends, one side of a line across the road being wet and the other side dry. As you travel north from The Hill, the annual average rainfall decreases considerably.

Living in the shed we came to accept the sound of the wind banging the large sliding shed doors. When the wind blew, we would get it just as strongly halfway down The Hill as on top of it. A few days before the builders were expected, I suggested we walk to the top to talk again about the location of the house. From here we could watch the sunset colouring the clouds pearly pink, deepening to orange, all fluffy and extraordinary – 'our slice of paradise', we called it.

'We bought this property because of the magnificent vista from here,' I said when we reached the summit. 'We know we get the wind wherever we are on The Hill, but we only get the full splendour of the scenery from the top.'

'Let's just accept the wind as part the natural order of things and build here then,' Jeni said.

As we learnt to work the vineyard, we came to see that the wind kept the vines healthy by moving on the mildew spores that develop in humid summers, and the frosts in winter and early spring.

~ * ~

Despite our first inclinations of talking with the experts on the matter of design for the house we decided we could save money by using the Brighton draughtsman to draw up plans based on our mud map, which would be checked by council for any problems with the regulations.

We searched design and architecture magazines for inspiration and inspected new housing estates in Aldinga and Moonta for ideas until we were ready to pinpoint the principles we thought important to guide the design for our special place.

It was critical to make the most of the vista while dealing at the same time with the orientation of the hot afternoon summer sun. The top of The Hill was flat and ran north to south, which dictated an oblong shape for the house. The back of the building facing west would receive the full blast of the late-afternoon summer sun and therefore should be windowless, apart from a small window in the laundry, and we would use Mt Gambier limestone because of its thermal qualities. This meant that the front of the house, facing east, would get the morning sun and therefore would require a large terrace with a pergola to shade the floor-to-ceiling-window walls.

Having decided to forgo the help of professionals, we had difficulty positioning the front door and a small vestibule. A main entrance in the back western wall would avoid having to make an opening through the eastern glass wall into the dining and kitchen area, but no matter how we manoeuvred and re-positioned doors and walls we couldn't make it work, so the vestibule idea was dropped and the main entrance was through a sliding door in the glass wall. Feng shui principles demanded that the front door should not align with the back so as to make it difficult for good luck and fortune, once having entered through one door, to leave by the other. Large money plants in pots grow happily at both entrances. The outer walls were to be rendered and painted off-white and the roofline to be kept low.

The other important variable was the very large glass-top dining table. Where to position this masterpiece in the large open-floor plan? A logical layout would consist of a lounge and television area at one end of the oblong, a winter snug around the wood-burning Coonara in the middle, and the dining and kitchen areas at the other end, the glass table contiguous with the kitchen area. But for some reason Jeni thought it best to have the Coonara at the end away from the kitchen and the table close by it for winter warmth. That was the mud map that I took to the draughtsman.

~ * ~

Our goal posts were now set and our run towards them steady, deliberate and without thought of failure. We knew we should keep our plans flexible for any required change along the way but failure was not something we contemplated. Our philosophy would see us be innovative, entrepreneurial and in charge of change and feeling good about it. Forget past difficulties, forge ahead with love, the kelpies and our dream.

The Hill had seduced us, and we tended it in summer heat and freezing winter rain, nurturing it with love and sweat. Our aching muscles and tired brains gave us a kind of pleasure in knowing that we were carving out the base for a new life together and putting down our roots for future growth.

~ * ~

For decades the soils of The Hill had grown grains and fed stock on the stubble. The tillage practices of our predecessors had resulted in the formation of a hard pan just below the cut of the plough disc causing a compacted clay layer that restricted water and root entry into the subsoil.

The layer can be ameliorated so that water can penetrate it by spreading gypsum, but to allow the rooted cuttings free root growth into the subsoil a metre deep furrow needed to be torn by a bulldozer dragging a huge metal hook. Rooted cuttings are obtained by taking cane cuttings from a mother vine of noted pedigree and health status, about 40 centimetres in length with a number of buds along it, and planting them in a nursery sand bed until they developed roots. Twelve months later they are dug up and tied into bundles of fifty, then placed in wool bales and stored in cooling rooms awaiting dispatch.

Our cuttings arrived on time, but the bulldozer operator, so critical to the whole operation, did not. The wool bales of cuttings went into a local coolroom and to save space, we were told, the contents of a small bale had been offloaded into a larger one. This must have been where the confusion lay: a few layers of Cabernet Sauvignon cuttings were mistakenly placed on top of a bundle of Chardonnay cuttings.

Six months later, during one of AK's monthly visits, we were walking the predominantly Chardonnay block with its small section of Cabernet Sauvignon vines at the bottom – frost-prone – end. The canopy was now well established and as we slowly walked along one of the Carbernet rows he paused and looked intently at some leaves. 'Hang on,' he almost shouted, 'this isn't Cab, this looks like Chardonnay and so does that one – and that.'

'How do you know?' I was flabbergasted.

'See the edges of this leaf – large indentations on either side. Now look at this, the edges are rounder, quite different.'

'So who knows what from what?'

'The experts – the ampelographers,' AK said. 'There's a whole mob of them dedicated to identifying grape varieties; there are some 4000 known *Vitis vinifera* – common grape vines.'

'A few Chardonnay in the Cab won't hurt, surely? The white grape will be lost in the red.'

'No, a few wouldn't,' AK agreed, 'but there are lots here – you'll have to dig them up and put in Cab.'

Lots there were – 150 in all – and the transfer was bloody hard work. It took three years before we had finally recognised the last one to be replanted.

~ * ~

You've got to decide your own fate and to do that you either develop your skills or modify your dreams. Our dreams were staying just as they were, so it was off to school for us. We enrolled in a viticultural course run by Nuriootpa TAFE, or rather only Jeni enrolled to save the cost of enrolment for me, but we both read our way through the ins and outs of growing wine grapes, making notes, reading references, planning and writing the various assignments. The intricate life of a grapevine is fascinating. Vines have a two-way flow system. Nutrients flow from the leaves to the roots, and moisture and micro minerals flow from the roots to the canopy.

'Listen to this piece about stigmata and photosynthesis,' Jeni said. '"The stigmata on the back of the leaves let in energy from sunlight and at the very point when the light enters the leaf the energy changes into ferredoxin, a gas which the vine takes in as nutrition. That's photosynthesis."'

'How about this bit dealing with fertilisation of the grape berry?' I said. '"At flowering, each little green hard berry sends out five tiny shoots and on the tip of each sits a finely balanced tiny white petal. One of these shoots will send down a probe that enters a seed and fertilises it. That's the story of what happens at the beginning of November in the Clare Valley, and if something affects the tiny white petals – if they're knocked or blown off by the northerly winds that blow in at that time, for example – the little berry doesn't develop. If all goes well, the berry enlarges into a grape as the pulp and juice develop inside the skin."'

We were fascinated by this information and the complexity of the inner workings of grapevines which, on the outside, looked to be such a simple process – you plant and water them, pick the grapes and then prune them for the next season. But no, you need to dig a lot deeper than this. So we did – or Heinrich's did with their machine, at sites we had marked over the entire 20 hectares eventually to be planted as vineyard.

These two-metre-square and two-metre-deep soil pits (into which we clambered with the instructions from the course) enabled us to read the soil's layers. First there was the surface layer of loam, clay, sand, or a varying mixture of each, then the hard pan, and beneath that perhaps gravel or stones, and the roots of previous plants, and so down to the bedrock. The thickness of each layer varied over the vineyard area, as did the soil's components. We were beginning to understand the term *terroir*. It is here that a wine's distinctiveness is born, in the soil and its characteristics and in its location – up hill or down valley bottom – as well as annual climate, seasonal variations, age of the vines, skills of the grower and, eventually, the skills and practices of the winemaker.

After one campus session, Jeni told the story of a field trip to the vineyard of an old bloke who had been working it for decades. He used Salvation Jane as a mid-row winter crop which, considering it had been declared a noxious weed, surprised the students. The lecturer had persuaded the grower to take part in a trial using triticale instead of Salvation Jane, which resulted in a much larger green mulch crop and consequent excellent supply of nitrogen. Given the favourable results, the owner, when asked if he would be sowing triticale in the future, answered no, he was used to sowing Salvation Jane, that's what he had always done and that's what he would go on doing.

Jeni's assignments scored reasonable marks and she was pleased to be awarded the graduation certificate.

Then AK suggested we enrol in the Property Planning and Management course. This was a Commonwealth-funded course that aimed at bridging the gap in farming practices between parents, who had been following the same routines for decades, and their offspring with new knowledge and ideas drawn from their university agricultural studies in the latest farming practices and understanding the new technologies available in machines and computers. A requirement of the course was to have as many of the family attend as possible. We acknowledged this by taking the kelpies and leaving them in charge of the ute, contentedly sleeping on the seats awaiting our return. As it happened, many of the families were blow-ins with only a handful of Clare originals, including the Wentworths. Their vineyard was on the other side of the ridge from ours and they sold fruit to the same winery we did.

The economist who presented the financial section advised that it was the use of machinery, not its ownership, which produced the best return on investment. This fitted nicely with our thinking. We knew nothing about farm machinery, or any other machines for that matter, and had written into our business plan the use of contractors, their knowledge and their machines. This was a convenience that would cost a bit more, but it also ensured that our scarce capital was not tied up in equipment that would sit in the shed depreciating every day for most of the year, and cost a hell of a lot more.

Financial considerations included learning to manage succession planning, allowing parents or grandparents – or both – to let go gradually and involve those offspring interested in maintaining the business, and deal with others who would move to the cities but still wanted their cut – which of course was running on a large overdraft. Family succession included the pros and cons of establishing family trusts to protect the enterprise and to apportion proceeds to members.

~ * ~

You might say we overdosed on learning. Perhaps it was because we knew nothing about this field of endeavour in which we were investing so much. In addition to the TAFE courses and AK's monthly visits, we attended field days, workshops and many conferences, most of which were about how to administer a vineyard and a cellar door, marketing trends, new concepts for cellar doors and suitable new grape varieties.

A short and stocky bloke from London kept popping up to talk about market trends. He was the wine buyer for the English Tesco supermarket chain who bought millions of bottles of Australian wine each year.

'You Australian winemakers and grape growers are a lazy bunch of bastards,' he would say in familiar Australian vernacular, before telling us that of the 4000 *Vitis vinifera* varieties, Australians were using probably thirty to fifty.

'Just look at the hundreds of varieties grown in Italy, Spain and France, to say nothing of those from Greece, Eastern Europe and Russia,' he said. 'Get out of your rut and plant some alternatives.'

This got us thinking, because in the marketing sessions of the many courses we attended we were told it was mandatory to have a point of difference to set our business apart from our competitors. I started reading about different grape varieties and the climate, soil type and terrain in which they blossomed in Europe and compared these variables with the soils and conditions on The Hill. From this small study we settled on planting Pinot Gris and Viognier.

A later decision to plant Nebbiolo arose from a conversation with an Italian friend who owned a marvellous Italian bistro in Adelaide. I had lunched there fairly regularly when working in Adelaide, and when I told him I was developing a vineyard in the Clare Valley he urged me to consider making Italian wine styles such as Barolo and Barbaresco. These wines turned out to be named after two villages in the Piedmont, just north of Alba, but the grape variety used to make them was Nebbiolo. My research suggested that this grape would be suitable for propagation in Clare and we were the first to offer this wine in The Valley.

At this time, Italian–Australian agronomist Dr Ron Bonfiglioni was consulting to a large vine nursery at Euston, near Mildura, run by Bruce and Jenny Chalmers. He suggested the Chalmers run a conference focusing on the benefits of growing Sangiovese, the grape used in famous Tuscan wines such as Chianti. Chalmers is a mate of Stefano de Pieri, the Italian chef living and working in Mildura in Victoria's north. He declared if the conference was run he would cook a grand dinner and serve it in the Grand Ballroom in Mildura's Grand Hotel.

This initiative was so successful that the following year the concept was broadened to include all varieties considered alternatives to the traditional ones widely used by Australian winemakers. From this small beginning the Australian Alternative Varieties Wine Show evolved. It was so successful that it is now held annually in Mildura.

Eggplant, capsicum, tomato and gruyere pie (without pastry)

Ingredients for 6–8 servings

3 medium-size eggplants, sliced lengthwise, 0.5 cm thick

3 large red capsicums cut into 4, seeds and white removed

olive oil

10 eggs

40 g parmesan grated

400 g gruyere grated

350 g of basic Italian tomato sauce (passata)

Brush eggplant with olive oil and chargrill each side until golden and tender.

Chargrill peppers and remove skin.

Combine eggs with grated parmesan and gruyere, mix well.

Line the base of a 26-cm-base springform pan with baking paper.

Place alternate layers of eggplant and red pepper in a radial pattern in the bottom. Place more eggplant and pepper slices along side of pan allowing tops of slices to overhang pan rim.

Cover the bottom layer with a third of the tomato sauce then top with a third of the egg and cheese mixture. Repeat these layers twice more, finishing with a layer of eggplant and pepper. Fold in overhanging eggplant and pepper pieces to cover the top.

Bake at 180°C for about 50–60 minutes, or until set. Stand 30–40 minutes before removing from pan.

Serve warm as a light lunch.

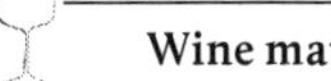

Wine match: Shiraz, Cabernet Sauvignon, Touriga

This was one reason – and an important one – we planted Viognier and not Riesling grapes, despite the Clare Valley's fame for this variety. But there were other reasons. When the Jesuits started their vineyard at Sevenhill they planted a grape called Crouchen, which they confusingly named 'Clare Riesling'. I've read that the Riesling wine in casks and flagons was made not from Riesling grapes, but from grapes of doubtful character that had been grown in widely differing regions of south-eastern Australia but the wine was still claimed to be 'Riesling'.

In the vineyards these grapes would have been pumped full of water to give a large yield but with little taste. A small percentage of genuine Riesling was added to the wine to give it flavour and to allow the use of the name 'Riesling' on the label. As a result, Riesling developed a reputation as a sweet and cheap white wine, and to some extent it begins to explain why AK recommended against our planting it. It would be a risk, he said, as the grapes would be hard to sell.

There were twenty-one cellar doors in the Clare Valley when we started, mainly selling Chardonnay, Shiraz and Cabernet Sauvignon to meet current demand. It was an obvious marketing strategy to choose to grow and promote varieties that would be original and innovative rather than to rely on a grape variety that produced a wine, which at that time, had a poor reputation.

It was the end of November and, a week ahead of schedule, the house builders arrived towing a very long caravan, which they parked near the ancient gum. There were three of them. The little bloke, Marty, held the builder's licence, his brother Jim did as he was told and Charlie, the big bloke, was labourer and cook.

The first thing they did was to fashion a fireplace from field stones. It consisted of a fire area and two other areas, one for warming and the other for resting food and pans. Completed within the hour this was most impressive and suggested they drew on camping experience.

Then they started on the ablution area. For the shower Charlie drove four very long droppers into the ground to support plastic builder's sheeting on three sides of a stone floor for the shower. The fourth side opened to the west looking over a vineyard at the bottom and rolling hills of grain just about ready for harvesting. A similar structure screened the portaloo. They were ready for business.

The top of The Hill, which we had dubbed our sticking place, was just about solid ironstone. This had resisted erosion for aeons and was contemptuous of Marty's efforts with the pneumatic drill, otherwise known as a jack hammer. The engineer's specifications called for a foundation block to be drilled into the rock to a depth of 20 centimetres for the sunken concrete slab. Little progress had been made at the end of the day despite constant attack with the drill.

What to do? To have the plan amended by council would take forever, but Marty didn't want to be responsible for non-compliance, Jeni didn't want to do the wrong thing and I didn't want the building to be held up.

'Will the house fall down for want of an in-ground slab?' I asked.

'Of course it bloody won't,' Marty said, 'it won't make any difference.'

'Then, get on with it.'

'Bloody, beauty!' Marty paused before making clear his position. 'Just remember, I'm acting on your instructions.'

As there was no travelling time required for the workers to get to the job, they started early each morning and finished at about nightfall, so the work progressed quickly. I observed, however, they were consuming a huge amount of beer each night.

'Well, they're working very hard and it's hot and besides they haven't got their ladies with them,' Jeni said. 'They need to relax somehow.'

'That's the problem. Three blokes living in confined quarters and lots of booze is bound to lead to trouble,' I said, little realising what a prescient remark it would be.

When it came to best canine dietary practice, Jeni was the last word. Previously she had bred standard poodles, helped along by her neighbour, a veterinarian, who set out his rules for her. For breakfast, he said, introduce the puppies to vegetables as early as you can, leaving some crunch and adding bran. He recommended raw meat and bones for the evening meal, but warned her she must never give the puppies cooked bones, especially cooked chicken bones. He said that he made lots of money extracting softened, cooked bones from puppies and older dogs when the bone turned at an awkward angle in the lower colon. But certainly feed them raw chicken bones, he said, to keep their coats shiny.

The kelpies had taken to *al dente* veggies with gusto and loved meaty bones in the evening. But a few days after the builders arrived, they went off their food. We thought they must have caught a leveret.

Jeni was talking to Marty about bathroom fittings and then drifted into chatter when I heard her decidedly irate voice. 'What do you mean, I don't feed my dogs?' she said. 'I'm very particular about their diet.'

'Yeah? You wouldn't think so,' Marty said. 'They come around every morning and evening to eat our leftovers. They love eggs and chops and spicy chicken wings. Charlie cooks a lot to make sure we don't go hungry and what's left over he gives to your dogs.'

'No wonder they're not eating my carefully prepared food. I feed them a balanced diet to keep their gums healthy and their coats shiny. You know it would be much better for your food budget if Charlie didn't cook such excessive amounts.'

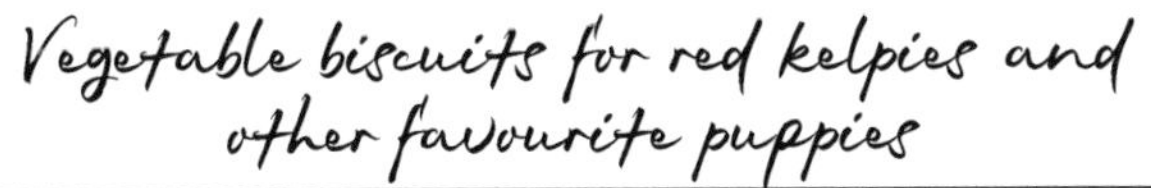

Ingredients for 4 servings

Finely chop up whatever fresh vegetables you have. Do not include garlic or onions. Add a few eggs and enough flour to form a dry dough.

Role the dough and form into individual sausage shapes.

Bake at 160°C until the biscuits are dry and crisp. Serve cold.

Biscuits for red kelpies and other favourites

Ingredients for 2 servings

25 g wheat bran
750 g wheat flour
750 g oat bran
12 g meat fat/lard
250 g milk powder
125 mL rainwater

Thoroughly mix all of the ingredients into a stiff dough. Put in the fridge for an hour. Roll out into a thick layer. Cut pieces and shape like a sausage. Place these onto a baking tray. Bake at 160°C for about 1 hour until dry and crisp. Allow to cool before serving.

Wine match: rainwater, before it has been turned into wine

'Jeni, those dogs are scavengers.'

'They are red kelpies, Marty, working dogs, not street mongrels. They have a lot of dignity and I won't let them lose that by becoming table beggars and scavengers. You never know what they'll pick up.'

The penny finally dropped with Marty. 'Sorry, Jeni, it won't happen again.'

Mollified, Jeni said, 'You know, Marty, we have friends up here who run sheep and only feed their working dogs every three or four days. They reckon they don't need more than that.'

~ * ~

We wandered up The Hill from the shed to see progress on the house. The frame was up, the roof stays in place and the large windows had been fitted. Marty was up a ladder with his head in the roof area studying the plan he held in front of him. I heard an unusual sound coming from the vineyard and looking down saw this large, noisy, twisting circle of wind and soil and leaves hurrying up towards us.

'Hang on to your hats,' I yelled.

Marty wasn't quick enough. As he grabbed for his, the wind whipped the large house plan from his hands shooting it up in the air. We watched as it was taken higher, higher still, ever higher until it was lost to sight.

'I wonder where that will come down,' said Jeni.

'Dunno, but I'm coming down from here before I'm blown down – and I'll need another copy of the plan.'

~ * ~

We were not the only residents on The Hill. The small menagerie included a kangaroo family which had taken up residence with the joey still in pouch. Other kangaroos visited from time to time. As they grazed they murmured to each other and as we approached they would prick up their ears and, interested, look at us. If we came too close they would gently turn and awkwardly, slowly and silently move away.

One Sunday morning we had decided to take the day off to go for an early walk around the vineyard and talk about where to go for lunch. The kelpies were busy running and jumping about when we happened upon two roos busily engaged in reproducing. The large male clutched his partner firmly around her chest and backed her onto his feet. This seemed to be acceptable to the female who showed no signs of struggling to free herself, just a few wiggles seemingly to make herself comfortable.

‘You know, Burtie, ’roos mate for life,’ Jeni said.

‘Yeah, and so do galahs and penguins, even stumpies – stumpy-tailed lizards.’

‘And do you also know that porpoises and anthropoid apes – no other animals – have sex just for the fun of it?’

‘I wonder if they stray as often as homo sapiens do?’

~ * ~

As we moved into February and harvest time was approaching, our excitement was growing. The bunches of grapes, spread lightly through the vines, looked promising as we wandered along the rows, observing that the whites were further advanced than the reds and wondering how many tonnes the yield would be, even speculating about our likely income.

‘I think you should drop it,’ AK said when next he visited us. ‘Drop the whole crop. It’s best to put the energy into developing the vine. The first fruit isn’t much good for making wine anyway.’

What a blow! After spending all year nurturing the vines with the promise of a crop, and dreaming of the first taste of wine made from our very own grapes, we now had to walk past every vine and cut off the grapes. We hated doing it, but we consoled ourselves that once this job was done the season would be finished for us. We could take time to try out some of the local eateries and maybe spend a few days in Aldinga walking the kelpies on the beach.

~ * ~

We decided on lunch in Mintaro. The most direct route would take us down The Hill, past the racecourse and through the Clare township. Cruising down the main street, we came to Knappstein’s Wines where we dropped in to taste their hand-picked Rieslings.

There were five all up – 'Ackland's Vineyard', 'Insider' and three others from different vintages. Although they were all made from the same grape variety, and had that characteristic Clare Valley crisp acidity, each was subtly different.

Back on the road, we headed out of Clare but deviated on the southern edge of the town to visit Tim Adams Wines. The first thing to greet you at Tim Adam's cellar door is a large, curly-haired hound with an effusive welcome, and then you realise the winery is immediately adjacent to the Riesling Trail, the old railway corridor now used as a walking and cycling track. The wines are impressive especially the Cab with its luscious fruit, ripe tannins and earthy overtones.

Tim grew up in Clare, left school early to work with Mr Mick Knappstein, then at the Stanley Wine Co., as his last apprentice. Many years later Tim Adams Wines bought the Leasingham Winery and vineyards and turned its cellar door into a bistro named Mr Mick, which specialises in a tapas-style lunch menu.

A kilometre or so past the Tim Adams turnoff we stopped to consider the choice: either follow the highly visible and abundant signposts and turn east to Mintaro, or continue on to the next little township of Sevenhill, with its venerable pub at the crossroads.

Sevenhill, the birthplace of the Society of Jesus in Australia, is named for Rome's famous seven hills. In 1848 – the 'year of revolutions' in Europe – two Jesuit priests accompanied Silesian émigrés to settle in the area. The first vines were planted in 1852 with cuttings from the Hawkers at Bungaree Station. The winery – the only winery in the world run by the Jesuit order – was developed to supply sacramental altar wine. Subsequently the priests built the seminary and the splendid St Aloysius Church, a celebrated example of Gothic revival architecture, with floors of Mintaro slate.

Faced with the choice of Sevenhill or Mintaro, we opted for the slate village. The road to Mintaro took us into one of the great wine-growing districts in the country. Discovered in 1839 by Edward John Eyre and named Hill River after fellow explorer John Hill, the district was first settled by Irish Catholics; the Silesians followed. The area came to be known as Polish Hill River. Pikes Wines, Paulett Wines, and the Wilson Vineyard are located here. Grosset Wines sources grapes for its Polish Hill Riesling from its nearby vineyard.

But with lunch firmly in mind, we passed them by and followed the road winding on to Mintaro. This settlement began life as a watering hole for bullocks hauling copper from Burra to the coast at Port Wakefield. Slabs from its slate mine are cut for billiard and pool tables – and church floors.

Mintaro is justly known as an historic township, its unspoiled handsome freestone buildings and triangle of leafy streets that nestle comfortably into the landscape. We arrived in Mintaro in the ute, with the kelpies on chains in the back letting us know that they were as pleased as we were to be off on an adventure.

In this delightful setting, Fran Gerard had established Mintaro Mews in an old freestone commercial building with a clutch of outhouses. The main building housed the restaurant and the outhouses had been refurbished as bed and breakfast units. Fran's generous figure and wide welcoming smile and the aromas coming from her kitchen let us know we were in the hands of a dedicated food lover. Having shown us to a table she said, 'I serve a set menu. Just leave it to me.'

A Mintaro Wines Riesling then, with its up-front citrus fruit characters so typical of the region, would be a good match for whatever was put in front of us. The waitress first served plates

Stuffed mushrooms Italian style

Ingredients for 2 servings

4 large flat field mushrooms, stems removed and chopped into small pieces
8 black olives, pitted and chopped
1 Roma tomato, seeds removed and chopped
2 spring onions chopped
1 rasher of bacon, rind removed, rasher chopped
4 heaped tbs fresh bread crumbs
2 tbs grated parmesan cheese
1 tbs chopped parsley
1 egg, beaten
freshly grated nutmeg
1 tbs dried tarragon
goodly sprinkle vinegar
cracked black pepper
4 ciabatta slices
olive oil

Heat oven to 190°C. Place the mushrooms downside up on an oiled oven tray.
Place all other ingredients (except the ciabatta) in a bowl and combine thoroughly. Divide into 4 portions and place firmly on top of mushrooms.
Cook for 12–15 minutes.
Brush the ciabatta with olive oil and grill or chasseur.
Place the ciabatta on a warm serving plate and top with mushrooms.

Wine match: Vermentino, Rosé, Malbec, dry Riesling

of large field mushrooms. What a taste sensation – the robust mushroom flavours beautifully balanced by the more delicate stuffing, and the whole dish matching the wine perfectly.

Sitting in the courtyard we watched as small parrots flew into the almond tree overhead. Duck featured as the main course, so we ordered a Stephen John Pinot Noir from Watervale.

'Is Stephen John the bloke who converted the old stables to a cellar door in Watervale, Burtie?' Jeni asked, as she contemplated her glass of red-purple wine.

'He moved from the Barossa to manage the Quelltaler winery at about the time we bought our land, and he and his wife later set up their own show with the charming stone cellar door.'

The duck breasts, served warm and thinly sliced, were set in a circle on the large plate with a generous sized fig which had been simmered in pomegranate juice as centre piece. This was served with a witloof, pear and walnut salad.

'This lighter style Pinot matches the intense duck flavours brilliantly,' Jeni said enthusiastically.

'It's interesting,' I said 'because I've read that Stephen regards it as a Gen XY wine, one that most of the older drinkers don't choose preferring those big-bodied, old-fashioned Australian reds.'

In the branches above us the parrots were loud in their praise of the almonds they were feasting on. The cracked outer shells gently dropped down around us, but flushed with bonhomie we chatted on over the last of the wine.

~ * ~

After the disappointment of dropping our first small crop, it was time to begin discussions about a contract for the sale of our fruit. In September, we talked to representatives from a number of the larger wine companies who were all eager to sign us up. Wine grapes – any quantity, any quality – were in great demand. Australian wines were knocking the socks off French, Algerian and Spanish wines in English supermarkets because the quality was superior at comparative prices.

But, in my view, the four largest Australian wine companies did not see small growers as equal partners. The list of demands in their contracts was long and one-sided, such as having to get their permission if we wanted to sell our vineyard. Where was the *quid pro quo*, I asked, and what about an equal partnership? The reps smiled indulgently, even smugly. One company agreed to what appeared to me to be important amendments, but the paperwork really had only one purpose, that of keeping the grower in line. When the downturn came, many large wineries in Australia broke the contracts leaving the small growers stranded, knowing their financial strength would result in a win in any legal stoush.

~ * ~

Construction of the house was progressing well and the crew had taken off only two days over Christmas. A few weeks before the planned completion date in early February, Marty reported that someone had disabled his electric saw and drill by pouring glue into the motors. He wouldn't mention the culprit, but Charlie was no longer present. So the bust-up had come, but it didn't amount to much as the tools were replaced and the job was finished just a few weeks later, which Jeni and I thought truly remarkable. Marty was extremely proud of the result, taking video clips for future promotions of his fledgling business. This was the first time he had built an entire house from start to finish.

The immediate task was to move the furniture from the shed,

a few hundred metres up The Hill to the house. I baulked at being involved in the lifting, pointing out that our small ute would mean many trips with no help for me to lift heavy items. What I really wanted to avoid was Jeni's method of deciding on the final resting place for each piece of furniture. I knew she would want to see each piece in every possible position and combination before deciding and the work-out would leave my back rooted.

Jeni reminded me that we went to the chiropractor each week to deal with the vicissitudes of vineyard work, so what was the problem? 'No, let's use the local removalists,' I insisted.

There were no local removalists. Right, let's ask the local furniture shop to send their men and vehicle. No worries, they agreed.

The poor bloody driver of the cumbersome furniture van wondered why he had copped the rough end of the pineapple as he tried to ease the top-heavy vehicle down the steep incline and turn it around at the shed. But the blokes knew exactly what was required to load everything in and then out again at the house. They also knew what Jeni wanted and after only a few adjustments it was all over – except for cold refreshing beers all around.

The logical position for the glass table had not won the day and it was placed at Jeni's insistence away from the kitchen. After a couple of years of living with this arrangement, however, Jeni was adamant that *we'd* got it wrong and wanted the whole area re-arranged. This meant that all the furniture and the table had to be moved – as did the Coonara and its flue, which extended right through the ceiling and roof.

The six men we coerced into helping to move the giant table top were quietened only with large quantities of Cooper's Pale Ale and then Jeni set about preparing a grand lunch to appease everyone. She decided on a BBQ but with a Mediterranean influence – to cook the food in the coals of our Italian-inspired wood-fired oven. The oven takes a fair amount of wood and time to get to the desired temperature, so we had fired it up a few hours before the weightlifters arrived to manhandle the glass top and four pillars of the table. Given previous experience this lift went very smoothly. As they relaxed with Coopers in hand the men got in the way as I swabbed the middle of the oven floor with a wet mop to have clean firebricks on which to put the food.

For entrée, Jeni impaled baby octopus on long metal skewers and chargrilled them by the side of the coals for a few minutes.

Chargrilled baby octopus

Ingredients for 6 servings as entrée

24 baby octopus
1 lemon for zest and juice
1 red onion sliced
2 garlic cloves chopped
4 sprigs thyme
4 sage leaves chopped
½ fennel bulb sliced into lengths
olive oil

Marinate the octopus in the onion, garlic, lemon juice, thyme, sage and oil for 1 hour.
Grill on the BBQ plate for about 3–4 minutes until change of colour.
Turnover once or twice to stop from sticking.
Place the fennel strips on the serving plate, put the octopus ingredients on top and dress with the zest.

Wine match: Pinot Gris, Riesling, Viognier, Chardonnay

'Out of the way, you lot, I'm bringing out some red-hot skewers,' Jeni announced.

She removed the octopus and set them out on beds of lettuce with lemon wedges and a good sprinkling of extra virgin olive oil. I served a chilled retsina to accompany them, which resulted in vociferous protest from Drew, but he was shouted down by the others who enjoyed its piny flavour and acid and loved the way it went so well with the octopus.

Next was a leg of hogget. To enhance the generous flavour of this meat Jeni cut small pockets into the flesh where she could insert cloves of garlic or rosemary, dribbled a heavy olive oil over it all and rubbed oregano and sea salt into the oily flesh. She put this in a roasting dish and lined it up next to the coals for an hour-and-a-half, turning the meat at half-hourly intervals to achieve a uniform crispness. In the last forty-five minutes, she peeled and cored quince quarters, which she added along with some unpeeled baby potatoes and onions. I served an old Cabernet Sauvignon to complement the dish.

The robust flavours of the hogget were pronounced a great success compared with the more delicate flavours of lamb. We adjourned once more outside to the oven with our reds to watch Jeni as she presided over the cooking of pudding. This was a galatoboureko, a Greek luscious creamy custard pie with a filling made from semolina, lemon zest, cinnamon and eggs and baked in a base of oiled sheets of filo pastry. Although the oven temperature was by now considerably lower, Jeni watched diligently over her pie so as not to burn the pastry. She finished the dish by pouring a lemon and cinnamon syrup over it, and I chose a late-picked Riesling to accompany it.

The lunch went on and on with much banter and noise. We started at 12.30 and finally staggered away from the table with glassy eyes at 5.30, all vowing never to help lift the table again.

~ * ~

The line of the eastern ridge emerged in the slowly intensifying dawn light. The floor-to-ceiling windows in the bedroom were without blinds and curtains so as not to impede the wonderful view. From my pillow I could see Venus, the morning star, its winking light seeming to invite me to come to grips with the new day. So I did – out to the kitchen to boil the kettle for the pot of jasmine and lotus root tea and then back to bed with the tray.

At times we would watch a fox slink across the slope giving the kelpies a wonderful excuse to bark their territorial ownership, or a pair of wedgetailed eagles slowly circle into view, hovering, watching. Rural sounds are natural, simple – birds calling, the wind sighing, the showy wagtail that visited each morning making demanding calls to its mate. The early mornings are our favourite time of day.

I remembered the bloke in the pub who told us not to build on the hilltop and wondered if he had ever watched in the first light of dawn as the sun etched the eastern ridgeline and climbed high into the flawless, infinite blue. The bright, glowing splendour of this spectacle had taught Jeni and me to avoid hangovers as these dulled the transcendence of those first awakening hours.

Mornings were planning time when, over our mugs of tea, we would talk through the jobs to be done and agree on the day's schedule. We had come to know that it was better to make small decisions daily than to let things drift and build – to break the bigger problems into their many small parts and deal with each in order so that we could correct any faulty decision before it escalated into a mini crisis.

At the end of each day we liked to know we had achieved something, not world-shattering, just a job that helped to clear the backlog which we could point to and celebrate at drinks' debriefing time. At night, as I went to sleep, I would assemble a mental 'to do' agenda, on the theory that my mind would conjure with its contents as I slept coming up with the agenda to tackle next day.

Jeni isn't really a morning person, so my outbursts first thing about plans for the day didn't always go down well. Jeni would rather come to wakefulness gently and then say good morning to the kelpies whose eagerness she finds much more acceptable. Leave room for serendipity, she would counsel. Gradually I came to adjust my ebullience and to wait for Jeni to ask about the day's agenda and what we might have for lunch and dinner.

~ * ~

Unlike the young blokes on our contractor's team, Jeni and I are not experienced farm machine operators, and I'm not really sorry about that. We had watched them in winter trying to maintain control of their machines on the sodden and slippery rows. They have to steer a tractor with extreme precision so that the pruning knives, for instance, were maintained at just the right level to cut the rods two to three buds above the top of the vines, while wrestling with the vehicle to stop it from sliding sideways. On a wet surface all this takes great skill, experience and considerable courage, and I'm happy to leave it to the blokes for whom it's all in a day's work.

If anything, it's still more heroic at harvest time in the autumn cool nights and very early mornings to be perched in the dark, a storey high on a harvester, traversing our hillside blocks. Even on a level surface the look of these machines doesn't inspire you with much confidence. One of the blocks runs along a spur, the eastern side of which forms a natural drainage dip and at the southern end, falls away steeply. The harvester straddles a row of vines and moves from side to side as it trundles along. The driver must then turn at the end of the row on this alarming slope and line up the turn into the next row without smashing into a strainer or letting the whole swaying machine tip over. To make a turning at the end of the rows easier, the driver executes a four-row circuit starting down row 1, then over to row 4, then back to row 2, and then 5, and so on.

While all that is going on, a tractor towing a bin that can hold 2.5 tonnes of grapes is two parallel rows away keeping exactly the same speed as the harvester so as to receive the grapes from an arm stretching across the rows. It seems a precarious arrangement and from time to time things do go wrong. The threshing rods of the harvester may tangle with and break wires. Sliding and slipping machines can snap off posts and vines, and sometimes the fish-tailing conveyor belt of the harvester collecting the falling grapes snags on the irrigation polypipe ripping out metres of it.

I'm more wary than Jeni when driving the old tractor we acquired from a neighbour. She became so frustrated about my slow pace that she decided to become the sole tractor driver. One day in November this country girl was clipping along a short row with the tractor towing a slasher and needing to turn adroitly at the end of it. I heard a scream and looked up to see her dashing out of the row and heading for the two-metre-high drainage bank. As she had tried to change gears, her foot slipped from the brake and caught in the accelerator pedal which increased the speed of the tractor so that it then easily climbed the drainage bank and came abruptly to a stop with its four wheels spinning in the air.

'What the fuck are you trying to do?' I yelled, running to help her.

'I didn't try to do it,' said a small, shaky voice, 'it just happened.'

I rushed over to help her gently extract herself from all the pedals and levers, which wasn't easy, and gave her an extended hug to help calm her.

What do you do with a tractor towing a slasher stranded on a drainage bank? We were disinclined to do anything, so I rang Mike, a man who had been riding tractors for the past forty years. But even Mike was momentarily flummoxed. With utmost caution he unhitched the slasher, then started the engine and gingerly waggled the machine until he got one wheel on the ground and then manœuvred it into a more manageable position. Sure enough, country blokes are naturals when it comes to taming machines.

~ * ~

Seasons repeat themselves in a continuous cycle, but only in broad outline. One summer is never exactly the same as another, no two seasons are the same. For all that, there is some order to them, even chaos theory acknowledges some order. They repeat themselves in ways that are marginally, sometimes radically, different, and to their characteristically routine manifestations they add the unpredictable and the unknowable. Farmers understand this intuitively, having learnt to live with the temperamental patterns, hoping this year's welcome bumper crop following last year's failure will keep the bank manager happy.

Cycles of nature allow for a fallow time for plants and animals and insects to hibernate after a burst of propagation. Only the surviving gums remember the itinerant travellers, the original inhabitants from long ago, following seasonal food sources. As they gently made their way, fossicking for honey ants, bees' nests, yabbies, lizards, snakes, and maybe a roo or two, they observed long-established rituals to ensure that seasonal food sources would endure.

The mysteries of our relationship with the natural world are not explained solely by a close association with the land along with its soil, the vines and the micro-environment of the block, but it helps because a vineyard certainly is a living organism pulsating to the rhythm of the vines as they respond to their physical environment. It's wondrous to see a block of hundreds of vines of the same variety all arriving at the same physiological point, as they do at budburst, all within a few days at the beginning of spring. I've read that the menstrual cycles of women sharing a dormitory become synchronised after a couple of months. What is the force at work here, the synchronising factor?

In the vineyard, as across all agricultural activities, is the always reliable, inscrutable but entirely indispensable rotation of the seasons. According to the season you prune or reap or plant or mow or patiently observe. If you don't get it right this time you have to wait until next year to have another crack at it, learning and building on your experience. No matter how you feel emotionally about the great movements of the natural world – its colours and drama, beauty and terror, its beneficence and its withholding – in the end you're stuck with its rhythms and realities. Rain or no rain, wind, humidity – you can enjoy or curse them, but at all times you have to bear with them so relax and do what can be done, but take care not to boast of good fortune, which can just as easily be lost in the next weather event.

We were developing a fairly sound understanding of the rhythm of the vines and the ensuing work to be done. I had written notes from AK's instructions and extracted items from the course work we had undertaken to draw up a twelve-month vineyard work schedule. The vines tell us when it's time to hand-prune the eight hectares. When the canes of the canopy have lost all leaves and hardened to rods, the vines will senesce – hibernate until September. The barrel pruner will arrive in June to remove the bulk of last season's canopy and we follow with a hand clean-up, cutting each rod to two buds to give an overall yield from the 1667 vines in a hectare of about eight to ten tonnes. The two of us had to keep at the pruning, day in, day out, seven days a week, no matter what the weather, to ensure we had it finished before budburst in early September.

Preferably we wanted to finish these jobs by the end of August, because August is what we call 'get ready' month; get ready for spring. Just as ants know when to get ready for a rain event by building up the breathing vents of their huge underground networks before the rain begins, so the vines know when to prepare for spring. Our readiness for spring is established by walking the length of each row to locate broken posts and wires snapped by barrel pruners or errant tractors or both.

Little green books are used to record these breakages by row number and later a list is typed to hand to the work crew to make it easy for them to locate and repair them. Broken posts will be removed and a new one thumped in and the wires stapled back into place. As we walk the rows, we also note any polypipe that needs repairing. When these repairs are completed, the filters are cleaned and pump seals renewed if necessary and then the whole irrigation system is tested to find any more leaks and to ensure the pumps and solenoids are operating correctly.

The midrow crop is slashed and later sprayed to remove regrowth and to ensure there is no vegetation high enough to impede air flow through the rows during September's frosty nights when only half a degree Celsius is the difference between no frost damage and facing a frost wipeout. All this work needs to be completed before the end of August to clear traffic from the rows before the vines start to burst in early September. We don't want the delicate emerging buds accidentally knocked off by heavy traffic.

~ * ~

At last, with the August work done, it's time for some relaxation. We started our welcome break by going to a wedding. Jeni's nephew who, in his early twenties, contemplated entering the priesthood, had met a beautiful Greek-Australian girl. Aphrodite triumphed; instead of entering the priesthood, he and his beloved entered into holy matrimony.

At the wedding reception, held in the function room at the Grand Hotel, Glenelg, and looking out over a placid spring sea, we found ourselves talking to two of her brothers. They knew we owned a vineyard and wanted to know if there were any rabbits, hares or foxes on our property. Their eyes lit up with delight when we said we had any number of them, not to mention the occasional visit from wild deer. They politely asked us for permission to camp in the vineyard in October for a couple of nights so they could hunt our feral visitors.

They took their role very seriously, arriving dressed in faux army camouflage fatigues, set up an impressive tent and unloaded a couple of rifles and much ammunition. The first night they asked us to go spotlighting with them. Jeni, the kelpies and I were in the ute cabin, while they stood in the back, rifles at the ready. I drove slowly down and around and into the vine rows where we surprised a few hares. Their shots were erratic because they said I was driving too fast, causing the ute to bump around. I slowed to a crawl, but hares are experts at avoidance and zigzagged off at great speed.

The next night they decided to walk and use their torches to surprise their prey and next morning presented us with a pair of skinned and dressed hares, keeping a few rabbits for themselves, and gave us all the details of their grandmother's recipe.

Greek-style hare ragout

Ingredients for 6 servings

1 hare, skinned and dressed
water and vinegar

Marinade

red wine
celery stick
carrot
cloves
crushed juniper berries
peppercorns
olive oil
1 large onion, chopped
2 cloves of garlic
thyme, oregano, parsley

To cook the hare

2 tbs tomato paste
1 can crushed tomatoes

3 large mushrooms, sliced

1 tbs honey

the hare's blood if you've caught it wild

1 lt strong beef stock

250 mL Port

thyme, sage, parsley or celery leaves

powdered sumac and coriander

salt and pepper

Soak the dressed hare in rainwater and vinegar overnight.

Discard the liquid and place the hare in the marinade for two days.

Discard the water – use the vegies to make stock.

Disjoint the hare and brown the pieces in oil in a large casserole dish. Remove.

Gently fry the onions, garlic, herbs and spices for a few minutes then stir in tomatoes, tomato paste and mushrooms. Stir the honey into the blood if available, otherwise add the beef stock and Port, stir in the honey for thickening and put the meat pieces in.

Put the lid on the pot and gently simmer for 2 hours or until the meat is tender but be careful not to dry the meat by overcooking. Stir occasionally and keep your eye on the level of the liquid. If it is too thin add a little more honey.

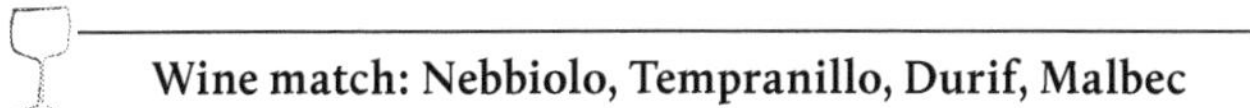

Wine match: Nebbiolo, Tempranillo, Durif, Malbec

Following the instructions assiduously the result was an amazingly rich sauce with tender meat, the flavour of which leaves beef and mutton for dead. You can use the same recipe for wild goat, they said, but best to use kid which is bound to be tender.

We really do get wild deer on The Hill, now and then, but at no particular or predictable time of year. One morning in November as I was having a shower, something caught my eye through the large bathroom windows. Six or eight deer were under the trees eating the grass. I called Jeni and she went dashing outside to tell them to move on. Another time we were in the bottom block and Jeni asked me to identify the animals further up the slope. Four deer were in the vine rows eating the young green shoots, having denuded the foliage over a goodly length of the rows. We rushed up the slope to shoo them away and watched as they nimbly dashed away in a delightful arc, jumping the fence into the neighbour's paddock as effortlessly as any bounding kangaroo.

So ended the year – with marauding deer repelled, our new house presiding splendidly above the rolling landscape and our learning curves as steep as The Hill itself.

6

September is the month of budburst during which we record the changes in the vines of each grape variety. Over winter the buds sit on the pruned spur as tiny hard bumps. At the end of August and early September the bumps begin to enlarge and start to open as a woolly bud that develops to a pink tip as it opens to reveal pastel-green leaves. This takes place over a couple of weeks and I marvel at this synchronised activity. It's extraordinary.

We go searching to observe these events and to record the dates when the buds are at the four-leaf stage. This is also the time to check signs of early mildew. Mildew spores spend winter in the bark and limbs of the vines. Should the weather become humid, the spores will burst into a new life cycle. Detected early enough, however, this metamorphosis is easily dealt with using a sulphur and copper spray, both of which are naturally occurring elements. The sulphur treats powdery mildew and the copper treats downy mildew. The latter is always present in the soil requiring only the right conditions – at least 10 millimetres of rain and a temperature of 10° Celsius over a 24-hour period – to burst into a new cycle. Raindrops falling on the soil will splash the downy mildew on to the vine's leaves. Because our hillside position is so exposed, however, humid air in the vines' canopies is dispersed by winds and breezes so there is little pressure from mildews.

This is also the time to keep an eye on water requirements.

After a wet winter the groundwater will have reached saturation level. This will carry the vines through to October but can lull one's thinking about the need for irrigation. Winter and early spring can be dry, and the month can get away from you, given all the other jobs that require attention. So we get out the dig stick, a metal rod with a runnel up one side, and bang it into the soil to half a metre or more, to estimate moisture content and the need or not for an irrigation event.

Weeds require attention at this time. Wild artichoke and scotch thistle seeds blow in from neighbouring paddocks and are best attended to immediately before they develop deep taproots, which can re-shoot no matter how many times they are cut back. Another troublesome invader is the paddy melon. These small, inoffensive-looking melons set down hundreds of seeds that quickly mature and produce their own crop of new baby melons, which can carpet an entire paddock with disastrous consequences. Then there is caltrop, commonly known as three-cornered jack, which is a bastard to eliminate.

We walk the property looking obsessively for these intruders. When we find them we drop to hands and knees to pick up every melon and every last seed that may have escaped from a broken melon and put them in plastic bags for disposal in the rubbish bin. The same with caltrop, digging out the plant and then using sponges in an effort to pick up all of the three-cornered seeds. This all sounds rather obsessive but so far we have kept the paddy melon and caltrop that inhabit a small patch near the Nebbiolo under control.

The weather at this time of the year can also pose challenges – frosts, especially the deadly black frost; rain so heavy and in such bucketing volumes that machines can't work the blocks; even early bushfires. Nature, with which you seek to work in harmony, always remains beyond your control. All you can do is be as prepared as possible for the unpredictable.

~ * ~

No wonder many painters have come to South Australia over the years. The light is translucent, the sky, so often a flawless arch of blue, is huge and all encompassing, seemingly infinite until it meets the horizon in a glowing straight line. As it so happens, there is no sun on this particular day. Instead, ominous, dark clouds move in from the northwest and, as I watch from our hilltop, another large front is building from the northeast.

It is a rare event to have two rain cells from opposite directions converge. The first had travelled all the way from Broome. The second had come down the east coast from Cairns flooding the coastal areas all the way to Victoria and then veering west into South Australia. In the next thirty-six hours these two intense systems dumped 63 millimetres of rain on The Hill, which bravely stood its ground under the onslaught.

The local Hutt River, which flows through the township, hidden behind buildings on the western side of Main North Road, usually looks more like a dry creek than a river, but today lives up to its grander title. Startling and destructive as some Mid North weather moods can be, it remains hard to imagine how tough life must have been for the early European settlers, one of whom – noting the searing summers, winter flooding, droughts, storms, hurricanes, soil erosion and fires – concluded that the place 'is more like Gehenna than paradise'.

In the hundred years to the 1980s, there were about a dozen serious floods in the Hutt River catchment. Flooding was controlled, more or less, by the flood mitigation scheme of 1984, which consisted of a number of dams developed to the south of the town to hold back water volume. We've seen only a couple of minor floods in the township but the collection of water to the south of the town means less of a supply to recharge the shattered rock aquifers to the north, including our Stanley Flat area. Interfere with nature and you never quite know the outcome.

Good rain years in South Australia in the middle of the nineteenth century led to farming settlements being pushed into northern parts of the state against the advice of Surveyor-General George Goyder, who recommended against agriculture north of his line of demarcation – Goyder's Line – mapped in 1865. In that year, however, and for a few years afterwards, good rains north of the line appeared to prove Goyder wrong; settlers built, farmed and established themselves in the northern saltbush country. When seasons reverted to their normal patterns, most of the settlers were ruined by drought and walked off their properties. The vestiges of their homesteads and abandoned townships can still be seen north of the line. Droughts are destructive in other ways. As the country dries out, whole paddocks can be blown away to become massive dust storms, several of which have reached Adelaide in past decades.

But good seasons also have their downside. Above-average rainfall produces grain for mice to feed on and then breed in their hundreds of millions. The massive 2010 mouse plague in South Australia wrought huge damage on crops and infrastructure. Some roads out west were so covered in dead, crushed mice that tyres wouldn't grip and mud flaps were thick with blood, skin and smashed bone.

As for locusts, ten plagues of biblical proportions and seven small ones have occurred in roughly the past hundred years. We've experienced two minor episodes on our property. Locusts swarm into South Australia from their Queensland and northwest New South Wales breeding grounds and head towards the sea as if on a mission of self-destruction. Those that land on your property are not the ones that will strip it of vegetation. Their task is to drill their egg cache into bare, hard soil; a week or two later the soil will start to heave as the eggs hatch out. These young will strip vegetation as they feed to gain the size and strength that enables them to move on to the next stage. As they begin to emerge from the ground they are easily dealt with if you are vigilant. Look for the moving soil, apply an insecticide and that's it.

Then there are bushfires. Details of many have been reported including the huge devastating ones of the mid-twentieth century. Some of these are caused by lightning strikes, which I assume caused our fire. There had been lightning activity for a couple of days leading up to the Sunday morning when, just before lunch, George Hill, our neighbour, burst through the door, highly agitated and loudly exclaiming there was a fire in our scrub.

Out the three of us dashed. George collected the wet sacks he had brought with him, Jeni filled a bucket with water and I collected a long-handled shovel. Jeni lost half of her water as we clambered through the wire fence to get to a patch of thick leaf matting under the gums, steadily burning downhill. Hilly started to beat at it, Jeni placed her water in a strategic spot and I tried to smother hot spots with shovelfuls of soil, but our efforts were ineffective.

Units from the Country Fire Service arrived, followed by utes driven by surrounding neighbours and equipped with fire-fighting gear, and then the squad car pulled up. One CFS unit took command directing the larger water units to move in from different sides. A mass of water was applied from the front and both sides of these vehicles and, as the larger units emptied out, the neighbours' utes were moved in. The fire front was not dramatic, amounting to just small flames, but it moved very quickly down the slope to stop just before reaching the irrigation polypipe, which surely would have melted. The whole event, which was over within an hour, was handled very professionally by the CFS and neighbour volunteers.

A week later Jeni spotted smoke coming from the same area. The thick leaf matting had blocked water getting to the dry material beneath allowing a hot spot to linger and re-ignite. The CFS unit again arrived quickly, and solved the problem – this time for good.

Certainly we were lucky, but luck really was on the side of our mate Mike McIntyre at his vineyard in nearby Penwortham on a blindingly hot day, a couple of weeks after our fire. The searing heat had everyone on the *qui vive*. The radio advised extreme fire danger. One spark and the entire area would go up. The fatal spark duly came – from an electric pump in the shed of a nearby winery. The fire exploded and raced up a steep hill fanned by a stiff southwesterly. It ripped over the ridge top and started down the other side towards Mike's boundary fence.

Local units were soon engaged, dozens of others kept arriving from distant towns, a helicopter took up a supervising role and crop dusters and a huge tanker helicopter provided a regular water bombing pattern, dumping their loads in precise positions. The blaze was stopped at Mike's fence just a few metres from his vines. New units of volunteers replaced exhausted ones over the next few days as ground crews continued to hose down hot spots. This vigilance went on for a couple of weeks, everyone fearful of another Ash Wednesday catastrophe.

It goes without saying that if the Clare Valley is a paradise, the CFS volunteer firefighters are its angels. We thanked everyone sincerely. I took the CFS leader aside to offer a dozen wines from our cellar for their coming Christmas party in a couple of weeks and another dozen to raffle as a fundraiser. The next time we drove past we left a dozen at Hill's house. It was his wife who had rung the CFS and police.

~ * ~

One day we had a visit from a different kind of fighting force – the Australian Army. Two officers arrived to propose the possibility of the army using The Hill as an observation post in war games to train troops and test strategic thinking. The Hill and another post on the ridge across the valley were the theoretical locations for artillery batteries to command activity on the plains to the north. These were designated 'the killing fields' across which an enemy force that had landed on the west coast was making rapid overland progress for its assault on Adelaide. This was the location for the last do or die stand. The only activity we saw, however, was the arrival of a staff car and several officers who spent the day on The Hill looking through binoculars and sending messages via their field radio.

This episode reminded me of the curious experience of a friend who told me of an occasion when, running sheep on a property up north, he was startled one morning to be accosted by two soldiers pointing rifles and telling him he was captured and would be taken to headquarters for interrogation.

Always ready for a challenge my friend responded aggressively, telling the two blokes not to be so bloody stupid and to get the fuck off his fucking property.

~ * ~

Jeni's sister offered us a midweek stay in her family shack in the Aldinga scrub. Delighted to have the opportunity for a break, we piled into the Brumbie ute, the kelpies in the space behind the seats. The puppies loved being inside on a long trip and anyway the back was loaded with our gear under the tonneau.

We were down to the beach very early the next morning for a five-kilometre walk. As we strode along the golden sands, the kelpies raced ahead, dashed back and around. Seagulls were swooping, swerving, screeching in the cool wind blowing in from the south and fighting the sun for temperature control. The Willunga Hills, noble in mien and wrapped in silence, rose stolidly in the distance awaiting their resolution. Along with every living thing they will be worn down and humbled, although this will take longer for them than for us.

We couldn't get enough of the kelpies, amazed at their loving, loyal ways, their energy and intelligence. And even though they were indulged we respected their integrity as *Canis familiaris* – never any tinned food to make their breath stink, no chocolate to rot their gums.

Janette, the larger, was a fighter. She would take an opponent full on. Jackie would wait behind to attack the opponent's unsuspecting hind leg. Left to herself she would have played a friendly game. I was fascinated by their behavioural traits and their very different personalities. When we saw other dogs approaching, we would call the kelpies to us and put on their leashes to ensure that Janette didn't race to them and challenge.

We sat in the water with them to introduce them to wavelets and salt water, but they weren't at all sure about either. They understood dam water, which was still and pleasantly muddy, not salty and rushing at them like this water, but they did like the wetness and coolness of it.

The beach was another matter. They loved the riot of smells, the stench of rotting organisms awakening deeply buried ancestral memories, masking their own smells by rolling neck and shoulders into decaying flotsam on the beach. And then there were the gulls – what great fun! Off their leashes, they would dash to the birds, race back, circle us and streak away again on another tack. When at last I coaxed them into deeper water to wash off the offensive odours and bits and pieces of rot, they protested loudly.

We walked the beach before breakfast and in the evenings at five we would be back for a swim and to have our cocktails on the sand. Moved by the beauty of the light, the rhythmic surge of water and the broad sweep of the sky, Jeni told me that the famous beach scene between Burt Lancaster and Deborah Kerr in *From Here to Eternity* had long been one of her fantasies. Very early next morning, long before anyone was around, we conjured up our own Halona Cove, Oahu, in the benign shallows of the Gulf.

We had read about an old kiosk in the dunes resurrected by a couple of young recent graduates of the Regency Park food and hospitality course. Rumour had it that they were doing interesting things with seafood, which is exactly what you want by the sea – and that's what we wanted for lunch.

We drove down a network of small roads looking for the kiosk and, eventually, there it was, hidden in the dunes close to the water. It was a small brick building that in earlier days had sold ice-creams and sweets but which had been empty for many years.

The young waitress, clad in crisp white, greeted us with a great smile, handing us the menu and wine list. Jeni immediately selected the bouillabaisse, which arrived steaming and chock full of prawns, green-lipped mussels, big pieces of white fish and a couple of crab claws in a wine-based broth. She pronounced it to be rich and indulgent – truly excellent.

I ordered the Italian seafood risotto. This was made in the Venetian style, with an almost soupy consistency, requiring fork and spoon. Biting into the chewy seafood pieces released their individual tastes, which perfectly matched the concentrated flavours absorbed by the creamy plump carnaroli rice.

Seafood risotto

Ingredients for 4 to 6 servings

250 g fresh prawns
200 g cleaned calamari rings
1 bay leaf, chopped
2 garlic cloves, peeled and chopped
salt
3 tbs olive oil
75 g butter, softened
1 onion, peeled and chopped
400 g carnaroli rice
3–4 tbs white wine
½ cup cooked green peas
freshly ground black pepper

Wash the prawns and put them in a pan with the calamari and water, bay leaf, garlic and pinch of salt. Bring to the boil and cook for 5 minutes. Remove seafood from the water with a slotted spoon, peel off the shells and put aside.

Return the shells to the water and boil for a further 5 minutes to add flavour, then strain and keep the stock hot.

Heat the oil and 2 tbs butter in a large heavy pan, add the onion and fry gently until golden. Stir in the rice, then add the wine. Cook gently for 15 minutes, stirring frequently. Add the stock a little at a time to moisten as necessary during cooking.

Add the prawns and calamari, remaining butter and salt and pepper to taste, then cook for a further 5–10 minutes until the rice is just tender. Stir in the cooked peas. Remove from the heat, leave to stand for 1 minute, then serve.

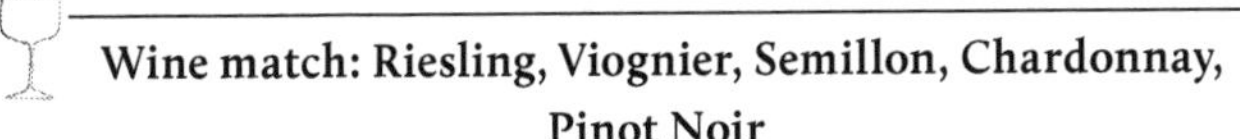

Wine match: Riesling, Viognier, Semillon, Chardonnay, Pinot Noir

From the rather limited wine list I selected a Pinot knowing that it would work well with the seafood.

'This is a great red, Burtie,' Jeni said. 'Whose is it?'

'It's from Magpie Springs, from that vineyard and gallery in the hills above Willunga where that famous artist has her studio, remember? We tasted it last year at their cellar door and were told that the light style went well with seafood – which is why I chose it.'

The cellar-door assistant at Magpie Springs told us their vineyard was the most southerly in the Adelaide Hills wine region and not in McLaren Vale area, as you'd imagine. The vineyard's elevated position ensured colder winters and cooler summers compared with those down in McLaren Vale. He said this protected the grapes from developing a 'jammy' quality, which they are prone to do in hotter locations.

To pay the bill I went to the kitchen, which gave me the

opportunity to tell the chef what a great effort he had made and what a great location for a café.

'You know, lots of our clients say something like that, but the council wants to close us down. We've been here for a year, but they say we're not HACCP friendly.'

HACCP is a quality control system established by NASA to safeguard American astronauts' food supply and was exceedingly complicated. He thought the council should just have been grateful that he was supplying a tourism service in such a great location rather than fussing over such exquisite quality control.

'That's local government for you,' I said. 'You should come to Clare Valley – we'd love to have you young people up there.'

~ * ~

Jeni finally persuaded me to let the kelpies sleep on the king-sized bed with us, but this lasted only one night. They insisted on sleeping across the bed rather than north and south as we did. When we sat up in bed with our early mug of Jasmine next morning I said firmly that it would never happen again.

'It was most uncomfortable, wasn't it, but I'm sure they enjoyed it,' Jeni said. 'I've got some old doonas somewhere. I'll buy some material and make covers for them. That'll be more comfortable than a rug on the floor. And next time we're in the Central Markets in Adelaide we'll go to that pet shop and buy a couple of trampolines for them.'

Talk about treating them like kids.

~ * ~

We took our car to the garage for a service. The mechanic later reported that the soft plastic seal under the bonnet had been eaten out along with a couple of plastic tops and he'd found a large charred rat's carcass under the starter motor.

Jackie must also have found a carcass. 'Why is her chest so swollen?' Jen said when we took her to the vet.

'Oedema,' he said. 'She's taken a bait.'

'Probably a dead rat,' I said. 'I've put out baits for the bush rats I saw in the compost bin. The packet claimed there was no secondary kill.'

'Bullshit,' the vet said, 'there's no product yet without secondary kill.' He gave Jackie an emetic to induce vomiting and kept her in overnight. We got rid of the mulch bin.

Later that week I let the kelpies out as usual in the early morning. It was wet and very cold. Jackie spotted sheep in the paddock next door and shot off barking vigorously, her tail thrashing, with Janette in hot pursuit.

'Come back, way back,' I shouted, to deaf ears.

Down the slope they charged, slithering under the fenceline, barking commands to the sheep they had soon gathered in a tight circle. I donned my boots, dashed after them, calling their names as I tried not to trip scrambling down the slope. As I neared the fence they broke off and came to me panting hard and very pleased with themselves, their large red tongues lolling out. I instructed them sternly that they must never herd the neighbour's sheep, then gave them a cuddle and told them what good dogs they were for coming to me. These are very intelligent dogs able to tell a scolding from praise – truly.

It had started to rain, a cold wind was blowing and I was naked except for the boots. Just as well there weren't any houses nearby. Mind you, there wasn't much to see given the cold. I hot-footed it back to the house and dived into bed for a cuddle to get the blood flowing again.

I reminded Jeni that the woman who had sold us the dogs told us that when they were about four weeks old their mother, Jac, had taken the litter on a midnight foray to the home paddock where a mob of sheep had been deposited that day. Jac showed her offspring how to round the mob into a tight circle to make it easier to move them along the track. 'We'll have to keep an eye on them. Their natural inclination is to work sheep into a controllable group,' I said. 'The paddocks surrounding us always have sheep in them after harvest.'

A week later Hutt, the neighbour on our western side, was monitoring the fenceline on his quad and stopped at the point nearest to our house. He climbed through the fence and strode over.

'Is he coming for a chat? I'll make some coffee,' said Jeni.

'G'day,' he said. 'I'm told a couple of dogs had a go at my sheep the other day. I asked Fawcett about it and he said you've got a couple of dogs.'

'We have, but we keep a close eye on them.'

'Like a coffee?' Jeni said diplomatically.

'No thanks. I think you should know I'm entitled to shoot any dogs I find harassing my sheep, so please take note – this is a warning.'

We saw Fawcett later that week and stopped for a chat. He asked us to give him a hand with drenching and dipping his lambs in a couple of weeks. And then he said, 'You know, I had to shoot one of my dogs. Killed a lamb. Do it once and they'll go on doing it for fun. Can't have that, so I shot it.'

Is that why he told Hutt we had two dogs?

~ * ~

Two weeks later we were out at six-thirty in the paddock with Fred. To 'give him a hand' meant helping him erect temporary fencing and a run leading to a deep, long trench, which Fred had dug in the place where the soil was softer and easy to work. The structure was made up of droppers, which had once been bent but he had straightened (no easy task), some salvaged reinforcing mesh, and galvanised-iron sheets. We were instructed to attach the various pieces to the droppers with coils of old wire.

With this done, we took up strategic positions to ensure the lambs didn't do what they wanted. Fred was in his element and knew what he was doing, waving his arms at the sheep and shouting invective at his barking, excited dogs to move the sheep into the race. We were told to prod those that resisted and, one by one, as they slowly moved along, Fred forced open their mouths to pump in a jet of drench, then made them jump into the trench with anti-parasitic wash and finally to scramble up a slope into the holding area.

Things went wrong. Part of the race was pushed over giving some lambs their freedom. As we scrambled to repair the breach, Fred and his dogs rounded the errant sheep to push them through again. His hand was jammed in the gate when it was flung open by a retreating upset lamb, but despite a bleeding hand and with the help of his blasphemous invective, Fred took it all in his stride. He was used to setbacks – he'd had years of experience.

Later I said to Jeni we had a lot to learn about sheep.

'How will we cope with our own?' she said, looking worried.

'Don't know, but if we keep helping Fred, he'll show us when it's time.'

Fred invited us for a barbecue that night, and I watched him playing with the minute steaks as we drank our red.

'Reckon our steaks are done, Fred.'

'Nah, you can't eat raw meat, mate. Gotta have some chew in it.'

When he passed us our dry, seared serves I lathered the wretched overcooked things in English mustard to try to restore some flavour.

'Great mustard, Burtie, what a trip.' Jeni was all smiles.

After a couple of glasses and a chat it was time for bed after such a strenuous day. 'Thanks for the tucker, Fred.'

~ * ~

Clare Riesling winemakers were concerned that the large wine companies were producing cheap white cask wine and labelling it Riesling. The argument over what was in the casks labelled as Riesling had disastrous effects on sales of premium Rieslings from Clare, the Barossa and elsewhere. The Clare winemakers started a campaign in the 1980s aimed at making it mandatory for a wine claiming to be Riesling to have its contents made solely from Riesling grapes.

Jeffrey Grosset was at the forefront of the campaign that eventually brought about a change in the law to allow the use of the word 'Riesling' only on wines made specifically from the Riesling grapes in Australia.

Grosset has long been an innovator, challenging tradition and questioning accepted practices. His decision to encourage Clare Valley Riesling producers to use the screwcap as bottle closures instead of cork was aimed at retaining the purity of fruit expression when a bottle was opened years later.

Such exactitude has seen Grosset develop significant national and international recognition. James Halliday calls him 'Australia's foremost Riesling maker', Robert Parker, an American wine writer, declares 'the Polish Hill Riesling ... is the finest Riesling I've ever tasted from Australia'; Jancis Robinson calls him 'Australia's acknowledged king of Riesling'.

Grosset's other accolades include being named International Riesling Winemaker of the Year at the Riesling Summit II in 1998 and *Gourmet Traveller Wine* magazine Winemaker of the Year in the same year. In 2005, *Wine and Spirits* magazine declared him one of the world's '50 most influential winemakers' and the 2006 *Decanter* magazine said he was one of the 'top 10 white winemakers in the world'. Such accolades are not only praise for the winemaker but also for Clare Valley's *terroir*.

Since 2000 the use of screwcaps as bottle closures has become widespread in Australia and overseas. In an attempt to contain this revolution, Portuguese cork producers countered that the pop of the cork as it exits a bottle is at the very heart of the romance of opening a bottle and drinking its contents. Grosset dismissed this claim with panache, observing that the crack of a screwcap when twisted is the sound of true romance because it is the guarantee that the wine will be fresh and true to the winemaker's quality and standards.

7

The Hill had been compromised with the clearing of its vegetation and we were planting a monoculture of vines – 20 hectares of them by the time we had finished the three development stages. We were nudging nature at the edge and so we needed to look for ways to compensate. A Department of the Environment advertisement in the local paper, *Northern Argus*, about control of Salvation Jane, led me to sign on to a program to test the use of the flea beetle.

This tiny insect, rather like a beetle but about the size of a large flea, lives on the small, succulent feeding roots of Salvation Jane and eventually results in the death of the plant by breaking its propagation cycle. The flea beetle's mode of operation is very similar to that of the phylloxera louse, which produces the same result in grapevines.

Nothing is simple when you deal with the government. Before I could participate in these trials I had to undergo a long interview and then sign a contract of agreement many pages long by which I would allow a pup tent to be erected on part of The Hill. I was not to interfere with it, and I was not to use a herbicide near it. Months later the outcome showed, that of the many sites chosen for this program, ours was one of the few that was successful.

From this small beginning the beetle has spread across the property and its work has resulted in very little Salvation Jane surviving; maybe the few plants we see from time to time result from seeds blowing in from our neighbours' properties. Apparently one plant can release 10,000 seeds to the square metre, and we found it had gone berserk in our irrigated area in the first few years, so this near eradication of Salvation Jane by the flea beetle was a real win.

We were also invaded by Portuguese millipedes. There was no natural Australian predator to control this particular millipede, but there was an Australian nematode that controlled Australian millipedes. Entomologists had genetically modified this creature to make it an attractive food to the foreign invader. We found an Adelaide agency specialising in the supply of these nematodes and once a year a number of Petri dishes arrived by post with a batch of embryonic nematodes on damp blotting paper. To set the eradication process in motion, we collected large living millipedes, put them in the Petri dishes for a couple of days until they had eaten the nematodes, and then scattered the millipedes outside, around the buildings.

The nematodes breed in the digestive systems of the millipedes with resulting offspring eating them from inside. These babies then spread out and are eaten in turn by other millipedes, in this way setting up the planned cycle of destruction. Remarkably, this work has succeeded in keeping the numbers of millipedes under control, but unfortunately it has not eliminated them. Millipedes still pour in to our property from the neighbour's hill next door.

We came upon another environmental program that was to fundamentally change The Hill when out of the blue we met up with an old colleague of mine.

'It's Christina Fink,' Jeni said, handing me the telephone. 'Do you remember her? She used to work with you, she says – well, she knows you from somewhere in the system. She's in the Flinders

Ranges and wants to drop in to say good day on the way back to Adelaide.'

Christina had spent a romantic week in the Flinders Ranges with her new boyfriend, Luke. I had no idea why she wanted to see me – it wasn't as though we'd been close friends. Maybe she wanted to impress her new man by visiting people with a vineyard in the Clare Valley. Just as well we'd moved out of the shed. Anyway, I asked them for lunch.

Starting work early so as to finish in time for a shower to spruce up our somewhat hillbilly appearance, by twelve thirty we were ready to receive them. There were hugs and kisses when they arrived and a glass of fizz all round. 'We'll sit out here on the terrace,' I said.

Christine and Luke were full of interest in everything we were doing, rushing us with their questions. The conversation was relaxed and lively although I must say I had some difficulty in recalling events from that earlier working life I had left behind.

For lunch Jeni had marinated a couple of pork fillets in Dijon and pomegranate syrup for me to chasseur with some large slices of red capsicum, zucchini, eggplant and red onion, which she later tossed in herbs, olive oil and vinegar. The meat, which smelt sensational, she served on a bed of couscous cooked in chicken broth with some roasted pine nuts and currants tossed in.

We had a Jim Barry Lodge Hill Riesling with its wonderful signature Clare Valley dryness and citric fruitiness to accompany the pork fillets and a bottle of Jim Barry Cover Drive Cabernet Sauvignon to have with a couple of cheeses and some crusty bread.

Luke was from New Zealand and knew nothing about South Australia's Flinders Ranges or Clare Valley and its wines and asked us about the unusual label on the Cabernet bottle.

Chasseured pork fillet with fresh pomegranate syrup and Dijon mustard

Ingredients for 2 servings

4 large pomegranates

½ cup fresh lemon juice

½ cup sugar

1 tablespoon Dijon mustard

1 tbs Canadian maple syrup (do not use a substitute)

1 large pork fillet, about 300 g

olive oil

parsley, chopped

Cut pomegranates in half horizontally and process in a juicer as if squeezing oranges.

Put 4 cups of pomegranate juice, ½ cup lemon juice and ½ cup sugar in a saucepan over a gentle heat and reduce to syrup consistency.

Store the excess pomegranate syrup in a jar in the fridge. (If you can't get pomegranates from Granny's garden buy a bottle of syrup from a Middle East food store.)

Mix 1 tablespoon of pomegranate syrup along with the mustard and maple syrup in a bowl. Cut pork fillet in 2 large pieces and coat with marinade.

Heat an oiled chasseur pan with olive oil. Cook fillets for 4–5 minutes each side. Rest for 10 minutes before cutting into thick medallions.

Meanwhile gently heat the remaining marinade.

Plate the meat, pour over the marinade and dress with chopped parsley.

Serve with Middle East-style cous cous.

Wine match: Cabernet Sauvignon, Pinot Noir, Durif, Barbera

Peter Barry, who now manages Jim Barry Wines, had expanded his area under vines and in one land purchase acquired a cricket pitch that he thought was a good basis for a back label story that might appeal to sports lovers. The label boasts a gentleman in 1920s cricket garb at the crease, his bat raised ready to cover drive.

You have to admire Peter's marketing initiatives. He was born in the Clare Valley, developed a country boy's typical rowdy, humorous streak and followed his father to Roseworthy. Maybe it was here that he learnt how to woo his beloved Sue; one day, seeing her walking across a lawn, he ran from behind and tackled her to the ground by way of introduction and to push his credentials as a potential husband.

A winemaker who exports will go anywhere and do almost anything to tell his story and to massage the potential of a market, constantly travelling to put a face to his label, to demonstrate the differences that make his wines stand out from the hundreds of others available. Good quality wines, those above certain price points, are bought as much for the romance of the story on the back label as for the contents of the bottle.

He took this same robust and innovative approach to marketing to New York to launch the new Cover Drive label. The launch took place in New York's Central Park. Peter rounded up a bunch of Aussies, including the Australian Ambassador to the US and the South Australian Trade Commissioner, to demonstrate to the astonished locals a game of cricket and the masterful cover drive stroke. At the end of the game onlookers were invited to taste the wine and the burgers – made with salt bush mutton and served with crisp fries that matched beautifully the Cabernet's background flavours of blackcurrant and dark chocolate.

Three Little Pigs is another of Jim Barry's labels. Peter runs a small piggery at his Armagh property as one way of relaxing from his high-flying duties selling wines on the international market. Once a year he holds a celebratory lunch at his property to say thank you to his Australian agents and sales reps. Lunch highlights are the whole spit-roasted piglets with potatoes roasted in duck fat. Peter also grows his own ducks – and you've never tasted potatoes like them.

The Three Little Pigs label arose from these celebrations. It's a blend of Cabernet, Shiraz and Malbec. If you hold the wine in your mouth for a few seconds your cheeks will experience the wine's consistency and your gums the drying sensation of the fine grain tannins. Once swallowed the flavours of the wine will linger at the back of your throat – what's called a long palate.

Luke was a volunteer grower for Trees for Life, an organisation committed to revegetating rural land under stress and for that purpose organises local volunteers in country areas to gather seeds indigenous to a region, while others, mainly based in the city, propagate them for a year for rural property owners to plant – 500 treelings are available each year to members.

I found this intriguing because I knew that after we had planted our full 20 hectares we'd have well over 33,000 vines, which is an unnatural monoculture on our small area. One way to balance this would be to plant indigenous trees – some TLC for The Hill with TFL. I thought we should be able to manage 500 a year although all would have to be planted in May when the volunteer grower handed them over, just before the winter rains start. I wondered about the effect on our backs this work would have, concentrated as it would be over just a few weeks.

You wouldn't call the scrub of the Mid North beautiful or enticing, but the local birds feed on it and nest in it and the wildlife uses the remnant treelines as movement corridors for security. We love the uncouthness of the Australian scrub and its determination to survive blistering summers and frost-heavy winters. My idea was that native scrub growing across our property would attract local birds and that they, in turn, would deter itinerant scavengers from congregating when the grapes were ripening. The water-seeking roots of the plants would help prevent erosion along water courses and the drainage banks we had created to take surface drainage to the large irrigation dam.

Another important consideration was that their canopies would leach the fumes from the air emitted by the machines regularly working our property. In line with this thinking we planted 500 trees each year for sixteen years until we ran out of space. Many species of birds flourish in them, lizards sun themselves on their branches, spiny anteaters track along their corridors as do the foxes.

The Trees for Life organisation claim that 200 trees planted in 2000 square metres of land will store the CO_2 generated each year by the average Australian household. In all we planted over 8000 trees and shrubs, which we hoped would take care of all the emissions associated with growing our grapes, including carting them to the winery and turning them into wine – with a bit over to cover exhaust emissions from our car and from the house.

~ * ~

One afternoon Mervin Munroe dropped in for a beer and a chat. Merv was the local gossip, or to put it more kindly, the custodian of local oral history. Merv knew everything and there was no way he'd let you beat him with earlier or better knowledge. He had the longest, shortest, oldest, newest, tallest, dearest, cheapest version of everything. He was very useful, however, if you wanted to know about sheep prices, or grape prices and contracts and he knew how to run a vineyard having been at it for decades. I quickly learned it was best just to listen to him.

'Them sheep of yours,' he said, 'you told me how many you bought and how many lambs they'd thrown. Well, that's too many for the number of acres you got them on. You started with sixty-three ewes and each threw twins.'

'But one died and the foxes got a couple of lambs,' I said.

'Like I say, too many – about 130 lambs and their mums, nearly 200 all up. It's too early to take the lambs off their mums just yet, but in a couple of months you should sell the ewes and rams, and then the lambs six months later to the Arabs. I'll give you the name of a bloke who'll buy them. He sends thousands a month to Saudi.'

Merv had introduced himself to us in the pub soon after we arrived. We were his neighbours, he said, or near enough, because his vineyard was just a few kilometres down the road. He told us he was the biggest grower in this part of the Clare Valley with 60 hectares, and we were just hobby farmers with only twenty. He offered to drive us around one Saturday morning to introduce us to the neighbours and their vineyards.

After the drive, we arrived at his new house, of which Merv was very proud, and stood outside talking with him and his wife. Later we learned the reason we weren't invited inside was because the carpets had not yet been laid. Merv, assuring us he was a fine shot, said he preferred concrete floors in any case because when he saw a hare or fox in his nearby vines he could fling open a window and fire his shotgun through it.

Merv has three features that strike you when you first meet him. He has a long torso, broad shoulders and short legs, so though he might not be able to run fast, he can sustain a hard day's work. Bushy grey hairs spurt out of his bulbous nose and, like many older country blokes, he has acute long vision and a long memory.

'How come they've got such good eyesight?' Jeni said.

'Didn't wank when they were kids,' I replied, rather too quickly.

Jeni just looked at me. 'What about their memories?'

'Regular practice in pub sessions,' I said. 'What they don't know, they make up to round off a good story.'

~ * ~

Fawcett came up to the house at about five o'clock and while drinking his second beer came to the point. 'There's a mob of one-year-old lambs up the river going for a good price 'cause they've been feeding on caltrop. Wouldn't be very popular if we brought them back with caltrop in their wool 'cause it's a bastard of a weed. Have to shear 'em up there and bring the bales back here for sale. So we bring 'em back, fatten 'em up for a year and sell 'em to the Arabs and make a decent quid. What d'ya reckon?'

'Sounds good – something wrong with it?'

'It'd take three days all up – one to get there, one for shearing, and one to get back. We'd split the proceeds.'

'What do you mean "we"?'

'That's my point. I don't have the finances to cover it. Need to pay for the sheep before they're shorn and the shearers once they've finished shearing. I need you to finance it and the two of you to help in the shed as roustabouts to save costs. It'd be about ten thousand all up.'

'How would you guarantee our ten grand?'

'Only my word, really.'

Jeni and I looked at each other – we had the finances to back the proposal and a day in a shearing shed would be a romantic experience for us, not to mention a break of a few days up-country. Jeni nodded, we all had another beer and then shook on the deal. We had no idea what we were letting ourselves in for.

A couple of days later we strolled down the track at six thirty with the kelpies who were to stay with Fred's wife and kids. Fred was waiting to leave, a large, caged trailer fixed to his old Holden, the engine running.

'I guess we could bring our ute to help with the wool bales, Fred.'

'No, mate, no worries, she may look old, but she's a Holden – got lots of guts. We'll save on fuel costs taking only one vehicle.'

Fred seemed to be pumped – full of energy and confidence. He did most of the talking as we set off and later he and Jeni hogged the conversation as we went along not allowing me to get a word in from the back seat.

'Don't open the windows so as to keep the car cooler,' Fred said. 'Now, we're buying the lambs from the Derwents who have offered us overnight accommodation in their house. They'll feed us along with the shearers and also tea at night. Mr Derwent will tee up the shearers and we'll be the roustabouts. I'll show you how to do it – easy really. The hard thing is the strain on your back.'

I asked a couple of questions which Fred and Jeni ignored – best to contemplate the scenery then.

Next morning, after a huge breakfast prepared by Mrs Derwent, we were off to an early start. You had to keep the floor around the shearers clear of cuttings and droppings, pick up the belly wool, which was always the first to be shorn, and remove the fleece immediately so the next sheep could be brought in. Throwing the fleece over the sorting table so that it spread out ready for 'skirting' – removing the dags, twigs and scraps – was an art in itself. We knew nothing about any of these shearing shed routines, and we had to work hard to maintain the hectic pace, disguise our ignorance, keep out of each other's way, stay calm and smile to show that we were. In short, the work was backbreaking and relentless, and we were hot.

Smoko. The shearers downed a couple of large mugs of scalding tea and lots of thick white buttered-bread sandwiches liberally filled with cold roast lamb and mustard pickles, and freshly made cakes; then it was back to the shed to lie on the floor to ease the strain on their backs. Even though they were using harnesses to take their weight as they bent over the sheep, the position is awkward, a backbreaker well before the end of the day.

By lunchtime, Jeni and I were rooted and grateful for the hour's break. Everyone from the shed and Mr Derwent and his workers took a seat around the huge kitchen table loaded with sliced meats, salads, pickles, bread, jams, cakes, bowls of tinned fruit salad, cake and a few large aluminium teapots, all prepared by Mrs Derwent and her daughters who acted as the waiting staff. As if this wasn't a feast enough the ladies served hot corned beef with mustard sauce, mashed potatoes and green peas. Crikey, real country people certainly know how to serve it up and put it away. The shearers bolted down vast amounts of food without much talk, seemingly more concerned to return to the shed to rest once more before the afternoon stint. I think I knew what they were on about.

Mrs Derwent obviously was pleased to be able to talk with a new adult female. She was interested to compare life on a sheep station with that on a vineyard and our previous work in the city. Jeni was in her element recounting how hard vineyard work

Mrs Derwent's zucchini cake

Ingredients

500 g grated zucchini

250 mL vegetable oil

375 g sugar

3 eggs, beaten

300 g flour

1 ½ tsp baking power

1 tsp bicarbonate of soda

1 ½ tsp ground cinnamon

grated nutmeg

180 g walnuts, chopped

Mix together zucchini, oil, sugar and eggs. Sift dry ingredients and add to zucchini mixture combining thoroughly. Stir in walnuts. Spoon into greased and lined 1 kg loaf tin. Bake in centre of oven at 180°C for 90 to 105 minutes or until a skewer pushed into the centre comes out clean.

Allow to cool in the tin for 15 minutes before turning onto wire rack to cool completely. Serve plain or buttered.

Wine match: sweet Sherry, Muscat, Petit Manseng

was, how much she loved it and how much she was enjoying the experience of working in the shearing shed.

'I'm also loving all the food you've prepared – such choice, so many different flavours,' she said.

Mrs Derwent's smiled broadly. 'Probably because you didn't have to prepare any of it.'

'Yep, everybody's pulling together.' Fred sat forward, looking around for approval, a wide smile on his broad face. 'Got it all together nicely, didn't I?'

Fred was cocky as he paid the shearers in cash. He was even more expansive over dinner. With cutlery held aloft in his large hands on the table he commented on the print on the wall opposite. Mrs Derwent fixed him with a cultured smile and said eloquently, 'No, it's an original, painted by my grandfather, but it does look modern, doesn't it?'

Next morning she insisted we eat a huge breakfast before departing, saying breakfast was the essential meal of the day, the only one you knew you were certain to have. We headed for Morgan, on the Murray, to a nursery with a reputation for its fruit trees. I wanted to buy twenty for the orchard we had started at the shed site, but there was only room in the boot for three. They were excellent small trees and putting them in the trailer I knew would have resulted in their leaves being wind burnt. Then off to tackle the long, steady climb from the banks of the Murray to Eudunda. We'd have lunch at the pub there.

Well into the drive I realised I was the only one talking. For once I was permitted to talk. Was anyone listening? 'What's wrong with you two, you're not interrupting me.'

Strange, I heard my voice, a little delayed, coming back to me. Something was awry. I was feeling wonky. Jeni was on the back seat fast asleep. At the steering wheel, Fred had an idiotic smile on his lips. The cabin felt very hot even though it was still early morning.

'I'm going to open my window, Fred, hope you don't mind. It's getting bloody hot in here,' I heard my echo say.

A few kilometres further on I was feeling decidedly groggy and asked Fred to pull into the next parking bay for fresh air and a pee. 'Yeah, I'm feeling woozy too,' said Fred, 'I'll find a stop.'

I had trouble opening the door and getting out, and I had to shake Jeni very hard to get her to stir. Having got her out, I watched her stagger toward the bushes. I made for a tree and noticed that I wavered as I tried to stand. Then I saw Jeni coming from the bushes with her gear still around her ankles, trying to steady herself but succeeding only in collapsing to the ground.

'Fred, help me drag Jeni to the car,' I called. 'Lean her on the bonnet.'

As I dragged Jeni along, I tried to pull up her knickers and once we had her on the car bonnet I gently tapped her face, then slapped it with a little more force and asked Fred to pour water on it.

'More, Fred, more!' I called. 'Come on, Jeni, for Christ sake wake up – take deep breaths,' I said, my voice getting louder and my tone more worried as she tried to open her eyes. 'Put some water in her mouth, Fred, that's it. Really deep, deep breaths, Jeni.'

She started to take her own weight, but her speech was slurring and half an hour passed before she was able to stand alone properly and to talk slowly enough to be understood.

'Must be carbon monoxide poisoning, Fred,' I said, 'your exhaust must be really shonky.'

'Yeah, well it's not too good. That's why I wanted the windows closed so as to stop anything seeping into the cabin.'

'It's had exactly the opposite effect – allowing fumes to build up in the cabin. Let's look in the boot. Jesus wept! What a bloody mess!'

The beautiful young fruit trees, so healthy and green when I put them in, were burnt dead, and the thick plastic mat under them was a melting, fuming mess. Suffocating, stinking fumes issued forth, among them carbon monoxide, the 'silent killer', which you can't see, taste or smell as it inhibits the body's uptake of oxygen.

'The load of wool would have put a strain on the old engine

coming up this long climb. Been meaning to get it fixed. I drive my kids to school in this with them in the back seat – never know what might've happened.'

I settled Jeni on the front seat and opened her window. 'I reckon we should call into the Eudunda hospital. Jeni's obviously copped a lung full.'

'Carbon monoxide poisoning, you say,' said the duty sister. 'Just sit over there and I'll take a few obs.' Nothing untoward was found, but we were asked to stay overnight, 'so we can keep an eye on you'.

We were up early next morning, but Fred was ahead of us. 'He's at the service station, just around the corner,' the discharge sister informed us. A mechanic was installing the new exhaust system.

'Luckily she's a Holden,' Fred said. 'Country garages always have Holden spares. I won't charge the cost of the new exhaust against the sheep expenses.'

'That's generous of you, Fred. Do you think we could afford hamburgers for breakfast?' I said, heading for the fast food shop.

Jeni said she felt anxious and nauseated for the rest of the week.

We had bought the lambs very cheaply because of the burr in their wool so we didn't make a hell of a lot when we sold it. Fred had located agistment for the lambs and having fattened them up, we sold them months later for a nice profit, which we split – after expenses were deducted.

~ * ~

Weeds were a constant problem even after the errant drip lines had been replaced. Our difficulties with weeds along the vine row could have been avoided had we used grow guards – metre-high plastic triangles – to protect each vine and freeing us to use spray guns to kill the weeds. But the guards cost $2 each and as there were about 13,300 vines I was reluctant to spend such a large amount on plastic.

We hand-hoed the rows three times each season for three years. The vines are spaced at two-metre intervals, that's about 27 kilometres in one pass. Over those three years we hand-hoed about 243,000 metres of weeds wearing out many metal hoes and breaking dozens of handles, to say nothing of the wear and tear on our backs, just to save a lousy $27,000.

This was stunningly hard work. We started off all right in spring because the soil was soft from winter rains, but the heat soon hardened the soil. We sweated buckets as summer moved in. To deal with the dehydration we would freeze water in plastic soft drink bottles and take it down to the vineyard with us. Morning and afternoon teas consisted of huge quantities of cold watermelon slices.

One Saturday morning friends we had met at the Property Management course arrived with a case of peaches freshly picked from their orchard and asked us to lunch the following week. After they left, we sat on the tailgate of the ute and devoured the lot – what luscious fruits, what sensational flavour, and what a truly wonderful way to rehydrate ourselves. Ecstasy!

Mind you, weeds aren't all that bad when you stop to think about them, it's just that they grow in the wrong places. To their credit their deep roots, especially those of Jane and wild artichokes, bring minerals to the surface, they hold the soil in place against running surface water and strong winds, and when they die they leave surface soil porous and provide nutrients for the vines. At the same time they compete with the vines so they had to go, especially the bloody Jane and wild artichokes and Scotch thistles, which will thrash a paddock in short time.

~ * ~

At times I would sit on the tailgate of the ute watching the ewes and their lambs graze. They moved as a mob, concentrating on eating, not interfering with each other. Sometimes they would kneel as they grazed, especially the lambs, as though praying to the grass and weeds not to be upset about being eaten. Content, as they slowly moved forward, they would raise their heads occasionally to sniff the wind.

The rams walked with the ewes, not trying to lead, just part of the mob. At times a ram would come upon a lamb directly in its path and butt it in the backside sending the small thing into the air.

On one such occasion of sheep watching Fred dropped by to say that with the money made from our joint lamb venture he had just bought another mob of lambs and had found agistment for them in the Skilly Hills. He boasted about the low price he had paid, giving me a funny little laugh as he said it, which made me wonder what he was on about.

The next day we were checking the yabby nets at the small dam in the south-east corner on the lowest point of our property. I love the view of The Hill from here, and I stood contemplating it, the kelpies rolling in the mud at the edge of the water.

'Burtie, look at the fence behind the dam. Someone's tied up the wires.'

'That'd be Fred, so his sheep can get to the water.'

'And our sheep to get out?'

I didn't mind Fred using the water, but he could have asked us first. The 12 hectares Fred rented had originally been set up as a horse stud so the fencing was inadequate for holding lambs. One morning his sheep wandered from his paddock into a neighbouring vineyard. Before we know it they'll be in the vineyard chewing the vines, I thought.

It was time to sell our ewes and rams. Merv had lined up a buyer for us and when we next drove past Fred's property we stopped for a chat to ask for the use of his holding yard for the buyer to inspect them and later the use of his loading ramp. No worries, he said. I then told him I had untied the fence wires near our dam to keep his sheep from wandering into our property and getting mixed with our lambs, and I also suggested he should get his sheep out of Hopkins's vineyard.

'Nah!' he said, 'They won't do much harm in the vines. The council charges me an agistment fee for this piece of government road, so I'm going to get me money's worth.'

'I hope they don't wander up to our place,' I said, 'where they can do a lot of damage if they get into the vineyard.'

The agent spent time looking the sheep over and then began the argy-bargy about the poor condition of the ewes and what he said about the rams was unpleasant. This really got up my nose. I pointed out the rams had done a great job with the ewes dropping so many lambs. Jeni quietly told me to calm down, that he was just trying to knock down the price.

This give and take went on for a while and then, out of the blue, he made me an offer that I immediately countered upwards. He grabbed my hand to shake it, saying we had a deal. I gathered from his eagerness that I could have pushed the price up higher. I guess that's the problem when you really don't know what you're doing. The sheep were left in the pen to empty out for a couple of days. Loading them wasn't altogether easy because of the inadequacy of Fred's makeshift ramp

Coming home from shopping in Clare we found the double

gates at the entrance to our land closed. This was strange. Who would've done that? I opened them and put large rocks against them to ensure they didn't self-propel shut. But mysteriously someone had closed them again

Next morning the large, long gas tanker arrived to fill our bottles and the driver wasn't pleased to have to stop to open the gates.

'It's bloody difficult to get this rig going again on a sloping gravel track,' he said. 'And I'm supposed to stop on the way out to close them. Like shit I will.'

I thought Fred must have something to do with it so I called on him to ask what the problem was.

'You told me not to let my sheep stray up to your place, and the easiest way to stop them is to close the gates.' I pointed out that it was his responsibility to keep them in his paddock. I wondered what we had done to upset him. This nonsense went on for a couple of weeks so I consulted the police.

'Nothing to do with us,' the constable said. 'There's no crime committed. Why not see the council about charging him an agistment fee.'

'Nothing I can do,' said the council officer. 'Mr Fawcett shouldn't have his sheep wandering over the road. He's only supposed to let them on it for a couple days a year to keep down the weeds. Actually he shouldn't have been charged in the first place because the road runs past his place to yours. We'll drop the charge next year.'

'If the council shouldn't have charged him in the first place why not give him his money back? It'd only be ten or twenty dollars.'

'The council can't do that. Isn't there another road?'

'Why not tell him to graze the weeds just two days a year.'

'Mr Fawcett is notoriously abusive – a trouble-maker – wouldn't want to get into an argument with him.'

On the way home I found the gates lashed together with stout rope. Right, I thought. I'll get some chain and padlock the gates to the piping of the fence that held them in place. But next time we came to them, they were closed again, bound together with rope. Fred had pulled the pieces of two-inch pipe from the fence assembly and slipped the chains off. I had to laugh.

'Christ, he must be a strong bastard,' I said to Jeni. 'Those pipes were well fixed into the strainers. You have to admire him. He's a very determined fellow.'

This time I padlocked the gates to the strainers and that was the end of the saga. Fred, however, had the last say. He instructed me to drive slowly past his house so that I wouldn't endanger his kids who played on the road.

It turned out that when we had rounded up our sheep to take to Fred's holding yards we had missed six or eight which turned up a couple of days later. I rang Earl's Transport to explain my difficulty. No worries, they'd collect them next time they had a mob to take out.

Then, would you believe, a squad car arrived and drove around the property. I waited for it to come to the house. A policeman poked his head out of the window and said, 'What's with the sheep down there. Where did they come from?'

'We've actually had them for the past year. I just sold the ewes but some were left behind. I've told Earl's to come and collect them.'

'There's been some thieving going on around here lately, and Fawcett tells us these could be some of the stolen stock.'

'What codswallop! What's he on about?'

'You've been buying sheep with him, haven't you?'

'Twelve months ago – from up the river – but we sold those a while ago.'

'All right, we're just checking. Seems you don't know much about sheep, do you?'

'Not really. Just use them for organic weed control.'

What was Fred up to, I wondered. What had we done to Fred to turn him against us – telling Hutt about our kelpies, then the gate nonsense and now dobbing us in to the police?

'How do we deal with this?' I asked Jeni.

'You're the planner,' she said, 'you've got to think of something. I really like his wife – poor thing, having to put up with him.'

As it turned out I didn't have to do anything. Fred was dragged up The Hill by his angry wife who instructed him in fulsome terms to apologise for telling the police that we might have stolen sheep.

When I was telling Merv the story in the pub, the men around us fell silent. Merv said Fred had been questioned about the new mob as they were similar to the description of stolen sheep from Hilltown, but the police didn't have enough evidence to charge him. He was probably trying to divert attention from himself by telling the police about ours, said Merv. The blokes listening couldn't believe it. Not that either of us might steal sheep, but that anyone would give information to the police about it.

Fredrick Farrington Fawcett must have realised this time he'd gone too far. He stopped going to the pub because the front bar boys gave him a hard time, and a couple of months later he moved his family up country to manage an isolated station.

~ * ~

You've got to find your own meaning in this world but when does the romance of running a vineyard shade into being a dream, perhaps a nightmare? Occasional renewal is necessary to keep things going well, as they seemed to be. So we would take stock at the end of each financial year to identify any risks lurking on the horizon and try to deal with these by going off to another course.

Such considerations informed our talk over five o'clock sherries over several nights. Grape demand was insatiable, kitty was still cashed up so was it about time to expand the empire and if so where were the workers to come from? We were able to do a large part of the work ourselves with only eight hectares but we would need someone to do it for us when we became too old for the hard slog. Our solution was to double the size and use half of the income to employ a manager.

The second stage of the vineyard development added another eight hectares, higher up The Hill, just to the north of the house. A winter creek bisects this area and in honour of our two wonderful companions we named it Red Kelpie Creek Block. To deal with water erosion we ran the vine rows across the steep slope rather than down it. The upper thinner soils would require more water than the deeper soils down the slope so the irrigation system was divided into six smaller areas by solenoids to enable more precise watering requirements.

This time we went directly to the Israeli company whose polypipe product was used as replacement for the first stage. These gentlemen were very easy to work with and, as we had agreed to buy their product, they would design the layout for irrigation system – mains, submains, laterals along the vine rows and solenoids – free of charge. This saved us thousands of dollars compared with stage one. All of the materials arrived on time and there were no problems with installation and testing.

The savings were used to buy growguards, half the price of three years earlier. These metre-high triangles of rigid plastic were placed over the vine cutting in the ground and attached to the cordon wire enabling the vine to grow inside up to the wire without us having to train them to do this. They saved us an enormous amount of work. In addition, because of them, we were able to spray the weeds growing in the mid row and along the undervine area. What a breeze compared with stage one.

There is usually a problem if things are going so well. Strong winds are a common feature of our hillside location and often these blew the guards from their position depositing them roundabout. We had to walk the property to collect them and replace them. But this was a small cost to pay and we were incredulous at the ease with which we got the whole block under control within a year.

It was about this time in the fourth year that the contractor we used for the machine work in the vineyard decided to shut shop because his partner had left. He was the only contractor in the Clare Valley to offer such a comprehensive service, so we were stuffed. We tried a couple of one-man operators, but we were not satisfied with their work.

We had decided to plant a mid-row crop of red clover in the vineyard because I thought it would look stunning when in bloom and at the same time it would help to set nitrogen in the soil. But the young bloke we employed to do the job sowed the seed too deeply, despite my instructions, and the seeds did not germinate. I still wonder, however, if he would have been better than the two blokes we ended up employing.

Experienced vineyard labourers were hard to come by and an experienced vineyard manager proved to be financially out of the question for us. I was not willing to pay the significant salary required and run the vineyard at a loss until income from the expansion was available in two to three years' time. It was back to school for me to complete a course in chemical use for weed and mildew control and on how to calibrate spray equipment with tractor speed.

Eventually Grantly Ovens came along. He had vineyard and tractor experience and was delighted when I hired him. He had decided to return home from the vineyard he had worked on in the Kuitpo Forest to his mother who lived in Jamestown and ran the pub there. She said she couldn't keep working seven days a week and wanted Grantly to help her at weekends.

Down to Wasleys we went to buy a tractor from the Ferguson yard, which was delivered the following week. After protracted negotiations, we bought the spray unit from the local supplier. This involved another raid on kitty. How far would it stretch, we wondered.

The second bloke we hired said he was an ex-roadie which, translated, meant he had been the sound effects and lighting man for an itinerant band playing in country pubs and clubs. I came to understand that it also meant he was a clapped-out dope smoker.

I now knew enough about working a vineyard to be able to draw up monthly detailed work programs. These were translated onto a whiteboard week by week setting out the work to be done. So far so good. To keep ahead, Jeni and I attended field days to gain an understanding of inter-row crops, which seeds to use, and useful tips about tilling, seed drilling, fertilisers, crop-spraying techniques, herbicides and synergy plants to compete with and defeat the weeds.

When looking for pruners that winter, people on unemployment benefits were sent out to us by Centrelink. Some only turned up to fulfil the requirement that they were looking for work, but there were some who really wanted to work and we managed to scrape together a team.

I must say hand pruning is a shit of a job. No matter the weather, it has to be done by the end of August so as to finish in time for budburst. Despite icy mornings, freezing fingers and toes, and rain for days on end, we had to be ready each morning to engender enthusiasm in our motley crew. Once they got down to work, we found we were able to complete the hand pruning in four weeks instead of the terribly drawn-out three months when Jeni and I did it between us.

Now we needed a new large shed to house the machinery and provide a base for staff briefing and a lunch room. Thirteen thousand dollars later we had a four-bay shed with concrete floor, electricity and water tanks. We were going against the financial planner's advice that it was the use of machinery not its ownership that optimised opportunities, and it was against our own business plan, but there seemed to be no alternative.

Judd, our roadie, was most inventive with reasons for being late to clock-on or not to come to work at all. At one stage he asked for a series of Friday afternoons off to take his partner to the fertility clinic in Adelaide and offered to work Saturday mornings to make up rather than lose pay.

One Saturday when he rocked up rather late, I allocated him a number of small jobs and off he went in the ute. A couple of hours later I went down to the pump house to change the irrigation schedule and then went looking for him to check his progress. There was the ute as far away from the house as possible, parked behind a group of small trees with Judd stretched along the seats fast asleep.

'Bit of a late night, Judd?' I said as I shook his shoulder.

He opened bleary eyes, blinking in the sunlight, trying to compute what was happening.

'How are the irrigation repairs going?' I said.

'That bloody dopey hare has chewed out the polypipe across a dozen rows,' he mumbled. 'Doesn't have enough sense to come back to the first chew to get its drink but has to go and have another chew each time it wants one. Or, maybe,' he said, with a bit of a grin, 'he's having a go at you – making work for us so we can earn a quid.'

'What a bastard,' I muttered.

8

You have to follow the rhythm of the vines to make the most of the opportunities they present. In the winter months they hibernate, dropping into a state that vignerons call 'senescence'. It's not that they are growing old so much as spending winter in a state best suited to deal with it. This hiatus presents a great opportunity – a time to prune when the vines are not active, so that when the canes are cut they will not lose sap, which is so full of energy.

The vines are not fully senescent until all their leaves have dropped and the soft canes have become woody. On The Hill, cold, windy weather produces this change by the end of May. Then it's pruning time.

We love working in the vineyard on a languid early morning bathed in sunlight and pleasure. When you are at the centre of that deep first-light silence, life's absolutes seem to stare you in the face. With the kelpies busy somewhere or suddenly appearing to lick an unsuspecting cheek just as you are on your knees engaged in a delicate repair, simple tasks like pruning, counting broken posts, or repairing the polypipe become a source of quiet joy. On a sunny day, rural sounds are simple and natural and so peaceful compared with urban cacophony. Birds call, winds sigh, the showy little wagtails flit about demanding their mate's attention, although I must say the strident, dry cacophony from the crows and galahs disturbs the harmony of the dawn chorus.

At times we hear an extraordinary buzzing getting louder and coming closer and know that this is a bee swarm looking to establish a new hive. I've seen an entire swarm – thousands of bees in one large cluster – land on a strainer post for an overnight rest, setting off again next morning when it is warm enough.

While we're working we come across bits and pieces of metal and stone – ancient artefacts. We have quite a collection of metal objects – a half dozen harrows that date from early last century, large heavy horseshoes thrown from plodding work horses, thin silver ones cast from prancing ponies, an ancient axe-head from some foreign land, and the bleached bones of a large hare brought down somehow during its last, headlong run.

We are really intrigued by the occasional birds' nests we collect from the vine rows. These have been woven ingeniously from strings once used for training the vines. We gather the strings after use, but not all find their way back to storage, some drop along the way. The birds unravel the thicker string into single strands and then weave these into round shapes with a shallow hollow in the middle. Wool pieces picked from a dead lamb carcass or caught on the barbwire fence are also knitted in. We marvel at the ingenuity and wonder at this innate response to fashion such materials into nests. But why do some birds site their nests in the vine canopy, which will ensure their certain destruction when the lumbering harvester thrashes through?

Another dimension of our artefact discoveries is that we have found several Aboriginal stone tools. Rocks, smoothed by aeons of running water and carried from some distant location to end up under an old gum tree where I found them. We can't read these objects as we would a book but, like the archaeologists, we must use our imaginations as to their purpose. Research would illuminate the provenance of the metal objects but only imagination would help in unlocking the intricate histories of the stone tools, birds' nests and the hare skeleton.

~ * ~

Our work over the past two years was reaching fruition and we were greatly anticipating our real first harvest. We thought we knew what hard work was until we joined the picking team. The two-year-old vines are not substantial enough to withstand the buffeting of a mechanical harvester and we were thrilled to be part of the contractor's crew of hand-pickers – a rowdy, bawdy bunch.

Jeni and I were slow to fill our buckets compared with most of the gang, but I saw some older couples really struggling to keep up. I guess they were earning pocket money for something special, but as they were being paid by the hour I wondered about our labour costs in view of the price per tonne of fruit we would receive. The difficulty was that pickers were in short supply.

The bloke who drove the tractor towing the bin that holds 2.5 tonnes of grapes was in charge. He and his offsider gave everyone a 10-litre plastic bucket and left spares along the rows. As the buckets were filled, one of the crew would collect them and put the fruit in the bin. When the bin was full, the tractor trundled away to the truck parked in the shade, manœuvred the bin so that it was beside the truck, and then used the bin's hydraulics to raise it and tip its contents sideways into the truck's capacious, leak-proof, freshly painted interior. The supervisor then dissolved a packet of potassium metabisulphite – 250 grams in 2.5 litres of water – and sprinkled it over the grapes to stop oxidation and the intrusion of vinegar flies.

We started at seven in the morning in order to finish by three, before the extreme heat of the mid to late afternoon sun sucked the essence and oomph from us. The full bucolic panoply came into play. Magpies carolled, a kangaroo family hopped away from the raucous mob, the kelpies chased galahs and the wedgetailed eagles slowly circled above us. Conversations were shouted across vine rows, one bloke was singing and the heat beat down. This was one hell of a hot day, way above forecast temperature.

You have to concentrate on holding the bunch of grapes clear of the canopy and your fingers away from the very sharp picking snips and ignore the flies and dripping sweat. Morning smoko couldn't come soon enough to relieve our aching backs, and when it arrived a really cold drink rehydrated our parched throats.

After lunch and into the afternoon it was clear that everyone's strength was being sapped. The heat was brutal, well into the forties, sucking out sweat and energy. Three o'clock came and went. The trouble we were now facing was that the winery expected delivery by three thirty and if we missed this time slot we would lose our spot in the receiving line; when our fruit eventually arrived at the winery it would have to wait for a new slot. This could damage the quality of the fruit. It was tough.

The contractor called it a day at four. The balance of the pick would have to wait. Meanwhile I had nicked into the pub to collect a half dozen slabs of cold beer, soft drinks and ice for knock-off. This all disappeared quickly as weary workers replenished their body fluids. Then they departed, buggered.

At six thirty the following morning, we were back to finish the job, all except the older couples. Our fruit was plentiful and prices were good so we made a good return and our cash flow was starting to look healthy, at last.

~ * ~

Flicking through a copy of *SA Life* in the dentist's waiting room I was stopped by an article on what the writer described as a 'memorable food experience' at Black Rock Bay. This is an obscure location about 30 kilometres north of our favourite beach at Moonta Bay. The nearest town is Tickera, I learnt from the article, a thriving settlement on the northern Spencer Gulf coast of Yorke Peninsula. Jeni and I played 'mystery destination' games with Mike and Liz McIntyre, taking turns to suss out an unlikely destination for a mid-week lunch, and I thought I was onto a winner with Black Rock Bay, but I had no idea how to get there.

Like all country blokes who seem to know every location, Mike thought he could get us to Tickera and we'd take it from there. We headed west from Clare to Lochiel on the A1 between Port Wakefield and Port Pirie, across to Alford on the B87 and then over to the coast. Tickera is a pleasant coastal village with a long history. These days it's populated by retired farmers and silver-haired retirees living in their caravans and travelling Australia.

We arrived at a car park with an abundance of noticeboards, including one detailing the history of a well that was used for supplying fresh drinking water to Moonta. This supply had arrived after the mine's establishment but not in time to save the lives of my great-grandfather's children and hundreds of others.

An unofficial handpainted sign pointed the way to Black Rock Bay; others appeared at intervals along the unsealed track that took us to a car park on the cliff's edge, packed with vehicles. Carefully we picked our way down a steep slope to a weatherboard house nestled into the hillside beside a small beach.

We made our way past tall leafy trees forming a canopy for the crowded dining tables and down to a wide verandah flanking three sides of the cottage. It was filled with the happy, satisfied sounds of eating, talking, laughing diners, and it was there our hostess greeted us. She explained that as the restaurant did not yet have a liquor licence we could take our champagne to the beach where we'd find a gazebo, and please return in about an hour.

At the south end of the sands, flat stones and some large hefty wooden boxes were set out for customers to sit on in the shade of the 'gazebo', knocked together from shade cloth stretched between four tall stakes driven into the sand.

What more could we want – the sun shining, small waves lapping the sand, a couple of fishing boats bobbing picturesquely on the blue water, and a bottle of Vouvray. This sparkling wine is made by Kevin Mitchell – the winemaker at Kilikanoon in Penwortham – on his annual visit to the Loire Valley, a region in France noted for its Chenin Blanc grapes used for making both still and sparkling wines. The Vouvray had the tastes of the more famous champagnes with lots of small bubbles and flavours of green apples and buttered toast. We were excited, full of anticipation – what would the mystery lunch offer?

We wandered back at one thirty to the glassed-in verandah boasting windows and ceilings decorated with an extraordinary array of flotsam and jetsam gathered from the shore, and a mixture of tables and chairs that appeared to have been assembled from other people's collections.

Our hostess showed us to a corner table. She was an older woman, tallish and thin, with a little stoop and a relaxed and welcoming air as she swapped easy banter with the happy diners. Her daughter and granddaughter were the cooks and her husband and son-in-law, who were the fishermen, also cleared the tables and did the kitchen chores.

The menu was a simple but different, an 'either – or' selection for mains, depending on whether you wanted seafood or not.

'Either' was a three-part degustation:

~ Italian omelet with spicy sausage and bacon
~ Peas and asparagus on Scottish potato cakes
~ Baked free-range chook, preserved figs and feta cheese.

'Or' was seafood:

~ Blue swimmer crab on olive-oil toasts
~ Local fish with potatoes, tomato and onion bake
~ Squid, prawn and wild rice with salsa verde.

Having spent forty years running a cattle station Mike said he was heartily sick of beef. Jeni, whose father was a stock agent with ready access to mutton, said how lucky Mike was to have had beef, which she much prefers to mutton. Not to worry, neither beef nor mutton was on the menu.

We had a couple of bottles of Riesling in the cooler bag Mike had put under the table so as not to be seen going against the restaurant's absence of a liquor licence. There were no wine glasses on the table, of course, but there were teacups into which Mike covertly poured the wine. I don't think for a moment that our hostess would have missed what we were doing. We all chose seafood knowing how well it would match the sharp and citrus-crisp Rieslings.

The Vouvray and now the Riesling were having a calming effect on us all, loosening our chatter and increasing our jollity. As usual, Liz was the first to comment. 'This crabmeat is so sweet, juicy and firm, tastes of the sea, and how about these crab claws to crack and suck on?'

'What about this firm, sweet flathead and the spiced black-butter sauce?' Jeni responded. 'And the wild rice that's giving a touch of Middle East flavour to the squid and prawns?'

Sunshine on the placid blue water, some inappropriate cowboy music in the background, and Mike telling us one of his unlikely bush tales all made for a most unlikely hillbilly lunch.

The son-in-law came over for a chat and from him we learned that the family had turned their backs on a dry inland country life near Coober Pedy in favour of this seaside paradise and the adventure of running a highly idiosyncratic restaurant.

Better seafood you could not find. It was stunningly fresh and so perfectly and imaginatively prepared. What a merry and unusual scene, an enchanting eating spot to discover not too far from Clare Valley.

Grilled calamari and prawns

Ingredients for 2 servings as an entrée

4 baby potatoes
fresh oregano, chopped
garlic, chopped
fresh zest and juice of 1 lemon
1 tbs good quality olive oil
cracked black pepper and salt
2 medium calamari tubes, about 200 g
8 medium green shelled prawns, about 140 g
1 medium red onion, sliced
fresh rosemary
4 lettuce leaves

Scrub the potatoes but do not peel. Rub them with olive oil, place them in a baking dish and sprinkle with sea salt and fresh rosemary. Bake in a 180°C oven for an hour.

Mix oil, garlic, lemon zest and juice, chopped oregano, salt and pepper in a bowl.

Skin the calamari tubes and slice into rings 5 mm thick and cover in marinade. Add the prawns to the marinade in the last 3 minutes before cooking. Mix well.

Heat the BBQ plate or chasseur until very hot, pour on a little olive oil and fry the sliced onion until well done and a little crisp.

Drain prawns and calamari and gently add to the onions. Cook for 2 minutes each side. Retain the marinade and heat gently.

Distribute prawns, calamari and fried onion onto the lettuce leaves on plates, spoon a little of the marinade over these and serve with oven baked potatoes.

Wine match: Sangiovese, Nebbiolo, Vermentino, Touriga

~ * ~

When we bought The Hill, there were three small stock dams, two of which we pushed in and over-planted with vines. The third, in the southeast corner near the big bore, we call our yabby dam. We put nets in it and the large irrigation dam in the months from September to April, during sunny spells.

The first thing to do this morning was to take the nets to the yabby dam. As a lure, we use fat cut from lamb or mutton with a certain pong that yabbies don't much like. It's said that yabbies are vegetarian and feed on grass and weeds growing around the water and that a bale of hay should be thrown into the dam now and again for them to feast on. Some silly sod told us that soap is good bait because it has a high fat content. We tried it once and found that the soap in the little bait net went sloppy in the water and was difficult to remove, and there wasn't a yabby in sight.

Our yabbies aren't huge and at times it takes a couple of days to get enough to feed two people. We put the really small ones back as we do the females with eggs clutched under their tails bent back to their bellies for safekeeping. The catch goes into rainwater in the laundry sink for a day to be purged.

To cook the yabbies put them into a pot of deep boiling water which kills them instantly. When they turn red, in a few minutes, tip them into a colander and allow to cool, then peel the shell from the tail meat and remove the flesh from the claws. The flavour is incredibly delicate, so be gentle with what you add. The sauce is poured over our homemade pasta with its soft and gentle texture. Homemade pasta is great to have with any sauce, come to think of it, if you can find the time to make it.

Homemade fettuccine pasta with yabby sauce

Ingredients for 4 servings

You will need a pasta-making machine

Pasta dough

250 g plain flour

1 tps salt

2 extra-large eggs

Yabby sauce

4 cloves of garlic, chopped

small fresh chopped chilli with seeds removed (optional)

250 mL dry white wine

fresh basil leaves, torn

freshly cooked and peeled yabbies

olive oil

Pasta dough

Using food processor, place flour and salt in processing bowl. Lightly beat the egg and oil together in another bowl. With motor running, add egg mixture through feed tube and process for about 5 seconds. Gradually add water until the mixture forms a ball.

Turn dough out onto a lightly floured board and knead briefly until soft and silky.

Divide the ball of dough into two, flatten one piece slightly and pass it through the roller of your machine, set at the widest setting. Flour the dough lightly to prevent sticking. Fold the dough into thirds, press down and pass through the rollers again. Leave the machine on this setting and repeat another 6 or 7 times to knead the dough. Sprinkle with flour as required. The dough will become very smooth.

To roll out the pasta: set rollers at next setting to place them closer together. Pass the dough through the rollers. Do not fold. Lightly flour the dough.

Continue to flour pasta lightly and pass though the rollers, reducing the gap each time until it reaches the desired fineness. Repeat process with remaining half.

To cut pasta into fettuccine noodles pass through cutting roller with wide teeth. Support the noodles with your hand as they emerge. Hang the lengths over a rod resting between a chair and the kitchen bench.

Cook the fettuccine in boiling water until al dente, about 4–5 minutes. Be careful not to overcook. Drain.

Yabby sauce

Heat olive oil in frying pan and fry garlic and chilli until garlic turns yellow.

Add the wine and cook to reduce slightly, add basil and yabby meat and cook for 2 minutes. Do not overcook.

Place the pasta into a warm serving dish and pour the sauce over.

Crack black pepper on top.

Wine match: Riesling, Viognier, Chardonnay, Vermentino

On the way back from the yabby dam, Jackie suddenly darted into the vine rows we were passing and moments later came prancing out shaking a dog's collar in her mouth. She was so pleased she ran at me, up my leg, into my arms, gave me a kiss and then down again. The collar was the reason for her ebullience because she had lost it a few weeks earlier, arriving home one day undressed. I hadn't realised a dog had so many ways of expressing pleasure. We both told her how wonderful she was, much to Janette's chagrin.

As we approached the large irrigation dam, Janette ran ahead, scattering a squadron of black ducks that had taken up residence around the water's edge. Returning with one in her mouth, she adroitly flicked it to one side to break its neck and then laid it at Jeni's feet. Great praise was lavished on Janette. The score was even.

That evening, with much anticipation, Jeni plucked, cleaned and roasted the duck for the evening's meal. But, after all her work the duck was very tough and a great disappointment. Perhaps we should have hung it for a couple of days or maybe just left it for the dogs to share.

We continued our walk, Jeni swinging the duck, up a bit of a slope to old gums slowly dying from mistletoe infestation. There we came upon a pair of wedgetailed eagles tearing into a rabbit or, hopefully, a hare. Taken by surprise, they paused, then, flapping their huge wings, took off awkwardly, one of them dropping a feather, which I picked up. I knew something of the story of this feather and a few others I had on my desk. I wondered if they would have made good quills for some writer or composer in centuries past.

We were heading for the northern boundary fence, the long way home, so as to get in a long walk in an effort to deal with our excess intake of kilojoules. Suddenly the kelpies propped, ears erect, snouts sniffing, one leg and tail raised. There, with its head through the square of the mesh wire, was a ewe, well and truly stuck and, given the furrow it had dug with its front feet, it had been there for some time. Jeni held the dogs while I went to help the ewe.

Urgently, she tried to pull back, but her ears and chin prevented her from moving her head at all. First I tried to pull the wire apart, widening the gap, but only succeeded in producing minimal movement of wire and maximum panic in the sheep as she pushed further into the mesh. Then I tried flattening her ears and levelling her chin, to no avail, as the more I tried to push her back, the more she pushed forward. But at last she got the message, pulling back as I pulled the wire forward, while holding her ears flat and her chin up. Soon she was free and immediately raced to the corner fenceline, again trying to push her head into a mesh square. It took some minutes for her to realise freedom lay behind her in all that open space.

The open space in which we were immersed was a huge bonus. On our walks down to the vineyard to work each day and back for breaks I marvelled at the openness and views surrounding us. The daily trudge down and up The Hill, along with our long leisurely walks for pleasure, resulted in fit, slimed-down bodies attuned to and enjoying the hard slog.

~ * ~

Over the lunch at Black Rock Bay, Mike had reminisced about their days working cattle in the northern pastoral country. He reckoned they were much easier to handle than sheep – no tailing or dipping, drenching and shearing, therefore less yarding required and therefore lower costs. In any case, he said, we really only wanted stock to keep the weeds under control to avoid slashing two or three times a year so why not try calves. He'd give us a hand in buying and selling and would talk with his mate about stock. Who knows, maybe we'd even make a couple of quid. And so we moved into Hereford calves.

The main requirement he said was a good-enough fence to keep them out of the vineyard; unlike sheep the calves were more likely to test their confinement. I helped Mike erect another fence, a different set up to a sheep and lamb fence and I must say it didn't look too professional to me.

Now we owned calves we decided to go to the annual Clare agricultural show to look at the beef entries and to talk to the people involved. But at the Clare show there was not a prize bull in sight; stock judging was kept for the major Adelaide show. There was a dog jumping competition, however, contested mainly by border collies and kelpies.

A flat-top ute was equipped with one hay bale atop another on top of which the dog owner stood. The dog had to jump from the ground onto the tray and up the bales into the arms of its owner to complete a successful round. This was very popular, with many young blokes watching, but whether it was interest in the dogs that held their attention or the shapely curves of one of the dog owners was a moot point. We watched because her dog was a kelpie bitch, full of energy and enthusiasm, really pleased with the applause as she demonstrated her jumping skills.

From this contest we wandered along and found ourselves in the beer tent. Chatting away over our draughts about the show dogs' abilities, and wondering if our two could be trained to achieve such feats, we found ourselves joined by a couple of blokes who also had been watching the jumping. They introduced themselves as Rodney and Ric, said they just loved the dogs and owned a schnauzer. They went on to talk about the former manse in Auburn they had just bought. We said we knew the former owners and asked why they had bought in Auburn. Over a few more beers they asked us would we like to join them for lunch in a couple of weeks. Would we ever?

The manse was a sandstone villa with slate roof and a plentiful supply of small rooms. Modern 'antique' furniture and many sterling silver artefacts gave it a somewhat grand style, though the kitchen seemed to be cluttered with different styles and shapes of woven baskets. The house had a rather cold feeling although open fires were burning in the sitting and dining rooms. One guest, a lawyer, suggested it was like the former rectors, all hellfire but cold as charity.

The guests were an eclectic mix of couples – the lawyer and an accountant, an obstetrician and an artist, a winemaker and a real estate agent, a pub owner and a cook, ourselves and our hosts. What a rowdy bunch. The food was somewhat overshadowed by the copious bottles of good wines, except for the eggplant fritters. Our social life was expanding with this bunch of really interesting people; the pub owner, who was chair of the Clare Racing Club, asked us to become members. Subsequently we did. We drove carefully home along the beautiful back track abuzz with what we had just experienced.

Eggplant fritters

Ingredients for 2 servings

1 medium eggplant
1 egg
spring onion, sliced thinly
salt & pepper
olive oil

Slice the eggplant lengthwise about 1 cm thick. Microwave for 2 minutes. Remove slices and gently score lengthwise with a fork.
Beat an egg (2 if using a number of eggplants) with salt, pepper and the sliced spring onion.
Heat olive oil in a frying pan. When very hot, dip the eggplant into the egg and then into the frying pan and cook until brown.
Drain on kitchen paper and serve hot as entrée or a side for the main.

Wine match: dry Riesling, Chardonnay, Viognier, Cabernet Sauvignon, Shiraz (depending on what meat you are having with your main course)

~ * ~

The sheep had been no problem staying within the fencelines and although their lambs slithered under to feed on green patches they also slithered back again as mothers moved on. The calves were a different matter altogether. The fencing we had erected was nowhere strong enough to deal with their habit of scratching along the top barb causing the fence to partially collapse under the strain, allowing the curious among them to explore for green grass patches and the succulent vine leaves. A vine can't ripen its fruit without leaves.

Each morning when I arose to get the early pot of green tea I would look down into the calves' paddock to check. It wasn't unusual to see part of it on the ground and the calves grazing among the vines. Quickly we would dress, hop down the slope to gently urge them back and to knock droppers back into place. Jeni didn't appreciate being so rudely awakened rather than slowly coming to with her mug of tea.

As someone wrote, when you have livestock you also have dead stock. That was our experience with foxes preying on the lambs, and it was also our story with the calves. One died from eating onion weed inconveniently dropping at the edge of the yabby dam. I rang Mike for help. He told me to dig a deep hole away from the water and arrived with his old four-wheel drive to drag it by the legs to the hole. We set about trying to eliminate onion weed by spraying at flowering time.

When the time came to sell the bovines, a couple of years later, Mike gave us the name of a buyer. This bloke arrived in the latest Range Rover decked out in crisp RM Williams moleskins and polished boots. He asked me how many hectares I owned and how many people I employed and scoffed when I answered thirty-six and casuals. He then proceeded to tell me the calves weren't the best he had ever seen and offered a very low per-kilo price. I defended the quality of the stock and tried to push up the price but he wasn't in a playful mood and wouldn't budge above ninety cents. Afterwards Mike reckoned it should have been at least

$1.10. Turned out the buyer was one of the biggest beef producers in the state.

We didn't make much on this little project but at least the calves kept the weeds under control which, in not having to slash, saved us a lot of effort, time and the cost of diesel. The experience of interacting with these animals was good, something different, but still compatible with our vineyard endeavours.

9

Our business was going well but how were we to distinguish productive equilibrium from stagnation. 'Disrupt the calm' is the mantra in business circles, to make the required mental adjustments so as to bring a creative approach to the task of strengthening, probably enlarging, our little venture. A romantic moment fuelled by Cornish Celtic Ale led to the light bulb revealing the next major stage of our dream – developing a cellar door and art gallery and bringing out our own wine label.

Our work program didn't allow for extended holidays so when we needed a break we would head to the coastal town of Moonta, about an hour's drive to the west. In the very hot months of January and February we would just go for a swim, leaving at 6 am, walk the kelpies for a few kilometres, have a swim then a cup of coffee at the Henley-on-George, and be back in the vineyard by about 10 am. This time, though, we would stay a few days and try the new Italian restaurant.

When the kelpies saw Jeni packing the bags that evening for an early start next morning they barked their encouragement for they knew they were in for another adventure. Jackie slept on top of a case that night so as to be sure we didn't forget her.

We had found a bloke who rented a few cabins and would allow the kelpies on site so long as they did not go into the cabin. This was fine by them as they loved to sleep in the ute. As a sideline he pickled onions, using his own secret recipe with just the right amount of spiced vinegar to produce a crunchy, well flavoured snack to accompany a hard, tasty cheese and a cold beer.

We were in Moonta by about 7.30 the next morning then drove on to Port Hughes for a long walk on the beach, a swim and a sunbake then back to the cabin for a shower and a change before heading off for lunch at the Seagate Bistro. I must have been in a very relaxed holiday mood to make such a dire mistake when choosing the bottle of fizz. There were only three on the wine list and I should have asked before selecting a Killawarra Dusk, assuming it would be a Rosé. Well, it was pink and it was plonk.

The bottle was brought to the table opened and artistically arranged in the ice bucket with crossed flutes. The waitress busied off allowing me to pour. The first mouthful was alarmingly bad. This was a gassed white wine to which strawberry syrup had been added. It was so bad we just had to laugh, but the lunch was great and made up for it.

Looking for a cleanser we wandered over to a nearby motel advertising a genuine Cornish Celtic Ale. In the front garden we sat under an umbrella enjoying the ale, looking down onto the seascape with a couple of yachts and a few fishing tinnies. Swoon! We just had to have another.

Jeni was talking about our friends the Goulburns and the activities room they recently had added to house their library, TV and stereo, bridge table and whatever.

'It's a great way of getting the books and the large TV out of the living area and a great place for piano practice and I like the idea of a winter snug with open fire,' Jeni chatted away.

'I could practice my sax there', I said 'when I buy a new one that is, and we could use it for learning how to tango, when we find someone willing to come up to teach us and enough friends to join us to help defray the costs.'

Another round of dark, fluffy draughts was poured, a welcome counter to the saltiness of the seafood bisque we had had for lunch. Suddenly Jeni chirped up, 'Hey Burtie, I've just had this marvellous idea. This Celtic drop has unlocked the right side of my brain. Now we have a couple of employees to help in the vineyard why don't we extract ourselves from that hard slog, and expand the activities room idea into a cellar door.'

'What, and bring out our own label?'

'Yes, exactly. We've been going to all of these conferences and workshops on the future of the wine industry and the financial planner said we had to value add or we aren't optimising our potential.'

'We couldn't build a winery on site because we don't have mains water and we have only single phase power. But, I guess we could keep back some of our fruit to take to a local winemaker with a good reputation,' I added, becoming intrigued by Jeni's idea.

Jeni was bubbling on. 'And remember that the pundits told us people wanted more that just wine tasting at a cellar door. There's the designated drivers to consider and some people won't be interested in wine but might like coffee and cake or a pruner's platter.'

'And, Jeni, how about this? How about designing the cellar door to be large enough to double as an art gallery? That would really give visitors something else to consider. Remember how we liked so much going to gallery openings in Adelaide and talking with the artists?'

Certainly we had the views to attract people and make them want to linger, and in the third stage of developing the vineyard we had been considering planting alternative grape varieties to provide a marketing point of difference. So, instead of the hard yakka of vineyard work we would swan on in our cellar-door gallery. Our fantasies were really off and away, expanding with each mouthful. Naively we were enjoying the lure of the quicksand dreams drawing in the innocents.

Jeni harked back to Charmian Clift on the island of Hydra when the Australian artist Sidney Nolan came for a visit. They were nicely away on retsina and Charmian was complaining about her lot and how she desperately wanted to get back to her writing. Nolan suddenly burst out, 'Bloody well fly then why don't you. It doesn't matter if you don't succeed, just so long as you try. Nobody can be blamed for trying.'

'I love it,' I said. 'Somebody said that life without risk is no life at all, so let's bloody well fly and just hope we get it right.'

We returned from our holiday brimming with enthusiasm to get the project underway. Over the next few days we sketched mud maps for the cellar-door gallery to be added to the northern end of the house with a large terrace on the eastern side of the house where people could while away time just sitting, contemplating the view. On the northern side the land fell away so that the gallery would have room underneath to use for wine storage but, more importantly, to build a studio apartment with en suite, private terrace and car park. At last we came up with a plan more or less drawn to scale and next time we were in Adelaide we took it to the draughtsman in Brighton for him to turn into building code.

I must admit that in thinking this through we did not seek specific professional advice about how to plan and present our new venture. Instead, we drew on the many courses, workshops and conferences we had undertaken to knock together our version of a business plan. This was a remarkable step for us to take, but then remarkable experiences do seem to come from small beginnings.

The project was dogged by setbacks from the beginning, starting, naturally enough, with the local council and the *Development Act*. The interpretation of this already complicated piece of legislation adds thousands of dollars to the cost of building. Why it is mandatory, for example, for the front of a house to face the street rather than allowing the orientation of the block to indicate the best environmental positioning for summer shade and winter sun, to say nothing of the view.

Our vineyard is situated in a zone labelled 'rural, agricultural', meaning that all activities apart from farming are subject to council approval. The only activity altogether banned is a conference facility. Maybe this is why the council would not approve construction of a religious facility for a non-conformist group just down the road from us near the racecourse, and also why the argument was taken by the proponents all the way through the planning appeals process at a cost to them of $90,000, so they said. They won. The message was clear, however: make sure there was no mention of a conference facility in our application even though cellar doors are favourite locations for such gatherings.

Progress through the council's system took months, though there was only one objection, and the delay stuffed up my arrangements with the stonemason and project manager. The objection was from the owner of Fawcett's old property, a former union official who had used the property as a country retreat but had now retired to a plush two-storey affair on the coast. His grievance was the possibility of the increasing traffic passing his property to our cellar door creating a troublesome level of road dust. In time his objection was thrown out.

At the time a friend of ours had decided to build a large, two-storey house on a tennis court in the Adelaide Hills. He had secured the services of a retired builder who now spent most of his time managing building projects. His job was to hire sub-contractors and buy materials at least at cost and ensure they arrived on site, on time and in logical sequence. As site manager he was also the quality controller. He charged ten per cent of the overall cost for his services.

I said to Jeni we should do the same. She said I had done a great job of managing our Seacliff rebuild and thought I should do it again now to save the ten per cent, but I thought I had quite enough on my hands managing the vineyard, teeing up a winemaker to process our grapes, arranging to have labels designed and printed, making decisions about bottle size and closure, finding someone to do the bottling, and so on it went. Unfortunately, we settled for the project manager.

The first problem was with the stonemason, by now the only mason left in town. Originally he had agreed to do the job, but because council approval was delayed he had started a long job at an old winery; he said we were next on his list. The other mason had retired aged eighty-seven and could not be talked into changing his mind even though I visited him several times in the pub to try to persuade him.

When the mason did arrive, the project manager immediately began an argument with him. The mason wanted the floor to ceiling windows to be put in place first by the project manager so the mason could snug his wall against them. The manager wanted part of the wall to be erected first against which the windows could be fitted. The entire length of the western wall and half of the northern was Mt Gambier limestone and part of it was double-storeyed. It was a huge job. Neither was willing to listen to my urging them to get on with it. On reflection, I think the project manager was overcommitted – he had a number of other jobs going on in Adelaide – and the mason wanted to fit in another small, long-standing commitment before starting on ours.

The argument about which should come first started in December and was not resolved before Christmas, and as all building trades down tools for holidays in January, infuriatingly we incurred a two-month delay.

Once things were underway though, they proceeded quite well for a time, but then the project manager brought in a carpenter, a dopey bastard who couldn't get started in the morning until he'd smoked a couple of joints, and who had great difficulty keeping going in the afternoon because he'd have a couple more at lunch; after a while his slow progress began to influence the mason. And then the carpenter made a dreadful balls-up of fixing the scenic windows upstairs on the eastern wall. Even I could see these floor-to-ceiling pieces of glass were not solidly attached and wondered how they would survive in the face of the very strong winds in this exposed location.

Fortunately, his mistakes were resolved by the welcome intervention of the cabinet-maker who was an ex-builder and took an interest in what we were up to. Construction was at an advanced stage by this time, and the project manager was absent on his many other jobs at crucial times, so we were very pleased to have the cabinet-maker to lean on. Maybe he took pity on us or his obvious obsession with precision and detail made him willing to intervene; we asked him to take over managing the final stages of the project.

The original time frame agreed on was three months and no more than four. The actual time it took was fifteen months and the cost overrun was double the original quote. We became disappointed wrecks in trying to deal with the constant problems and in desperation turned to our kelpies for solace; they were understanding and comforting.

Taking the cellar door and gallery to extreme possibilities, we applied for and received a Special Circumstances Liquor Licence. This allowed us to make our own wine, run a cellar door and a restaurant that would seat a hundred people, and sell other brands of wine and alcohol. But it also meant we had to redevelop our kitchen to commercial standards. Back to TAFE to be accredited to HACCP standards for handling food and we both enrolled in the 'how to run a cellar door' course to get our 'responsible serving of alcohol' certificates.

Next we enrolled in a 'small winemaking' course, again run by TAFE. Twelve of us were enrolled but only eleven turned up. Each person was required to bring in a hundred kilograms of red grapes, preferably Shiraz or Cabernet Sauvignon. The winemaker supervising all of this ran one of the smaller wineries in The Valley where we assembled for most of the classes.

We each tipped our grapes into the receival bin, which trundled them into the de-stemmer, from where the grapes were transferred to the press – a large stainless-steel cylinder with an inner membrane which, when inflated, gently presses the fruit against the steel sides, allowing the free run juice to drain into a tank. The slow release of the juice is a finely balanced process to extract flavour from the skins and to eliminate the possibility of over-extraction, which could result in the production of harsh tannins from the skins and seeds. Once completed, the 800-odd litres of juice were then transferred to an old fermentation vessel made from slabs of Mintaro slate.

But this was only the start. Dutifully we participated in the ensuing complex stages of the winemaking process and found it taxing but fascinating. The grapes underwent fermentation (a process which converts sugars in the grapes to ethanol and is assisted by the addition of yeast) to gently extract colour and important soft tannins over eight to nine days. The skins float to the surface and, unless constantly plunged, will form an impenetrable barrier blocking the escape of CO_2 and the ingress of oxygen, all of which may stall fermentation. Many readings were taken and analysed during the process to gauge progress and guide decision-making.

Hand plunging isn't easy work and has to be undertaken twice daily. Each of us took turns to do this. In a very large winery it is most often done automatically by machine. After fermentation was completed, secondary malolactic fermentation takes place to convert harsh or strong malic acid to lactic acid, which has lower acidity. The fermented juice was then transferred to French oak barrels to mature for 15 to 18 months.

During this wait the wine must be racked a number of times to eliminate sediment that gathers in the bottom of the barrels and replace contents lost to evaporation as the wine seeps into the wood leaving an increasing surface of wine exposed to oxygen. Some air is required for the wine to mature but too much may cause spoilage. Racking is undertaken by transferring the clear wine via a hose from one barrel to another. It's a rather messy process, especially the washing out of the empty barrels with hot water under pressure to eliminate the possibility of any nasties developing in the wood. The process must be undertaken a number of times whilst the wines is still ageing in barrels.

All of these laborious processes convinced us we were right in wanting to use an established winemaker and his winery to make our wine. Not only would we save ourselves from all this heavy work, but we would also avoid expensive investment in plant and equipment that would only be used for a short time each year. So we thought our decision to call upon an expert winemaker's surplus capacity was the right one – but at a cost, of course.

Building and equipping the cellar door to be run also as a reception and conference centre meant taking out a large overdraft. For the first time we were in debt, but we were consoled by reminding ourselves about the advice remembered from the financial course; if we were not gearing our investment we were not fully using our asset potential. So the debt didn't really trouble us. We had a strong income stream from the vineyard and behind our romantic whim was the prospect of our kids one day taking over. One son already had his viticultural credentials from Roseworthy Agricultural College, another was a qualified chef with international experience, and a third was a born salesman. All that was needed was a strong administrator who knew how to keep the books in order, which sounded just like the chef's spouse.

Mind you, this was just part of *our* dream – so far there had been no consultation with the offspring. We weren't endeavouring to create a dynasty, just revelling in our new-found freedom and way of life.

How do you go about designing a label for a wine bottle, I wondered. Given the hundreds you can see in any bottle shop we thought ours had to be distinctive. We decided that a purple for the red and a canary colour for the white would do just that. We had previously discussed labels with the proprietor of a bottle shop in North Adelaide. We decided to visit him. He told us he was an expert on labels so we thought we'd run our choice of colours past him.

'Look, mate,' he said, 'yellow would look like a "two-buck chuck" bottle from the US. And as for purple for the reds, only gay blokes would buy a bottle of red wine with a purple label.'

'Right, we'll sell our reds in Auburn then,' I said.

'Don't be ridiculous, Burtie,' Jeni said, ever practical, 'even that bunch of wine connoisseurs couldn't drink our entire vintage.'

We paid a visit to the leading label printer in Angaston to talk to a young designer with years of experience. I had come up with a basic line drawing of a mount, representing The Hill, a fish impaled on the mount, representing Jeni, who was born a Pike, and a bunch of grapes underneath, representing the fruitful outcome of this impalement. Crude, you say? Well, yes, it was, but fortunately the young bloke pushed those images around and came up with a rather conservative but thoughtful design to incorporate all the ideas.

Next we had to find a bottling plant. The only local one was much more expensive than the itinerant plant that came right to the winery, saving the cost of moving the wine from winery to the bottler and back. The manager of the mobile plant was hard to pin down, but when he did arrive we had a great time helping him to load the cartons. This was an amazing factory on wheels starting with a bottle wash, an assembly line to fill the bottles and apply labels, a printing facility to mark and then assemble the cartons and, after we had filled them with bottles, an apparatus to seal them with glue. My job was to stack sixty-four cartons onto a pallet whilst a bloke on a front-end loader hoisted them back into the winery where they would rest for a few weeks to recover from 'bottling shock'.

~ * ~

How to attract customers to buy our products? We concluded, in the time-honoured manner, that you give them away in free tastings. But how do you get customers to attend free tastings? You invite them to an art exhibition opening, we decided, and that's just what we did. A hundred and thirty turned up to our first event. They drank our wines, ate our home-made hors d'œuvre, then bought a number of paintings and many cases of wine.

We asked a local politician formally to open the exhibition and we invited the editor of the local newspaper to come and hear what she had to say, resulting in a half-page write-up the following week. Being billed as the only purpose-built art gallery in the Mid North enticed many locals to visit, so we were off to a good start.

Then we were faced with the question of how to get publicity for the studio apartment? It so happened that our politician friend's daughter was to be married so we invited her to use our accommodation unit on her wedding night. As a result we later hosted many honeymooning couples and many wedding celebrations with sit-down diners.

The next trial was to work out how to sell wine in a crowded market where nobody knew our label. Why not just hit the road on a sales campaign, get people to taste what we're offering and, hey presto, there's a sale. We planned a massive campaign – several journeys, each lasting a week, to visit every pub and licensed eatery in every town in the Mid North, Upper North, Yorke Peninsula and Eyre Peninsula. We wrote and printed our tasting notes and price lists, thought through a tasting procedure and the accessories required for this, and wrote out a patter that we just knew would convince a host of buyers. Talk about clearing our thinking and preparing for the unknown. How you deal with change will govern your future – or such was the received wisdom – so off we went with a few dozen cases and the kelpies.

We were well received. Owners, cooks, bar staff and waiters were all interested in tasting our wines, and even a few customers in the pubs joined in, self-invited. The staff all liked our wines, the cooks were interested in our food match suggestions but, no, the owners wouldn't buy. They relied on agents working for the large wineries to fill their shelves and to write the orders for replacements. Demand for wines in the 1990s in most country pubs wasn't high and the little that existed was in the low-cost, commercial category.

The quality of our wines was much higher, but so was the cost, because small quantities of each variety were produced. We sold very little on our initial excursions so tried again the following year, but with similar results. We also tried advertising our cellar door and romantic studio apartment in the small regional newspapers, again, with only limited success.

Canvassing within the immediate Clare area produced much better results, but was not without its problems. The usual terms for wine sales included payment on delivery, especially to hotels, but a popular one demanded sixty days, and even then was slow in settling.

Restaurants often ran 'winery of the month' programs, but some demanded fourteen bottles to the dozen and then sold each bottle at two to three times the price they paid for them. We were competing against larger wineries with their widely advertised and much lower cost products. Even with generous mark-ups, the restaurants wouldn't pay the account for two to three months.

From these experiences we concluded it was better to sell only through our cellar door, selling fewer cases but at a price higher than wholesale. And so we circled back to the original problem:

how to get people to our winery. We decided that because the occasional art exhibition openings, with tastings of our wines, attracted a good crowd, we should hold an opening every five weeks. There would be one week to assemble and hang the pieces, develop the catalogue, mail out invitations and then we were ready for the four-week exhibition. This worked, allowing us to sell not only the art but also our wine and at times our food platters. We were certainly giving it our best shot – trying new ideas and harnessing new opportunities.

It was now necessary to develop a website to keep up with new trends in selling our offerings. Jeni was an excellent typist, but knew nothing about computers, so it was off to TAFE yet again, to the beginners' courses, then the advanced course, and then to master spreadsheets and computer publishing. We had outside help to design the engine room of the web and to give Jeni the skills to conquer the intricacies of updating the contents of our website, all of which became another demand on her time. We also set up a system so that our customers could order our wines and book our accommodation and pay online, although most of the accommodation bookings arrive via a search engine, for which we pay a reasonable commission.

In these various ways we were plunged into the new and complex technological demands of the online retail world, a startling change for us from the simple demands of the vineyard. No one could say we were stagnating. We were constantly on the lookout for new ways to make ourselves of continuing interest to our customers.

When Australia's winemaking pioneers planted their first vines they chose varieties popular in their home culture, those from France mostly, and Spain, but when it came to planting our third stage the thoughts of the Tesco buyer and my chats with Secundo came to mind. Along with the traditional varieties we added small blocks of Viognier, Pinot Gris and Nebbiolo. It took the Mildura Wine Show to bring these varieties to the attention of the wine writers and it took wine drinkers somewhat longer.

While all of this was going on, we still had to manage the demanding work in the vineyard. Of late this hadn't been going well, possibly because we weren't in the blocks with the workers. On Fridays at knock-off we would have a meeting with them over a couple of beers to talk about the program for the next week, and then each week morning I would discuss the day's schedule with them. Eventually this level of supervision proved to be insufficient.

Serendipitously, at this time we were invited to a grower's get-together by one of the smaller wineries that bought some of our fruit. We got chatting to a young man called Adam who, a few years back, had worked with a gang installing trellising in our Red Kelpie Block. He was a personable young bloke who often broke into a large cheeky smile while talking. He had established his own contracting business and was offering full vineyard services.

On our way home I suggested to Jeni that our two workers had lost interest and perhaps it was time to make a change, to 'disrupt the calm'. Why not engage Adam as contractor? Let him find the pruning and harvesting gangs, do all the paperwork and deal with the hassles of the public servants for information about tax and the endlessly changing rules of superannuation and occupational health and safety regulations. Although there would be a cost for doing this the change would mean that the administrative demands on us became much simpler.

Adam readily agreed, 16 hectares was a good-sized area to add to his growing business. This meant dismissing our two workers, which didn't seem to upset them as there were lots of jobs available in The Valley. We had no trouble selling the tractor, spray unit and slasher, and so we circled back to our original business plan.

Our lives were to be entirely altered by the changes we had introduced to life on The Hill. The Hill had been our sanctuary, a retreat where we were in control and most ourselves. Now, our new personas began to emerge with insights about business life and changing technology, and open to new experiences as we interacted with those who heeded our call to visit our cellar-door gallery. These experiences were positive, on the whole, with the return of many guests who appreciated our wines, food platters and the great views.

~ * ~

One thing that didn't change was our attendance at the races. Our property overlooks the Clare Valley racecourse and we had become members of the Race Club some time after we arrived. Unlike the Balaclava course, which is flat and large, the Clare racecourse brings you closer to the horses both before and during each race. It's a compact, small track with a gentle slope to its west, allowing for easy viewing.

Racing in Clare began in the 1880s when Easter weekend meetings were held at various large properties in the district. From this beginning a number of people provided finance to establish the course as one in the South Australian circuit of annual events, holding picnic meetings a number of times each year. For racegoers in the Mid North, gathering at Clare for the Easter Saturday meeting before moving to Oakbank in the Adelaide Hills for the larger Easter Monday event became the thing to do. Now, most of the older people remain for the Clare Easter Monday meeting, not wishing to become stuck in traffic jams along the miles of narrow roads leading into and away from the Oakbank course, and wishing to avoid police breathalyser screenings. But the younger ones camp in their swags under their utes and take off on the Sunday for Oakbank.

We became part of the group gathered under the trees at the southern end of the course among the utes and four-wheel drives laden with picnic hampers and local wines, especially Clare Rieslings. Jeni's mother would join us for the weekend, betting on each favourite and able to claim by the last race she had backed many winners and come out ahead, though not by much.

After I was invited to become a committee member of the Race Club I found myself acting as a volunteer labourer to get the grounds and pavilion in order before each meeting. One item on the agenda I found interesting was the question of what to do with the old grandstand. It was a lovely piece of early twentieth-century architecture and age was its problem. It had not been lovingly maintained and now featured unsafe railings and a bit of a wobble in high winds due to the activity of white ants, a pest in this area.

To knock it down was an easy matter but what would replace it? I had previous experience with state government grants for all sorts of things including amenities for sporting groups. I contacted the Department of Recreation and Sport to obtain the lengthy paperwork required for the competitive bidding process and applied for $10,000 to replace the grandstand with a concrete pad and sun sails.

A couple of months later at the next race meeting I saw the newly elected South Australian premier at the bar. I button-holed him over a beer, and explained about the grandstand and the application.

'Right,' he said, 'that's got my support. One of my ministers is over there, go and tell her the same story and say I said to do something about it.'

The $10,000 duly arrived. Committee members helped to dismantle the old stand and the thing that surprised me that day was the large number of populated rabbit burrows in the ground under the floorboards. The occupants scattered; after a few months we didn't have the same trouble with rabbits in the vineyard.

It was at one of these meetings that Rodney and Ric from Auburn introduced us to Robert, a former actor and a wonderful pianist. His most recent claim to fame was ownership of Wolta Wolta, the elegant 1860s homestead just off Horrocks Highway, a little to the west of Clare township. This property had been destroyed in the 1983 bushfires but had been lovingly restored and now was filled with antique furniture and an exceptionally large collection of glassware.

Robert wanted to revive the English high tea tradition and so began monthly meetings in the homes of the five couples involved in this delightful practice. The first was at Wolta Wolta, with Robert's partner buried in kitchen preparations while Robert regaled us with resounding flourishes on his grand piano.

We in turn introduced our friends from Burra to the group and included Portuguese cinnamon tarts when it became our turn to do the afternoon spread. At the time we were advertising in *Blaze*, the Adelaide magazine of the gay community. This led to a new friendship when Francis and his partner, Putu, arrived at our cellar door for coffee and homemade cake.

Portuguese custard tarts

Ingredients for 12 tarts

125 g caster sugar

2 tbs cornflour

3 egg yolks

1 ¼ cups milk

2 tsp vanilla extract

2 sheets butter puff pastry sheets, frozen

1 tsp ground cinnamon plus extra to dust

Heat the oven to 220°C.

Lightly grease a 12 medium-hole muffin tray.

Combine sugar and cornflour in a bowl. Whisk egg yolks and milk together in another bowl until smooth. Pour into sugar mixture and whisk until combined.

Transfer to a small saucepan and stir constantly over medium heat until the mixture thickens. Remove from the heat and stir in vanilla.

Transfer to a bowl and leave to cool, completely covered with cling film.

Lay one pastry sheet on a lightly floured bench top. Sprinkle with cinnamon and lay second sheet on top. Cut in half. Roll up tightly from short side to form a log.

Cut into 2 cm thick slices. Lay cut-side onto lightly floured surface. Roll out until 10 cm in diameter.

Line each muffin hole with a round of pastry. Fill each with custard and liberally sprinkle cinnamon on top. Transfer to oven and reduce temperature to 200°C. Bake for 20–25 minutes, or until the pastry is golden and custard has set. Cool in tin for 10 minutes. Transfer to a wire rack and cool completely.

Wine match: Spanish Pedro Ximinez Sherry, Muscat, Petit Manseng

Subsequently Francis and Putu invited us to dine in their small restaurant in Burra. Putu cooks an excellent Indonesian menu. As their restaurant at the time was unlicensed, we would take a bottle or two and sit with our friends in the back garden while Putu created his grand banquet which Francis served so elegantly. The dishes, cooked at the last minute to order, were beautifully fresh and filled with interesting spices and herbs. It was surprising to find such a gem in rural South Australia and what a delightful difference from the usual pub fare.

~ * ~

Unfortunately the restaurants and caterers in the Clare Valley are forever changing, although this may be more to do with burnout than moving to greener fields. Take Billy and Brie for instance. This vibrant young couple put a huge effort and no doubt much money into redeveloping the Citadel in Clare. This former Salvation Army HQ, next to the bridge at the southern end of the town, had been empty for years and was now reborn as a modern bistro. How innovative.

Business must have been good, for eighteen months later they moved to larger premises on the southern edge of town. Here, the verandah, running along the front of the building, offered great views of the opposite ridgeline and provided outdoor dining at its best. Then a couple of years later they suddenly sold up and moved on. Was it burnout or something to do with this building, we wondered.

The original owner, an electrician, had resurrected the old farmhouse from dereliction to open it as a coffee shop and installed a large outdoor screen facing the verandah for film shows on Friday evenings. After Billy and Brie's incumbency, the place then emerged as a Greek bistro with an adjoining cellar door.

Now, a few years later, it has been rerun as a bakery and the cellar door rebadged by one of the local wineries. What a marvellous combination – an eclectic offering of daily-fresh bakery products, a glass of premium wine from the next-door cellar door, and a verandah to lounge on while contemplating the simple enjoyments that The Valley has to offer.

10

The early 2000s saw the wine boom starting to falter. It was an obvious move for us to keep back some of the fruit grown on The Hill to be made into wines for our own label. Prices for grapes had levelled off and the large wineries that bought our fruit were trimming their requirements. Some of the smaller vineyards had their contracts cancelled and we wondered when this might happen to us.

Keeping up with the demands of the vineyard kept us connected to the natural world and working in cellar door, we concluded, connected us with the social world; not only in our local community but also with South Australian visitors and people from interstate and abroad. The art gallery would connect us with the art community in South Australia, something we had missed since our relocation to The Valley.

The name for our label seemed obvious – Mt Surmon Wines. We were the Surmons living on a 400-metre mount. The play on words was irresistible.

We named the gallery Scarlattis after father and son Alessandro and Domenico Scarlatti. Alessandro, who lived in the late seventeenth century, is credited with laying the basis for the development of the modern operatic form. Domenico contributed greatly to the development of modern piano technique. The name

Scarlattis came into our heads one morning listening to their music on the radio.

We visited all the cellar doors in the Clare Valley to see what each had to offer and how they conducted their sales and soon realised that our building on The Hill was a very different milieu. Wendouree had its ancient vines, slate vats and old field stone buildings, Crabtree and Jeanneret used restored old villas, whilst Taylors had adopted a Spanish façade and Wilson's is an earth-covered army transit hut decorated outside with large, disused railway artefacts. None of this seemed to fit with what The Hill had to offer. How to reach out to attract customers to our brand-new venue?

The design for the original house and now the gallery was modern minimalist. The long outside western wall we decorated with large sea creatures worked in metal and floodlit at night. These were created by Gerhard Ritter, a sculptor, artist and a Fellow of the Royal South Australian Society of Arts. Subsequently we presented an exhibition of his watercolours.

We commissioned Bruce Tolley, a South Australian landscape and figurative painter, to decorate the outside northern wall with a *trompe-l'oeil* of Jeni and me surveying our realm, overlooking the Red Kelpie Creek block.

As visitors approach the main entrance, two sculptures of exotic female forms made from cement fondue and executed by Graham Kenefick, another South Australian artist, gaze down on them. The female figure with her eyes cast down and with rich blue streaks through her garment we have named after the Egyptian god Ptah, the patron of all arts, the creative urge. The other figure, wearing a commanding turban and casting a challenging look, is called Hathor, for the Egyptian god of joy and music.

At the side of the steps leading from the car park to the gallery front door is a series of ascending, large clay bowls from Bennet's Pottery in Adelaide, from which fish forms leap out, catching the rain from a downpipe and discharging it among rocks retrieved from the vineyard. We commissioned Jane Layne, a farmer and metal artist from Lochiel, to create small trees, shrubs and animal forms, fashioned from old metal pieces found on her farm, that now sit on the southern area of the terrace.

Inside, we treated the gallery walls with textured paint in a startling Madras to echo the deep orange colours in the large rocks scattered around the edges of the car park and unearthed when the parking area was gouged out of the hillside.

The fabric tones we chose for our sofa covers were also drawn from the hillside environment – a lightish green, the colour of newly emerging Shiraz buds, brown-red for the soil, canary yellow for the paddocks of canola in bloom, and gold splashes, which I likened to the coin we hoped would accrue from successful trading, all woven into an unusual whole by Designers Guild Fabrics in England. Each was chosen to provoke discussion. Whether people liked them or not didn't matter very much as long as they talked about them. We hoped our visitors would take pleasure from making their own connections. These colours didn't clash with the exhibited paintings because of their natural hues. Only one artist refused to have his works hung on the Madras-coloured walls, though he changed his mind for a later joint exhibition.

Such was our interpretation of what constituted drawcards to bring visitors to taste and buy our fine wines, to take coffee and homemade cake and to feast on our food platters on the terrace. Our advertisements in local tourism publications and newspapers and our highway signs invited people to come and sample our offerings as we naively opened our sanctuary for business. Running a boutique enterprise set us off once again on a steep learning curve.

Cellar door work is far less physically arduous than vineyard work but far more brain strain is required in dealing with customers and in sourcing artists to fill an annual exhibition schedule. The difficulties in dealing with visitors came as a surprise to us. Finding the energy and push to develop and work in a vineyard is one matter; developing the skills set to run a successful cellar door is a very different proposition.

In a supermarket bottle shop a customer walks in, selects a bottle, often without much advice or guidance from the sales assistant, pays at the counter and walks out. A completely different approach is required in a small cellar door where effectively we were hosting an 'occasion'. To make it successful we must establish an emotional connection that gives the customers the feeling that they are in a personal and well-informed exchange. That, at any rate, was our aim but experience showed visitors' responses differed widely.

Some people are very serious about a visit to a winery, some may be a little timid about exploring new territory. Others just seem to pop in to break a long journey. They interrupt each other to talk to us about their odyssey or anything other than the wines they are tasting. Some simply accept the wine in the tasting glass and then turn their backs to gaze out the window at the views, not at all interested in interacting with us. Best of all are those who just want to talk about the wines, the vineyard, how the wines are made; they're the customers who make it all worthwhile.

One model for selling wines is to appoint agents in the large cities and have their reps call on retailers, pubs and restaurants, but given our experiences in hawking our wines through the Mid

North we decided to stay small, confident that those visiting our cellar door and art gallery would be impressed enough to talk to their friends about a worthwhile experience.

We have had many discussions with people tasting our wines, of course. Many say they don't know how to analyse what their palates are telling them, so we talk about the tip of the tongue being the principle point for assessing sweetness, the gums for picking up on tannins, the sides of the tongue for saltiness, and so on. But the main point we try to establish is that their palates are as individual as their fingerprints, making it really important to keep tasting, trying new varieties and retrying those they think they don't like because every winemaker will produce something different, even from the same grape variety. Most importantly, we urge visitors to think about choosing wine to match with food and give them examples.

The art gallery side of things is a completely different matter. Word soon got around among professional and emerging artists that a purpose-built commercial gallery was open for business in the Clare Valley. Some phoned to ask for an appointment to show us their portfolio, others just turned up with examples of their works, to look us over and have a chat over coffee.

The first exhibition featured Philip Pike, Jeni's brother, a then emerging artist. From him we garnered the names of a few of his artistic colleagues and we looked at the artists in our own painting collection and contacted those living in South Australia. After a few exhibitions we were fully booked two years in advance, thus allowing the artists time to create a sufficient number of pieces for a solo exhibition.

We scheduled exhibition openings for a Sunday, from two to four in the afternoon so as to give people in Adelaide time to drive to Clare and have a leisurely lunch before heading for the opening. Of course you have to learn the tricks of the trade by trial and error. To schedule an opening on significant days, such as Mother's or Father's Day, meant that the hoped-for gathering had opted for pub food instead. The footy finals mob, on Grand Final Day, was glued to the big screen. Sundays on long weekends were out, as were any Sundays in December when Christmas thinking takes over. We learnt this the hard way.

Scarlattis Gallery was the first purpose-designed commercial gallery to open in the district. Some wineries display local artists on wall spaces between doors and windows, and some artists have their own studios. There were a couple of galleries in former government buildings, but we were the only purpose-built gallery for a long time. Then a spate of small galleries opened, scattered around the area. Many of these people frequented our openings; some were up-front enough to tell us they attended to learn how to do it, even down to poaching artists at our openings. They survived for a few years, but I think they are now all closed.

The arty group in Auburn appreciated our efforts right from the beginning, attending openings and buying pieces and we became friends with many of the buyers. We started mixing couples from the south with our mates in the north for convivial long lunches. Many of our friends had developed old farmhouses as their weekend retreats and out buildings as bed and breakfast facilities. Indeed, these B & Bs, which were feeding off tourists visiting the wine region, were popping up throughout the valley. The wedding trade was also attracted to wine venues. In truth, much of the historic fabric of the area has been preserved by the hard work of city people retiring to the country, reinventing themselves and celebrating the spirit of their new environment.

Bruce Tolley and his wife Julie from Adelaide had come to see us about an exhibition and to do some preliminary sketches in The Valley as a basis for future works. This was the beginning of a long association; Bruce presented several solo exhibitions with us over the years. His paintings seem to invite viewers to share his gaze, to see the vineyards and buildings of the Clare Valley as both sensual and material. Eschewing a photographic interpretation, he conjures an abstract vision of reality that is rich, colourful and bountiful, inviting us to experience the intensity of the natural world. It is an invitation many accepted; his works sold very well.

According to Charles Le Brun, France's seventeenth century master of the arts: 'Paintings have but a single instant and must compress everything into a single view.' That fleeting moment is one of the reasons we buy a painting – so we may look at it again and again. It's what we do with Bruce's vinyardscapes that hang in our house; we like them so much that we have hung one in the public toilet.

A young couple – expatriates living in Hong Kong – who visited our cellar door were captivated by Bruce's painting of a paddle-steamer. Before coming to Adelaide for their holiday they had watched a television series about paddle-steamers on the Murray River and were so struck by the painting and the nostalgia it evoked that they just had to take it back with them to Hong Kong.

John Illsley, an excellent artist working with watercolour and pen, popped in to talk about an exhibition. As a former stock agent, John travelled widely throughout South Australia, sketching homesteads, shearing sheds, out buildings, ruins and pubs. He exhibited with us a few times, on each occasion drawing large numbers of visitors, many of them the owners of the buildings who came from all over the state to purchase the drawing of their property.

Another artist with whom we developed a lasting relationship is Roe Gartleman. We happened upon her in Neagle's Rock cellar door where she was preparing an exhibition. It transpired that she and her husband Stu owned Magpie Springs Winery in McLaren Vale, where Roe had her studio and where we had tasted their excellent Pinot Noir wine.

We staged a memorable exhibition in November 1998 to coincide with the Wagner *Ring Cycle* season at the Adelaide Festival Centre. We arranged with a tourist company in Adelaide to bring a coachload of Wagner aficionados to our winery for lunch, and invited a friend, a psychoanalyst, to deliver a paper on his psychological interpretation of Wagner and his works. This exhibition by four artists attracted many opera lovers, including the then chair of New Zealand Opera who bought four small paintings depicting scenes from the cycle.

We have sold many works to international and country visitors. A Swedish couple bought three paintings of scenes in the Clare Valley and solved the problem of transporting them by removing the canvases from their wooden frames and rolling them up for the journey home in their suitcases.

One couple who booked our B & B provided us with a pointed and encouraging example of how our many offerings worked to reinforce each other. They came to the Clare Valley for the race meeting to be held on Saturday. Arriving on the Friday evening they ordered dinner and a bottle of wine. Next day, after the races, the wife came to our cellar door and gallery to talk about the races and to look at the exhibition. She bought two pieces – perhaps they had backed a few winners – ordered dinner, and bought two dozen Mt Surmon wines.

She said friends had come back with them for a couple of drinks. Next morning Jeni took the breakfast tray to their room and there were their friends with their baby asleep on the floor.

'How did you tell them the room is only for two?' I asked Jeni when she returned from delivering the tray.

'I didn't. Sometimes you just have to accept a *fait accompli*,' she said.

Within a little while we were receiving enquiries for wedding receptions, conferences and private celebrations. To cater for such events we purchased furniture, crockery, cutlery and glasses sufficient to serve a hundred seated diners. Interestingly, the number of patrons a venue is licensed to hold is based on the number of toilet seats available.

One conference we hosted gave us new insights in sales technique. The after-lunch speaker was a confident and erudite gentleman from the US; we slipped into the gallery to listen. His message was that Americans are conditioned to listen to a sales presentation and then to buy, and he gave examples of how to pitch for a sale.

As a bonus to the conference organisers, we offered a formal wine tasting, which a number of people accepted. As Jeni was taking people through the tasting, I went over to chat with the guest speaker and put to him my view that Australians were more resistant to a hard sales pitch than he had suggested Americans seemed to be. He listened politely and I invited him to allow me to take him through a tasting. I gave him a pitch that followed closely what I had just learned from his presentation. I described each wine, emphasising its qualities and suggesting foods to match and before moving to the next wine asked how many bottles he would like to buy. He bought several dozen.

In 2008 a group of young musicians provided us and our wine tasters with a wonderful and unexpected treat. They were members of the Australian Youth Orchestra. When the Adelaide season finished, orchestra members split into small groups to provide performances and master classes in country locations. We attended a concert in Clare given by four string players and afterwards, while chatting, I invited them for a wine tasting.

They were on their way to Broken Hill for performances and master classes and to our surprise, on their return journey one Sunday morning, they came in, and spontaneously took out their instruments to play string quartets for the next hour. People arriving for a tasting sat down quietly to enjoy the wine and the music, grateful for such a professional performance.

Thanking us for the chance to play in our winery, the players said the acoustics of the gallery were superb. We responded enthusiastically, assuring them that their performance matched it and gave them half a dozen bottles of our *méthode traditionnelle* Mt Surmon Sparkling Pinot Gris.

At one conference in the gallery a participant came to Jeni, apologised for what she was about to say, and told her how she had been idly playing with the sides of the chair when she felt something move over her fingers. She stood up and looked under the seat only to find a red-back spider and its nest. She suggested to her friend beside her to do the same – and there was another nest.

After the conference, when everybody had left, we inspected each chair and found yet another nest. Next morning we returned the chairs to the storage shed and inspected all the remaining chairs, of which there were a hundred, and found more nests of red-backs. And that's not all we found. Several of the chair covers and under-sponges had been eaten by bush rats. We had the chairs and shed fumigated, but we knew this was only a temporary step in removing the pests.

This was when I was a member of the Clare Racing Club committee and it was from a discussion about replacing the old implements shed that I remembered talk of shipping containers. The design of shipping containers seals them from invasions of any kind and would certainly keep out spiders and rats. We started to track second-hand containers and discovered many types and sizes available. To get an approximate size we went to our big shed and measured the area taken up with the chairs and tables used for functions in the gallery. We soon found one the correct size, for $1600 including delivery. (It's a pity we didn't have this idea when we built the large shed, which cost us $13,000 but now seems to be used only for storing firewood and accumulated junk.)

Scarlattis became a popular venue for conferences, private celebrations and weddings. We would prepare the food ourselves for smaller events (up to thirty people) but bring in a local chef for larger ones. Plating up eighty to a hundred dishes of hot food on warmed plates, with six or seven different items on each plate, without dribbling or spoiling the plate's elegance and attractiveness, and delivering them all to the tables within ten to fifteen minutes was an exercise we weren't willing to get wrong. Foremost, we embrace quality in our offerings.

One memorable wedding brought together a doctor from Darwin and her groom, an oil rig worker from Moomba, and their hundred guests. Both Darwin residents and oil rig workers have great reputations for enjoying themselves. We brought in a chef for this event and supplied the beers and wines for the wedding and the recovery lunch next day. The party was loud and jolly and the takings were bountiful.

Then there was the young couple from up north. The parents of the bride ran a business with offices in the Alice and Darwin. When they came to Scarlattis to arrange the wedding, the bride's father was very taken with the current exhibition by an Englishman living in the Adelaide Hills. He thought they would look excellent on the walls of his offices and bought several. It was a large and expensive wedding and he took home several dozen wines.

The wedding was booked about a year ahead and mother and daughter called in many times on business trips to and from Adelaide to talk to Jeni. The daughter was most excited, Jeni said, asking the same questions over and over. She called in again several months after the wedding to talk to Jeni about her new husband leaving her for a much older woman. And a few months again after that to show Jeni her baby girl. She was a happy young mother despite everything.

~ * ~

The Clare Valley was slow to warm to farmers' markets, but when Phil and Amanda from London Hill Caterers organised the first in 2005, the idea quickly spread through the district. That first market was beautifully positioned – in the Madonna Hall, Sevenhill, right next door to the pub – and well timed, being held on the last Saturday morning of each month.

The Madonna Hall is abuzz as people wander past tempting goodies in an array of jars, pots, open boxes, bottles, vases and tins. When you enter, the first items to take your eyes are Phil's artisan wood-fired breads, quickly followed by Amanda's array of Danish pastries, fresh out of the oven, and rows of fruit cakes and cupcakes. Further along is a generous display of pies and pasties made by Louise and Ron from the Sevenhill pub.

Among the many available products are olive oils and olives offered by our bookkeeper Ros from her property on Emu Rock Road, next to freshly laid hen and duck eggs, fish fresh in from the coast, pickles, conserves, preserved fruits and vegetables, and so it goes.

Estela's Filipino fried rice

Ingredients for 4 servings

2 tbs cooking oil

1 rasher bacon, remove rind and finely chop

2 spring onions, chopped

2 garlic cloves, chopped

2 white celery sticks, chopped

1 red capsicum, deseeded and chopped

1 or 2 red chillies, sliced, for those who like it hot

1 Chinese pork sausage, thinly sliced

150 g dried shrimp soaked in warm water

1 cup frozen green peas

1 cup tinned or frozen corn kernels

salt

2 cups steamed jasmine rice, cold

Heat the oil in a wok or frying pan until hot, add the bacon, spring onion, garlic, celery and capsicum (and chilli) and stir fry for a few minutes until al dente, add the sausage, drained shrimp, peas, corn, and salt, turning the ingredients all the time.

Add the cooked rice and combine all ingredients and toss over a high heat until heated through. Serve immediately into a warmed bowl.

Wine match: Semillon, Pinot Gris, Petit Manseng, Vermentino

Just by the entrance a lady from the Philippines has large spring rolls ready to pop into sizzling oil as well as exotic fried rice and chicken kebabs. Ros's young son is playing his sax, for practice or pennies. Next to them is Peter Barry, from the famous Jim Barry Wines, cooking up a storm with bacon and egg rolls on a barbecue.

This is what Jeni and I have come for. We eat junk food only when we're in a holiday mood and this is early Saturday morning; but in any case this is far from junk food. The eggs were laid only yesterday and the bacon is home grown and smoked in Pink's butcher shop – an absolute treat, fresh and full of flavour. I have tomato sauce on mine; Jeni prefers the hot English mustard.

Peter takes time out of his hectic schedule for a couple of hours on these Saturday mornings to volunteer his services to raise funds for the Sevenhill Country Fire Service, located next door to Madonna Hall on the other side from the pub.

We sit in the sun consuming the monster rolls, trying not to dribble sauce or mustard on our clothes and, at the same time, taking the opportunity to catch up with friends, or strangers who have come from Adelaide on a weekend visit. And then, it's inside again, for a couple of Amanda's Danish pastries and a plunger of Rio coffee, Royal blend. On Sevenhill market days, there is no need for lunch.

This market has become so popular in the Clare Valley that traders now come in from fifty to a hundred kilometres around, which makes you wonder just how local a farmers' market should be. Stalls have spilled out of Madonna Hall and fill the surrounding car park.

Following this success another food, art and craft market began, this time on the middle Saturday of the month in the plaza next door to the Clare town hall, and it was followed by another, this one held at the showgrounds.

Tourists and locals flock to these markets, especially city people. It reminds Jeni and me of the produce markets that pop up in country towns all over Italy. There are no chain stores in these small towns to dominate, just small, home-based producers pleased to be able to sell their wares and to become involved socially and commercially in an organic way. With some goods you may taste before you buy; with others there's no need to – the artisan fresh quality is immediately evident.

In a complementary move, in the laneway besides Jason Matthie's Meat Shoppe in Clare, some blokes from Apex are sizzling up Matthie's award-winning sausages with fried onion on a slice of bread, tempting passers-by to stop for a chat and to make a donation to the primary school attended by Jason's children.

Such scenes, both busy and relaxed, add a new dimension to the pleasures offered to visitors to the region, the markets adding to the clean, fresh image that winemakers foster and giving visitors another reason to linger in the romantic Clare Valley.

~ * ~

In more ways than one, this time was probably the height of our success, depending on how you measure success, I guess. If it is in terms of dollars to be taken out compared with dollars put in, this was the peak. We could have sold the whole lot for three million about this time.

We were at the peak of our physical abilities and so loved what we were committed to that we had no thought of stopping or selling. We had a feeling of belonging, of knowing who we were. This story would have had quite a different ending if we had sold then.

11

Management of the vines (the amount of fertiliser applied, the manner in which the vines' canopy is dealt with, the amount of water applied, pruning methods and so on – all part of the vine's *terroir*) helps to determine the chemical components of a grape (colour, aroma, flavour compounds, pigments, tannins) and to a great extent depends on the vigneron rather than the work of the winemaker.

The manner in which these compounds are handled, to produce distinctive tactile sensations of the wine on the tongue and cheeks of smoothness, body, viscosity, dryness or sweetness, stems from the knowledge and scientific manipulation, or the art, of the winemaker. But of course it is the wine drinker's personal preferences, expectations, cultural and regional background, and ability to pay that determine the wine to be drunk and matched with food on a specific occasion.

The natural tannins of grapes help to age reds and add critical colour and sensory properties. Sensible handling of tannins is essential to optimise quality and character. In the making of whites and Rosés, tannins are mostly excluded by minimising contact with skins, seeds and stalks. Wine with a higher concentration of tannin has a noticeable gripping or drying effect in the mouth. Wine with a lower concentration of tannin will give the wine a soft and supple feel. Grapes that are not ripe enough when picked will have tannins that give the wine a green, coarse, bitter or unripe sensation in the mouth. Grape varieties high in tannins include Nebbiolo, Shiraz and Cabernet Sauvignon. When these components are all balanced – the right amounts of tannin, acid, sugar, alcohol, and so on – the finished red wine will have a silky, velvety and ripe finish. In simple terms wine is composed of eighty to eighty-five per cent water, ten to eighteen per cent alcohol or residual sugar, acid about half a per cent, and only a tiny proportion is responsible for the extraordinary variety of aroma, taste, colour and feel.

The Australian Wine Research Institute in 1998 developed a Mouthfeel and Astringency Wheel for use in describing these sensations. For instance, the term 'complex' is posited as soft, subtle, fleshy, rich; whilst 'weight' is given as watery, thin, full, viscous.

The different oak types used for making the barrels in which the reds are aged also contain different types of tannins and these have most effect on the wine when the barrels are new. The way they are handled by the winemaker is critical in making the most of the wine's character and longevity. The aim is to achieve a well-structured wine with a balance of fine grain tannins, full fruit flavours, a long acid spine backed by discreet oak flavours that add depth, complexity and finesse.

Jeni and I came to a better understanding of the significance of the term *terroir* when we visited a ridge-top village to the south of Turin in the Piedmont. Barbaresco and its neighbouring village, Barolo, are homes of the Nebbiolo grape. These villages cling to the ridge-tops of steeply incised valleys. The only cellar door we found open was that of Carlo Boffa. Here we sat on the terrace overlooking the Tanaro River, running way down below us. We talked with Carlo for a couple of hours – he in hesitant English, we using an Italian–English dictionary – about the five versions of the one vintage of his Nebbiolo with the grapes grown on five separate blocks on one hillside, three with a southerly aspect, one with an easterly aspect, and the other a westerly.

Each wine differed; one had a little less mouthfeel, another showed fuller fruit expression. Those from the south and southwestern blocks were considered the most desirable, showing more fullness of flavour and aromatic complexity with higher natural acidity and tannins. One, without oak, was a softer, less assertive version and the last was medium bodied with nicely balanced aromas and flavours.

With each wine Signor Boffa served some food – small portions of black olives, a hard cheese, smoked pork sausage slices, thin strips of prosciutto and lightly pickled zucchini – to match. The difference between the wines, Carlo assured us, resided in the vine's individual response to its *terroir*. 'Let the wine do the talking,' he advised.

We would loved to have bought a dozen of each of Carlo's wines to help pay him for his time in interacting so intimately with us, but this was not possible. We bought a couple of bottles for the evening's meal and six of his aprons for gifts back home.

Ted Lemon, a viticulturist in Sonoma County, California, is more effusive and outspoken in maintaining that 'great *terroir* does not exist in a vacuum'. In his view it is built from historic, cultural, economic, scientific and agronomic blocks, and the winemaker's job is to reveal this uniqueness, to craft the wine as the most honest expression of 'a noble and distinguished place'.

Our Nebbiolo vines seem to have found a noble and distinguished place growing near a small stand of very old gums on a rocky spur. A favourable critique by a wine writer in the

Australian Financial Review of our 2003 Nebbiolo spoke of the 'deep in-your-face brick dust ... fabulous texture with dry, dusty, chewy tannins ... [which] finishes with smoke, dust, chew and peel'. We were delighted by the critic's enthusiasm, creativity and chunky prose, which clearly struck a chord with readers as the article led to a sales frenzy during which we sold the entire Nebbiolo vintage in three weeks.

Many wine writers talk about the necessity of removing the mystery from wine drinking but unfortunately in Australia much of the advertising and writing about food and wine endeavours to develop cult followings – chefs creating extraordinarily complicated dishes and wines selling for hundreds of dollars a bottle. In Italy and France, for instance, there is no mystery about eating excellent, slow-cooked food and drinking good wines. That is taken as a matter of course.

There isn't much mystery in our cellar door, or most small cellar doors, for that matter. Some people will arrive for a tasting and say they drink only 'savvy blank' (Sauvignon Blanc) or a big, gutsy Shiraz. There's no point in arguing with these opinions. When it comes to taste there can be no argument; each person has his or her own sense of what constitutes good taste in a wine.

Whilst we discuss taste, we may not prescribe it, but we think that part of our mission is to suggest that visitors try wines they have not tasted before on the grounds they might just find one to add to their repertoire. Beware of the palate rut, we say, keep pushing the envelope to see what happens. No expertise is required.

~ * ~

Zac arrived on The Hill in a circuitous way. He sourced fruit and made wine for a large winery in another region in South Australia, and rang, one day, to ask the price of bulk Viognier we had for sale, saying he wanted to blend it with Shiraz grapes. This is not a new combination. French winemakers along the Rhône, the home of Shiraz grapes, blend the white Viognier grapes with the red to give more character. Shiraz often struggles to produce fulsome flavours in the cool summers of the Rhône Valley. The earlier ripening Viognier fruit, added to the Shiraz, helps to extract colour from the Shiraz grapes and imparts softening fruit characters to the wine. The French often grow the white vines in among the red vines, treating them as one fruit and harvesting and processing them together.

Australian wine regions usually don't have trouble ripening the fruit so I puzzled about why Zac wanted to add the Viognier. I wondered if it was to add softer flavours to inferior fruit. Whatever his reasoning, we decided to make a deal with Zac for the sale of the bulk Viognier.

I asked him if he was also interested in buying Nebbiolo grapes surplus to our requirements that season, and he was. He said he had participated in a number of vintages in Italy, including making Nebbiolo.

'It's a very interesting grape and can make great wine if handled properly,' he said. 'I've got my own small label and I'd be interested in adding neb to my range.' He asked us to recommend a local winery where he could process the fruit.

We introduced him to Moby who managed a mid-sized winery, nothing like the behemoths run as modern factories with their gushing waterfalls of commercial-grade wines for sale in supermarkets and chain stores. Despite its small scale, Moby's winery still looked like an oil rig, all steel walkways, pipes, cables, ladders, stainless-steel vats, and gantries and their hoists. In the halls, hundreds of barrels lay in their cradles stacked six high, dwarfing the winemakers and 'cellar rats' – the fledgling young cellar workers – dragging hoses to rack the wines or working the forklifts, many from abroad on working visas.

Only the racket posing as music blasting out of a radio disturbed the romantic spell of the red-stained barrels with their odour of maturing wines, about the only similarity to a French limestone cave you are likely to find in The Valley.

We introduced Zac to this, at least we introduced Zac to Moby, who was in charge of all this. Zac and Moby were completely different. Zac was a small man who spoke rapidly in staccato bursts. I could understand individual words, but it was difficult to make sense of what he was saying. He repeated sentences several times, each time, it seemed, with a slightly different message because of the change in speed or emphasis of delivery.

I soon came to realise this was Zac's way of getting your interest. He would lay down a barrage of possibilities, each one expressed slightly differently although, on the surface, all appearing to say the same thing. The result was you thought you had grasped his meaning, but in fact it turned out to be different from what you had tentatively discerned.

Zac came a number of times to inspect the fruit on our vines, never enquiring about the price but claiming, 'It's better to do something with this fruit rather than leave it unsold,' – and later adding, 'I don't know that I could take it all – there must be eight to ten tonne here – it would depend on the price.' Clearly Zac was strapped for cash and it soon became clear that a tight rein on expenditure was part of his management strategy. When eventually he asked about price for the Nebbiolo grapes it was my cue to voice an idea I'd been considering.

'I've listened to all you've had to say, Zac, and the message I get is that you haven't got much spare cash You probably won't want to pay what it costs to produce the crop. You're very interested in what can be done with the grapes, and so am I, so why don't we set up a partnership for this particular crop. I'll put in the cost of the fruit plus the harvest and freight; you put in the winemaking expertise and the barrels. We can make a spreadsheet to keep track of things. When the wine is ready we'll work out how to divvy it up.'

'You mean a partnership *just* for this project? Then right,' and we shook hands on it.

It was some months after harvest before we heard from him again. He phoned to say he wanted us to join him to taste the wine. Zac had assembled twenty barrels, all different – some French others American, a couple of new ones, the rest of varying ages, a few having been re-burnt and shaved a couple of times.

Some held free-run juice, some light pressings, the rest also-ran pressings. In some, malolactic fermentation was complete; the others were at various stages in this process. Spurning computers, Zac held all of these variations in his head and with a wan, half-smile he described for us without reference to notes the history and contents of each of the twenty barrels. He was in seventh heaven.

He noted the different fruit characters of each barrel – raspberry, roses, violets, liquorice, gamey notes – and explained that fine-grain tannins made this a very dry wine, but that the sweet fruit flavours were coming through. In describing his approach, he said, 'The differences between the barrels give me opportunities to blend so I can optimise outcomes. We could take some of your last year's stock and blend it in to see what we get, and we could hold back some of this year's to blend with next year's. That way we can get consistency of product.'

Moby Swan couldn't believe this approach to winemaking,

the intricate analysis and the fiddling with the juice. His own winemaking style was one of minimal intervention, using only the finest fruit along with yeast and the oak that he thought was the best for the fruit variety.

Our association with Zac set us off on another learning trajectory. From the beginning we had told him we would enter barrel samples of the Nebbiolo in the next year's Alternative Varieties Wine Show in Mildura. When the time came to draw the samples for the show, Zac arrived with several samples very different from the original barrel tastings. They really weren't good enough in our view, and we didn't enter them.

Zac's explanation was that they still had a long way to go, but we stuck to our guns of wanting to enter them in the show. But no, that didn't happen and I reckon he had deliberately botched the samples so that we would not enter them.

When the time came to divvy up the bulk wine, we entered an extraordinary period when it was impossible to get him to state or to accept a solid proposition. Eventually Jeni and I decided that we should get out of the partnership before we developed stomach ulcers. Zac agreed.

'Right, I'll take all the wine and pay you for the fruit,' for which he offered us a very low price. *Snap* went the trap.

The punch line to this extended and increasingly unfunny narrative was that he didn't have any ready finance to settle the deal on the fruit. It took him another nine months of juggling a full hand of credit cards before he could settle.

~ * ~

We had eliminated the spiders and rats from inhabiting our chairs but not the rabbits, not altogether. They took longer to eradicate, although getting rid of the grandstand helped a lot. We didn't want to use baits because of the kelpies so we relied on traps, setting them where we saw evidence of warrens.

A friend had given us some traps, and I set one on the heap where a pile of old tree trunks and soil had been pushed together. This resulted in a number of catches, but nearly one victim too many. That day, we had finished our work in the vineyard and set off up The Hill at five thirty for something in a glass. It was rather dark when we sat down with Janette, but where was Jackie? Certainly it was odd for Jackie not to be first home as she vied with Janette to race up the slope. How come we hadn't noticed her absence? As we puzzled over where she could be, Jen thought she heard something odd and went outside to listen. She returned and in an agitated voice said, 'I can hear her whimpering somewhere in the vineyard. Get the torch.'

Down the three of us went and sure enough Jackie was sending out distress calls, which we followed to the rubble pile. She was on top of it with her front paw caught in the trap.

Jackie behaved very well as I tried desperately to open the jaws without getting my hand caught, which was far from easy. It was dark, very windy and I couldn't get a good grip as she insisted on licking my face. Levering a trap open is always difficult, but with a dog's paw in it, it was a great challenge keeping the jaws from snapping shut on the paw and my hand, especially for one who knew little about rabbit traps.

Jackie was very grateful for her release, her tail making fast circles, her tongue licking my hands and face repeatedly, and then Jeni's, while barking her thanks. Janette added a few celebratory barks to endorse Jackie's successful release. I couldn't see any damage to the paw, but I'm sure it would have been bruised.

~ * ~

It was about this time that we attended another growers' meeting organised by the large winery to which we sold some of our fruit. There was the usual morning conference, then the tasting and discussions about growing grapes and wine quality, followed by a hearty lunch and as much and as many wines as anyone wanted to drink. Afterwards we sat in the sun with some other growers, an opportunity for old timers to yarn about what things used to be like.

Slow-baked beef short ribs with piquant chocolate sauce

Ingredients for 4 servings

salt and pepper
3 bay leaves
olive oil
2 sticks celery and tops, chopped
1 carrot, chopped
1 onion, chopped
3 cloves garlic, chopped
2 kg small beef short ribs (without the joint end)
1 litre beef stock

Heat a baking pan on the stove top. Add pepper, salt and bay leaves and heat until they start to pop, being careful not to burn. Add oil, celery, carrots, onions and garlic and sauté for a couple of minutes to brown a little.

Add the ribs, fat side down first and brown. Add the stock, seal dish with alfoil and bake in oven for 2 hours at 160°C.

Drain vegetables and liquid and reserve. Put ribs aside.

Piquant sauce

1 tbs olive oil

1 onion, finely diced

3 cloves garlic, diced

2 cups Shiraz

1 tbs fresh oregano, chopped

1 tbs tomato paste or puree

good dash Worcestershire sauce

salt and white pepper

1 tbs cocoa powder (2 if you want a richer sauce)

freshly grated couverture chocolate

Heat olive oil in a frying pan and sauté onions and garlic until soft. Add red wine, tomato paste, oregano, Worcestershire sauce, salt and pepper and simmer slowly for ½ hour. Add the cocoa powder and some of the reserved liquid and keep simmering until thick and creamy. Put the ribs on the bbq and grill for 5–10 minutes to crisp. Cut into single ribs and place on serving dish, smother with the hot sauce. Grate couverture chocolate over each serving and serve with your favourite vegetables or salad.

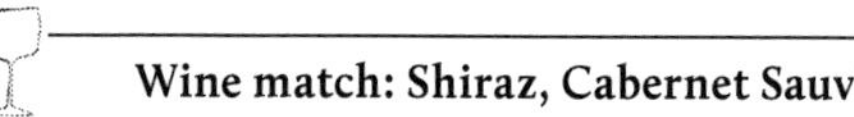

Wine match: Shiraz, Cabernet Sauvignon, Mataro

Into his fifth glass of red, from the best label of course, Harvey Ord was reminiscing. 'Did you ever meet old Ned?' he said to those around him. 'Ned had a block at the northern end of The Valley. He lived in one of the original cottages with his old kelpie who, in human terms, was as old as Ned himself. The kelpie was nearly blind, quite deaf, and overweight. Ned was overweight too and rather slow but his health was okay. The dog would follow Ned whenever he went into the vineyard. Up and down the rows they would go and at times the kelpie would wander off to follow a trail and roll in something really rotten. In summer she'd jump into the dam to cool off and roll in the mud, kicking her legs in the air, really contented.

'By this time she could no longer hear Ned's call so Ned would bang his secateurs on a steel trellis post to attract her attention. The flies would buzz Ned's face looking for a bead of sweat and swarm all over his back so Ned would take off his old floppy hat and thrash it about to get rid of them. You always knew it was Ned from a distance by the way he would flail about with his hat.

'This day the dog wandered down to the dry creek which ran across the property. The banks were steep, probably two metres deep, and the dog must have been on a scent and, not seeing too well, fell down the bank and tumbled into the thick weeds at the bottom. Ned eventually realised the dog wasn't with him so he called and banged his pruners, but no response. So he went looking for her and picked up her tracks in the long grass, following them to the edge of the creek. There she was, lying at the bottom, not moving. Ned shouted and whistled to no avail so he started to pick his way down the steep bank, slipping on the dry grass but steadying himself by clutching at tall weeds.

'Then he lost his footing, slipping and tumbling down to land at the bottom beside his dear old kelpie. Ned saw she was panting lightly and started to pick her up wondering what was wrong. As he moved, the long brown snake struck at his wrist, claiming its second victim. They lay there together, the old man and his faithful dog, the venom slowly and fatally relaxing their muscles. Ned's son didn't find them until a few days later.'

After a silence I asked quietly, 'So, what's the message, Harvey?'

'Buggered if I know, just a bit of history I suppose.'

'Beware of brown snakes in summer, I guess,' his wife, Gwen, said.

'Beware the snake in the grass, more likely,' Jeni added, thinking of Fawcett, she told me later.

Speaking of the dreaded Fred Fawcett, a young German family had rented the Fawcett property. They had visited Australia a few years earlier and had now returned to settle with their two beautiful young kids. The father was energetic and ambitious. He was a chef, worn out from working long hours in the family's large restaurant in Hanover. Now, he had visions of making smoked wurst from home-grown pigs, cheeses from goat's milk, and buffalo milk too if he could find such an animal in the Mid North.

He planted vegetable seeds, and dope, which was potent apparently with a disastrous effect on the his energy and ambitions. We learned about their plans and how things were going for them when we invited them to our house for a barbecue, and later they invited us for dinner. The chef found employment at a local pub but didn't last long. He was critical of the cook in charge of the kitchen and they ended up having a blue.

His wife defended his dope smoking saying he needed it to calm himself from the stress of the long, constant hours worked in Germany. Whatever the truth of that excuse, he planted very few vegetables and the piggery and cheeses did not eventuate, but the dope flourished. Her parents came out for a visit and we had great times with them all, eating German food, drinking local wines and comparing them with wines from Germany, especially the Rieslings, and singing enthusiastically.

The young chef couldn't or didn't want to find a job locally, and we could see his dynamism ebbing away as the months passed, and their nest egg must likewise have inexorably diminished. Eventually, they left for a look at north Queensland where he thought he would find work in one of the resort hotels. We didn't see them again.

It is interesting to look at the rich cultural mix developing in The Valley these days. The early days of white settlement saw Irish, Scots and English along with Polish and German settlers. Today this mixture is being enriched by local men marrying women from the Philippines, and the arrival of a number of Chinese and Indian families.

There are Chinese and Thai restaurants and now an Indian one called Indii. We took the breakfast club there for something different. Sri, the owner, was surprised that we would want Indian foods for breakfast but obligingly opened early at eight to accommodate us – and, yes, he did have a stock of champagnes.

Three Filipino women work for our vineyard contractor and have been dubbed 'The Three Fillies'. You know when they are in the vineyard by their constant chatter and contented laughter.

~ * ~

I received an email from KT, a work colleague in a previous life, inviting me to a reunion. I said to Jeni that I wouldn't mind catching up with her, but the rest of them represented a past I had left behind. Anyway we couldn't have gone because we had booked a cabin at Moonta Bay that week, and walking the beach was preferable to trying to chat to people with whom I now had nothing in common.

I had got on well with KT and we had swapped yarns about our predicaments. It was she who told me that you could always win a woman's heart with a bunch of flowers and as a result I sent flowers to Jeni in an effort to win hers. I would meet up with KT after work for a drink and later she and her new bloke visited us at Seacliff a few times. We decided to ask them to come and stay with us for a couple of nights and we used their visit to take a couple of days off and join them as tourists.

KT's husband, Waz, knew the Burra mines from childhood visits. Jeni and I had never been to the mines, so Waza's description of them sparked our interest. Today Burra is a well-preserved township, attractively nineteenth century in architecture and ambiance, with a calm and solidity that belies its somewhat chaotic beginning.

From 1843 pastoralists grazed the land still inhabited by the Ngadjuri people, who had long valued the territory around Burra as a reliable source of water. The Ngadjuri word for water – *cowie* or *kowi* – is enshrined in many Mid North place names, such as Yarcowie, Canowie, Caltowie, Warcowie, and Booborowie. Their peaceful ways were interrupted, however, when two English shepherds independently discovered copper deposits near the Burra Creek in 1845. Two mining companies were established: Princess Royal by a group of pastoralists and the owners of the Kapunda mine, and the Burra Burra Mine Co. by Adelaide traders in 1848.

And thus began one of the important migrations into South Australia. Miners from Cornwall, Scotland, Wales and Germany were soon on the scene. Owing to the lack of housing in the early years, hundreds of miners and their families lived in dugouts stretching over several kilometres along the banks of the creek. Eventually they moved into the first company-built houses in

Australia with separate nationalities in different villages, some on mining company land and others on government land.

The output of copper was prodigious – eighty-nine per cent of South Australia's output and five per cent of the world's for fifteen years. The mines closed in 1877 and reopened again between 1970 and 1980. One was dubbed 'The Monster Mine' for obvious reasons.

Burra is also famous for another monster – *Diprotodon optatum* – or giant wombat, some four metres long, two metres high and weighing in at 2800 kilograms. Fossils of this animal, which became extinct about 25,000 years ago, along with those of giant kangaroos and cats, were found in Baldina Creek just 10 kilometres east of Burra in 1890 and are still there today for the avid seeker.

At the opposite end of the scale you can also search for the pygmy blue-tongue lizard, which is about 20 centimetres long, in the Tiliqua Nature Reserve. It was considered to be extinct until a population was discovered in the reserve in 1992. A 'citizen science' event, held on Threatened Species Day – 7 September – is an opportunity for the public to work with academics to help locate and protect this living fossil.

Waza was a treasure trove of knowledge, and his stories made us keen to repair what had been our inadvertent neglect of this fascinating region. We were able to introduce them to a newly opened café, La Pecora Nera, housed in a ramshackle building clad mainly with corrugated iron – a quintessentially Australian rural building housing traditional Italian cuisine. So off to Burra we went, 43 kilometres to the northeast of Clare and, after a tour of the mine sites, we turned our attention to an Italian lunch.

Herbed pizza base

Ingredients for 1 base

2 cups plain four

1 x 8 g sachet of dry yeast

1 tsp caster sugar

½ tsp salt

2 tbs olive oil

¾ cup warm water

1 cup of chopped fresh or dried herbs: rosemary, thyme, oregano, mint, sage

tomato paste

Combine all ingredients except the herbs and tomato paste in a large bowl and mix to a soft dough.

Knead on a floured surface until soft and pliable. Return to the mixing bowl and cover with cling wrap and leave in a warm spot for 30 minutes. The dough should double in size.

When it has risen, punch the dough once to remove air bubbles.

Remove from bowl, sprinkle with herbs, fold in and gently knead for 1 minute.

Roll the dough out to desired size and spread tomato paste over the top. Bake for 10 minutes at 240°C.

Cut into triangles and serve warm with an aperitif.

Wine match: brut sparkling, Viognier, Chardonnay

The ambiance of *La Pecora Nera* – The Black Sheep – is beautifully warm and friendly. The front half of the store, partitioned and set with odd tables and chairs, is dominated by an indoor wood-fired oven made of house bricks with a cement dome.

We were greeted effusively by Claire, a tall, thinnish woman in her forties who later told us that she was born in Adelaide of Italian parents. Before setting off on a trip through Italy to trace her heritage, Claire had bought the Burra building that would become the restaurant.

Claire travelled more or less aimlessly but pleasantly in Italy until she discovered Paolo and brought him back to her Burra building to open it as a traditional Italian village trattoria. I don't know which one was the black sheep, Claire for abandoning Adelaide, or Paolo for forsaking Italy, but together they provide wonderful hospitality and fine food.

After eating we waited until other diners had left so we could have Claire's full attention. We asked if she would like to taste our wines, and she asked Paolo to join us. I dashed outside to collect the tasting kit – six bottles, glasses and napkins. Their comments about the wines were very favourable, but Claire said she would only take the Nebbiolo because their plan was to market their café as a *trattoria rustica tradizionale*.

Lunch at La Pecora Nera was a fortunate, thoroughly delightful experience which we owed to Waza's passion for the mining history of Burra and the news on the grapevine about the delights of La Pecora Nera.

'*Ciao*,' we called, self-consciously experimenting with vestigial Italian, as we waved goodbye to Claire and Paolo. '*Alla prossima*,' they responded – 'Till next time' – and assuredly there would be a next time.

12

The world was changing around The Hill, and one of the changes was significant but controversial – the spread of wind farms across the Mid North. We were fascinated by these monumental structures, or so they appeared from a distance. Their actual size in and command of the landscape only really becomes evident closer up. Despite wind being our constant companion on The Hill, unfortunately the size of our holding is minuscule compared with the area taken up by a wind farm. There are many of them in the Mid North – one a little north of Burra, three east of Jamestown, and a huge one on the Barunga and Hummock Ranges to the west of Clare, which started with forty-seven wind towers and added another ninety by 2015.

The closest town to this Barunga forest of towers is Snowtown. Here one of the blades is on display, all 54 metres long and 10 tonnes of it; three of these are attached to one tower. Literature detailing design of these towers states a wind strength factor of four metres per second is required to begin the blades' rotation and the best wind speed is between 20 and 26 metres per second. Over this speed the device will shut down until the speed drops to 22 metres when it will become active again. The blade head turns automatically to face the oncoming wind.

Standing up close to one of these monsters would have shaken even the redoubtable Don Quixote's mad resolve. Rearing skywards from their anchorages deeply buried in the earth, each juggling its giant blades, the towers stretch along the ridge for kilometre after kilometre, usually facing south to collect the Antarctic winds that have travelled vast distances to keep this appointment. The blades circle with statuesque deliberation like an endless animated succession of those mysteriously propeller-like Isle of Man logos, choreographed to turn ever so slowly, over and around in a clockwise direction, geared to an exact beat no matter what the wind speed, around and around, only their rhythmic swooshing disturbing the rural silence.

Overwhelming an ant-sized human standing beneath them, the wind towers are a fantastic sight, I love them. I think they are awesome – in the true sense of the word – but inevitably they are controversial. Many people vigorously oppose them, citing possible noise and health problems. From a distance, you wonder how their smooth, elegantly turning blades could be noisy, but closer up, the resonant humming is loud and constant, and it is this eerie, thrumming song that is regarded as a threat to the health of those in the vicinity, either by depriving people of sleep or by slowly driving them mad, so they say.

Supporters argue that, from the point of view of both economy and efficiency, wind farms are worth the risk when it is a question of saving the planet from fossil fuel-fired electricity generation and worse still, they argue, from a nuclear solution that many others argue is the one technology that would eliminate coal emissions at a small fraction of the cost of both coal and alternative technology.

For Mid North landowners, however, there is one incontrovertible fact about wind farming: those who host a wind farm receive a generous annual rent for the use of their land. This economic buffer means they obtain relief from the traditional threats and problems of rural life – fickle weather and the volatility of local and world markets. Does this explain what is really at the heart of some of the neighbours' complaints about noise and health risks, simply another face of envy?

Wind generating is not only a matter of giant structures marching across rolling hills. At the opposite end of the windy scale are the fans used on some vineyards in frost-prone areas. These devices are simple two-bladed affairs that automatically come into action when the air temperature drops to two degrees Celsius. At this point the blades start to turn, not to produce and store energy but to disperse it among the vines, to move cold air on and out through the rows and onto lower ground. Just keeping the air moving, preventing it from dropping below two degrees, is sufficient to dispel the frost threat.

For several days in late October and early November of 2012 our property was in the grip of a black frost that spread not only through the Clare Valley, but also across much of South Australia and into Victoria and New South Wales. There was no relief in the following winter when it happened again. It's heartbreaking to look down into the vineyard first thing in the morning and see the healthy canopy burnt black. Black frost is deadly not only in vineyards, on roads it is invisible even to the most alert driver.

Vine leaves engulfed by black frost are burnt to a crisp as are the florescences, the tiny potential grape bunches. The scene is devastating. All of the work and resources put into getting the vines to this point have been wasted. But the vine has a survival mechanism called the basal bud, which sits at the bottom of the cane where it joins the arm of the vine, awaiting just such an emergency. When all other buds are gone, this bud will be activated to put out a new cane. The result is foliage that will take the vine through the season; it may even bear some fruit, and the vine will survive. That season the vines already had survived the hot northerlies but these winds were a half-hearted attacker compared with the frosts.

When we first arrived in The Valley a study into the use of mulch under the vines was in progress. It concentrated on variations in worm activity and rates of moisture retention in soil shaded from the summer heat by straw, and the impact of frost. The virtues of increased worm activity were confirmed as was the superiority of dark mulch over lighter coloured mulch. The study also concluded that the lighter coloured straw mulch should never be used with Cabernet Sauvignon vines as it would stop the movement of cold air along the rows from higher to lower ground.

Cabernet Sauvignon vines are often planted in frost-prone areas because they bud late, usually about a month after Shiraz and, therefore, they will escape the September frosts. Our large Cabernet block is at the very lowest part of The Hill and in past years has seen only minimal frost damage, just a few vines nipped.

The young contractor suggested the use of straw mulch for soil improvement and hence a better yield. The soil in this block is somewhat thin, shaly and of low fertility. I listened to him and, completely forgetting the results of that study many years before, followed his advice. The mulch, when first applied, was knee high around the vines and protruded into the inter-row impeding air flow. Impeded air flow, in this case, also impeded cash flow.

Frosts are taken for granted in the early part of spring in Clare Valley, but you never know. The old timers say you can't be sure there won't be a frost until after Armistice Day, just as they say not to plant your potatoes until after Anzac Day, because that's when the autumn rains will start.

As I looked down into the vineyard on this gelid, still morning, I saw a fox waiting in the vine rows, close to the southern fenceline, eyeing the neighbour's sheep, biding its time. Now that we no longer ran sheep, we weren't bothered about foxes or onion weed. Onion weed and sheep don't go together and we had tried to eliminate the weed because it can cause scouring in sheep, what the locals so accurately describe as 'shitty bum'. But no matter how hard you try, some of the weed population always survives, as does Cape Tulip.

The other pests we had to deal with early on were flocks of starlings that would come up from the plains when reaping was finished for a season of grape feasting after 'veraison', beginning at the end of December. Veraison marks the beginning of grape ripening. Hard small, green berries begin to expand, soften and change colour as internal pulp volume increases and acidity decreases and turns to sugars. The starlings eat the grapes, transforming each bunch into a skeletal framework and galahs strip off emerging buds.

In the early years I mounted dawn and dusk patrols, driving the ute to tree clusters to raise a horn honking hell in an effort to persuade the invading birds to go elsewhere. This strategy had some success. Various devices then started to appear on the market – one made of nylon, shaped like a large black hawk and attached to a cord at the end of a high pole. As the wind catches hold of it, the black hawk shape would be pulled out to hover, swoop and dive.

Gas guns became popular for a while. The guns would fire at timed intervals to scare the birds but the birds simply became used to the time interval and learned to ignore the sound of 'gunfire'. Some neighbours, however, did not share the insouciance of the birds. Mike told me about a friend whose gas gun disappeared. Mike was helping him to install a new rainwater tank a couple of years later, but first they had to dismantle the old worn tank, which was still half full of water. There, inside it, slimy and rusting, was the missing gas gun.

One winemaker, a Scot and an intrepid piper, took to playing his bagpipes at dawn and dusk to scare birds away from his property and across the road to his neighbours. I asked him jokingly which was the better deterrent, the pipes or the gas gun. He answered in all seriousness that neighbours seemed to dislike both, but the birds seemed to be unperturbed.

I came up with a double-barrelled solution. First, planting trees under the Trees for Life program to encourage local populations of birds to inhabit The Hill and thus as the resident population be seen to 'occupy the corner' and so deter fly-in-by-nights. And second, in December, we tie lengths of red and silver tape to the canopy throughout the vineyard. The theory is that a passing flock, seeing the dynamic glitter of the tapes, will be deterred from landing for a feed not knowing what is causing the glittering aberration and instead land in a vineyard without the glitter. The tape is biodegradable.

While the efficacy of these various schemes is debatable, they do seem to have a cumulative impact and we experience very little bird damage these days. Even the crows that used to live in the scrub next door have moved on.

~ * ~

Country communities love to gather for all sorts of reasons, including those of an arty nature. For example ACDC – the Auburn Community Development Committee – has long celebrated

Auburn as the birthplace of C.J. Dennis in September 1886. This favourite son became one of Australia's best loved poets. Each year the festival in his honour presents his verses, about the simple pleasures of life, as readings and cabaret stage events.

There is a claim that C.J. was conceived at a spot in Penwortham. It is said by some that a mile post on the Riesling Trail used to have a copper plate attached reading 'C.J. Dennis conceived here 1875'. Thinking this was too valuable to be left for someone to souvenir, the walker detached it and gave it to the C.J. Dennis Society for safekeeping from where it subsequently disappeared. So, a local known for leg pulling (just look at the dates), fashioned a new plaque with the same inscription and attached it to the same milepost. To mark this important occasion the local had his Riesling grapes vinified by Ben Jeanneret and labelled Conception Riesling. It is not known if this drop is for public consumption.

But times are changing. There is an awareness in the Clare Valley, especially perhaps among the winemakers, of the entertainment possibilities and value of art, music and performance. Greg Cooley Wines, on the Main Road just to the south of Clare, presents regular stage shows – live bands, singers and actors, such as the *Me and My Mates* performance of retro Australian ballads and folklore in 'colourful and humorous language in an irreverent but affectionate way', according to the winery's publicity.

The Clare Valley Film Festival of short films started with local filmmakers but soon blossomed into an annual event of international importance with entries from twenty-five countries. The organisers, Chris Bishop and Seeta Indrani, chose Ian Roberts's Blyth Cinema as the venue for the screenings.

And there is the Clare Writers' Festival organised by ex-journalist Nan Berrett and her friends and colleagues. The patron for the first of these was Clare's very own author, Fiona McIntosh, who was full of praise for the organising committee.

Another bestselling author, Dr Sean Williams, was so impressed with the quality of the offerings he offered to sponsor future presentations of *The Write Week* to help to place the celebration of words firmly on the calendar of arts and events in the region. Mt Surmon Wines was a minor sponsor offering a dozen wines for a fundraising raffle.

Then there is the recent opening of Clare Aerodrome at Anama, a twenty-minute drive to our north, where local plane enthusiasts now organise fly-in visitors from around Australia. We have painted 'Mt Surmon Wines' in metre-high letters on our very long roof to aid aerial navigators and have had the pleasure of hosting a number of fly-in groups for wine tastings.

A Melbourne company, Air Adventure, is offering Victorians 'luxury air travel' to Clare with a private tour of The Valley, Riesling tastings and lunch at Skillogalee. They advertise a four-day tour to the Flinders, Clare, Barossa, Coonawarra and back to Melbourne for $4900.

Spring and summer have become colourful, stimulating and exciting times in the romantic Clare Valley in the Mid North of South Australia. Fine wines, excellent food, art galleries, music, literature and drama attract the full range of tourists from the amiably curious to the serious patrons of tastings, and the freewheeling visitors alive to good times and high-class enjoyments.

~ * ~

We were invited to help celebrate Paulett Wines thirtieth anniversary at their party for friends and workers. A few days before the event, some of Australia's most influential wine communicators (what the local paper reported as 'wine royalty'), including James Halliday and Ralph Kyte-Powell, arrived at the winery for a vertical tasting of Paulett Rieslings from 1983–2013.

Most wineries retain a few dozen of their wines each year for their museum and use these occasionally to taste to see how they are progressing. Such occasions are usually reserved for a formal gathering of wine writers to expose them, say, to the past ten vintages of a particular variety. In the case of the Paulett Rieslings it was the past, or the first if you wish, thirty vintages.

The event to underline how important the Clare Valley is in the Riesling wine world was a remarkable achievement indeed and James Halliday was most effusive in his appreciation of the occasion. He wrote that the Clare Valley 'was his favourite Australian wine region' both from a winemaking perspective and because of its history, its villages and the beauty of the region. 'There is a palpable sense of history mixed in with the quintessential bush and each of the small valleys being unique with a different feel. Clare Valley hasn't fallen prey to big, brash *corporate* wineries. Very few regions could compete with Clare when it comes to giving a totally authentic wine growing experience.'

The wine writers commented that as 'well as displaying Neil Paulett's fine winemaking skills the vertical tasting showed the wisdom of the Clare Valley winemakers when the region changed from cork to screwcap closures'. Chef Louise Haines served a lunch featuring local foodstuffs for the wine writers, many of whom also write about food and restaurants for their publications, so this was great publicity for the Clare Valley wine region.

Patatas bravas

Ingredients for 6 servings

6 medium potatoes

50 mL olive oil

Hungarian smoked paprika

grated nutmeg and coriander

½ cup tomato sauce and

½ cup chilli sauce mixed in a squeeze bottle

a small carton of sour cream

salt, grated black pepper and nutmeg

Heat the oven to 180°C. Slice the potatoes to 2-cm triangles.
Cover the bottom of a baking dish with the oil and put the triangles into it.
Sprinkle the spices over and mix the potatoes to coat with oil and spices.
Bake for 45 minutes until the potatoes are browned and al dente.
Place the potatoes into a warmed serving dish.
Distribute the sour cream, sufficient to your taste, over the top and then squeeze the sauces to cover. Serve hot with main course, or as tapas.

Wine match: dry Sherry, Viognier, Cabernet Sauvignon

It was a salutary occasion for this small winery, which like many in the Clare Valley is a family affair. Neil looks after the winemaking, his wife Alison runs the cellar door, their son Matt manages the vineyard, and Matt's wife Ali sees to sales and marketing.

We felt very privileged to be part of the occasion. In the speeches Neil told us that he had just realised that it was the thirty-first year since he and Alison had arrived in Clare. Mayor Alan Aughey, locally renowned for his ready wit and eloquence, suggested that Neil must be a pretty slow mover having taken thirty-one years to ask the Mayor to officially open the winery.

Unseasonable December weather – a cold wind and lashing rain – forced us to congregate inside the winery rather than sitting on the terrace with its breathtaking views, but did not in any way blunt the wonderful bonhomie and joy of this very jolly affair. At this same event, Paulett Wines became the third winery in Clare Valley to launch a locally brewed beer following in the footsteps of Jeanneret Wines and Knappstein Enterprise Winery and Brewery. Strange how winemakers love their beer.

About this time we were also having a smaller celebration for Jeni's birthday. We were having a bit of a craze on Spanish tapas and Italian starters, and for a bit of fun I had bought a bottle of Saint Hilaire Brut with which to toast this important occasion because the qualities and history of this relatively inexpensive wine are quite interesting. We found the Saint Hilaire to be a crisp, lively and sparkling wine with elegant aromas that reminded us of the taste and smell of pear and peach.

This Blanquette de Limoux ('blanquette' being, literally, a 'little white') made from Mauzac, Chardonnay and Chenin Blanc grapes cannot claim to be a champagne even though it was made by the *méthode traditionelle* with two years on the lees in the bottle.

Legend has it that Dom Pérignon and his clerical winemakers at the Abbey of Hautville near Epernay, Champagne, found that some of their bottled supposed still wines were in fact sparkling. The province of Champagne has claimed the intellectual copyright over the term 'Champagne' and under French law and international treaty only champagne wines made in Champagne may use the

Italian broad bean bruschetta

Ingredients for 4 servings as entree

50 g cooked skinned broad beans
100 g cooked green peas
2 tbs grated parmesan
1 tbs extra virgin olive oil
1 tbs wine vinegar
juice of 1 lime or lemon
a few dashes of Tabasco
white pepper and sea salt
4 slices ciabatta

Combine all ingredients except the ciabatta in a bowl and crush with a fork to a rough, wettish mash.

Brush each slice of ciabatta with olive oil. Brown on a hot chasseur.

Spread the bean mixture onto the slices and add salt and pepper.

Wine match: Semillon, Riesling, Viognier, Rosé

word on their labels, thus stealing the thunder of all other sparkling wines.

Limoux is a small town in the eastern Pyrenean foothills just to the north of Catalonia, a natural home of the cork tree. The Saint-Hilaire people suggest the romantic Dom Pérignon story is probably false because the cleric's central interest was in making the province's still wines, not sparkling wines. They claim that sparkling wine originated in the Limoux region in 1531, produced by the monks at the abbey in Saint-Hilaire, and using cork from Catalonia for bottle stoppers long before it was consciously used in Champagne.

The story on the back label of the Saint-Hilaire bottle and the contents of the bottle got us off to a fine start to our celebrations. The forebears of Jeni's mother (Molly Pike) were buried somewhere in a small cemetery in the Clare Valley. We decided to go on a history tour to find their graves, but there are twenty-one cemeteries in The Valley, a number of them still active.

There is a small one just down the track from us, a former Methodist Chapel with a graveyard, and another on the ridge to our east on Square Mile Road called The Gaelic Cemetery. We set off to visit this one first. This cemetery is dedicated to those immigrants from Scotland who arrived on the sailing ship *Hercules* and farmed the Mid North in the early days – the McKaskills, McLeods, Campbells, Morrisons and Nancarrows to name a few. One McLeod interred in this cemetery was born in 1796 in Scotland, travelled to the Clare Valley to settle with his family and to make his fortune. His descendants are still working the land today. The earliest interments date from the 1870s and the cemetery is still extant.

Not so the very small one on Spring Farm Road where Molly Pike's ancestors were laid. Spring Farm Road runs parallel and a little to the east of Main North Road, and the cemetery is just to the north of Artwine Vineyards. There are thirty to forty graves in this plot, overgrown with wild olives and almonds, the roots of which have no respect for the dead or their gravestones.

There we found the headstones of Jeni's ancestors – John Dunstone who died in 1891 and whose son, John junior, married Maria Jane, the daughter of Samuel Bray, who was interred in 1892. John Dunstone was Jeni's great-grandfather. And here was an oddity; the grave of Mika, 'a converted native of Samoa', who died on 16 September 1891 aged twenty-one. How intriguing to ponder the story and implications behind this headstone and its inscriptions, 'a converted native'.

Then, on to the hotel in Manoora. The reason for this visit arose from the presentation to Mayor Allen Aughey by Commander Alan Williams, Royal Australian Navy, of a memento from HMAS *Manoora*, which had been decommissioned. Manoora is a village in the Clare and Gilbert Valleys Council area, which lies to the southeast of Clare on the Manoora Road running past Grosset's winery.

The present site of the village was once a camping ground for the local Aboriginal people, whose word *manoora* probably referred to a source of fresh water. The village grew up as a result of the Cobb & Co mail service when its horse-drawn coaches used it as a water stop, but it really developed after 1870 when steam trains began running from Adelaide to Burra.

HMAS *Manoora* had originally been named TMVS *Manoora*, a merchant vessel on which my father served. There is a photograph of the vessel hanging in the bar of the local pub and a history of its service in the Manoora Institute.

We intended to have lunch in the pub only to find lunch wasn't served midweek. Well, why not try something entirely different in Sevenhill. On the way there we called into Annie's Lane Winery to look at their new Riesling. The winemaker was Alex MacKenzie, to whom we had sold fruit in the past. Alex had started as a youngster at Annie's Lane making red wines. Now, years later, as the chief winemaker, he was producing Clare's iconic white wine.

The winery is situated in the village of Watervale, originally a European settlement dating back to 1847. In 1889, Carl Sobels and his brother-in-law, Herman Buring, bought the winery and changed the name to its German equivalent Quellthaler; the 'h' subsequently was dropped. Quelltaler was sold to Wolf Blass in 1986 (and renamed Eaglehawk), and when Wolf Blass became part of Mildara Blass in 1991 it adopted the name Annie's Lane, supporting a sales story with a youthful ring about a young woman who delivered lunches to vineyard hands working on the winery's blocks in the Polish Hill River area. Annie's story had prompted the council to name the road running past the blocks Annie's Lane.

So here was a turn-up, a young Scot interested in making Riesling with a clear nod to its German origins, with one of the Rieslings being made from a single vineyard planted in 1935 with a clone from Geisenheim on the Rhine.

In 2011 Alex made an extensive tour of Germany's wine regions and included Alsace in France. He worked as a picker during harvest and undertook extensive tastings in the cellars.

Alex says he works at the drier end of the Riesling range, looking for balance rather than working to a formula as he deals with grapes from different vineyards and different seasons. 'It's a matter of balancing the components – fruit weight and flavours, alcohol level, structure and sweetness all come into play. I think people like my style, which is a little more full bodied and generous than others from the same area.'

Off then to the Little Red Grape at Sevenhill, just across the road from the pub. This is a somewhat unusual combination of cellar door, modern homewares and an up-market bakery. An unusual feature of the wine tasting is that you are able to taste and talk about wines made by a number of very small wineries that do not have their own cellar door.

A young Canadian bloke serving us said he had just finished working a vintage at Skillogalee Winery. He and his wife had travelled to the Clare Valley from Winnipeg in the very middle of

Canada. His wife was on a year-long teacher exchange program in the Clare Primary School, so he had taken the opportunity to look into how things were different in an Australian winery.

He took us through a tasting of a number of Rieslings until we came to one called 'The Mad Bastard', Mark Barry's label. We thought the wine delicious and just what we wanted to go with our light lunch from the bakery of a pie and a large roast lamb roll with pickles and salad, which the waitress had cut in half for us so that we could share. We sat in the garden crunching on the roll, drinking the Riesling, absorbing the ambiance chatting with the young Canadian.

~ * ~

At that time Swans was a delightful place to eat on the outskirts of Mintaro. Marjorie Moncrieff, an innovative Scot, started with the skeletal field-stone walls of a former farmhouse and lovingly restored them into a modern bistro offering fusion food styles for discerning palates. It was a delight to sit inside in winter by an open fire or on the deck in summer and take in the peaceful surrounding fields along with a scrumptious menu. A bonus for us was that Mt Surmon Sparkling Pinot Gris was very popular in her restaurant.

We received good reviews and won medals for this offering, with Marjorie's young waitress singing its praises to guests who were unfamiliar with our label. We produced only 300 cases so our production costs were high – one year to grow the grapes, six months to make the base wine, then two years in the bottle to give it its sparkle. Given the size of the run we didn't make a huge profit but it certainly brought the customers back for more. People still come in asking for it. Subsequently we made a Sparkling Nebbiolo, our last champagne-style wine because the champagne maker who spent two years nursing it for us died in tragic circumstances.

Marjorie closed Swans, bought a set of old buildings in Auburn and opened up as Cygnets. Her ebullience as hostess, her love of cooking and the warm, relaxed ambiance was again apparent in this new location. But the life of a restaurateur is a hard, constant grind and people move on after a few years. Later Cygnets closed and fortunately reopened as Terroir in the expert hands of chefs Dan Moss and his brother Rohan.

13

Chardonnay was becoming hard to sell because New Zealand Sauvignon Blanc had knocked it off the top shelf. Much of the New Zealand wine was a light, sweet affair tasting like a passionfruit soft drink. The light, low-alcohol Italian-style wine Moscato was also making inroads into the white wine market. Chardonnay had been the biggest selling white wine in Australia for decades and it's hard to understand why these sweet, light alternatives replaced it in popularity. Some say this was because the piss was taken out of it by TV shows and Chardonnay lefties, would you believe.

It seems that many people start to appreciate wine via a sweet white. As their appreciation develops they move to dry whites and then into reds. I can understand Moscato and 'Savvy Blanc' being popular with beginners but why should Chardonnay drinkers abandon it for this 'passion pop'? By comparison the French wine Sancerre made with Sauvignon Blanc grapes is a fine example of what can be done with this fruit and it is worthwhile paying a few dollars more to taste the difference.

The winery taking our Chardonnay grapes gave us the flick at the last moment. Usually Chardonnay grapes are picked at about 13° to 13.5° Be, but these grapes were left hanging, the sugar level reaching 15^ Be. We had finished a small job in the vineyard and I stopped to taste the grapes, then called Jeni over to try. The fruit flavours were generous – nectarine, peach, spicy and sweet.

We picked a sample bagful and took them to Donna Stephens at Kirrihill Wines, who, as contract winemaker, had made such excellent Viognier and Nebbiolo for our Mt Surmon label. She suggested we add a little Muscat Blanc au petit grains, which Australians call Frontignac after the name of the town in France where it is grown, to produce a wine approximating Moscato (Italian for Muscat). In an expectant mood we picked the Chardonnay and sent it to Donna for her insightful treatment.

The result was beyond our expectations. The generous fruit flavours of the Muscat grapes give a pronounced flavour followed by the rich mouth feel and acid spine of the Chardonnay fruit. We started to experiment with food matches and found great rapport with Asian food, especially Thai dishes, with the sweetness of the wine picking up on the spices and chilli heat. We called the wine 100 Blossoms to suggest an affinity with Asian food to those tasting it.

~ * ~

Three French couples arrived at the winery one morning excited and talkative about their planned trip north through the rugged Flinders Ranges and Uluru. They told me they had intended to hire a campervan or Winnebago-style motorhome for their four-week trip, but were horrified to be told the cost would be $25,000. Instead, they bought an old Holden station wagon and camping gear and were looking forward to some rough and ready camping.

They enjoyed our wines but were especially taken with 100 Blossoms and declared it an excellent wine to drink with pâté and soft cheeses.

Avocado pâté

Ingredients for 4 servings as hors d'œuvre

For the pâté:
2 avocados, peeled
zest of 1 lemon
1 garlic clove, finely chopped
salt, fine grind black pepper
4 pickled eggs, sliced and chopped
fresh thyme leaves
2 tbs Madeira or Marsala
chopped parsley to garnish
fresh crusty bread or ciabatta slices browned in a chasseur with a little olive oil

Place all the ingredients except parsley and bread into a serving bowl. Mash with a fork to combine. Spread generously onto the ciabatta and sprinkle the parsley over.

Wine match: late picked Riesling, Gewürztraminer, sparkling Riesling

That afternoon Jeni went to Clare and bought a pâté and some white and blue Costello cheeses for us to have with the wine as an aperitif. We certainly agreed with their judgement on the match. Now we had another great food and wine combination to suggest to guests.

Two young men, who had met at the International Terminal in Brisbane and decided to partner-up for their Australian odyssey, came in for a tasting. The shorter, more ebullient Frenchman was from the Rhône Valley; the taller more reticent fellow was from

Stuttgart. I struck up an instant rapport with the German because he was appreciative of and more open to consideration of our Australian styles. The Frenchman, on the other hand, had definite opinions about what constituted a good wine. He was taken with our Cabernet Sauvignon, saying of all our wines it came closest to what he was used to in France. The German enjoyed the sweetness of our 100 Blossoms.

Jeni and I enjoy these sessions and often find that customers teach us something, especially if they're from a different country. So it's *suum cuique* – to each his own – after all.

The 100 Blossoms is one of our most popular wines but it was evident to us that the glory days of Chardonnay in the Clare Valley were over and, would you believe, those of Cabernet Sauvignon were returning. We drew up a three-year plan to graft our 4000 Chardonnay vines to Cab Sav. This is a complicated process. First, ordering the grafting material, as it's called, from the nursery. This consists of rods with four to five buds, cut from last season's Cabernet Sauvignon vines before they are pruned. These are tied into bundles of fifty and placed in a stout plastic bag with a sprinkle of water and put into a coolroom awaiting delivery to the buyer.

When we received them we put them into our coolroom awaiting the arrival of the grafting team. Tony Hoare and his people are in great demand and have to be booked months in advance. Other vineyards are taking out their Chardonnay, Sauvignon Blanc and Pinot Noir, which after decades have been found not to do well in particular regions, including Clare, as Australian winemakers come to understand the European emphasis of the right vine for the right place developed after hundreds of years of experience.

In the Clare Valley it's best to graft in October and November so we booked the contractor to lop off the Chardonnay vines a couple of weeks before Tony and his team were due. The vine trunks are cut off at about knee height by huge hydraulic loppers attached to a tractor, and then cut from the cordon wire along which they are wound. The top of the trunk is painted with a sealant and the lopped vines taken to the burn-off site awaiting a winter bonfire.

The day before Tony was due we removed the grafting material from the coolroom and placed the bundles of sticks at the edge of the dam water to give them a soaking. One of the grafting team retrieved these and had the job of cutting the buds from the rods with a little of the wood attached as a base, which he then placed in a small container of water. The grafter took the container, strapped it to his waist and moved along the vine row making two slices into each vine trunk, slipping a cut bud into each slice, then binding it with a light tape to ensure it stayed there. The cost per vine is less when over a thousand vines are grafted at the one time.

We had booked David Meanie, our neighbour on our southern boundary, who is the regional fencer, to replace the cordon wires between strainers cut off with the vines' arms wound along them. Then a team, probably the Three Fillies, arrived to tie a string around the vine trunk under the graft and to fasten it to the new cordon wire. This has to be done before the buds burst. Once this happens they will grow quickly and will need to be supported by being taped to the string to avoid being blown out by the wind, or knocked off by passing roos, or maybe David's sheep, which sometimes find a hole in the fenceline and wander in for a feed of vine leaves.

Then our work begins. The Chardonnay vines in their effort to survive will send out water shoots at ground level. These grow very quickly because the old large root system continues to provide energy to the vine. We pass each vine and detach most of this growth to decrease competition for the new bud growth, but we leave a little, mainly at the top of the severed vine trunk, to keep the nutrients flowing. We pass each vine many times over the coming months cutting off the water shoots (which keep coming until senescence in winter) and winding the new shoots around the string, and stripping off lateral growth. When the new trunks reach the cordon they are crossed over and wound along the wire to form arms.

Hard at this work one morning I could hear an unfamiliar sound, which I took for the movement of a roo in a nearby row. I heard it a few times so I stopped and had a look – nothing. There it was again, this time with some snorting included. I started to trace the noise, down to the drainage bank with Trees For Life growing along it, and there, nearly concealed by the growth of the bushes, was a large something. At first it looked a little like a giant wombat. But moving closer, slowly, so as not to frighten it away, I could see it at last – a bloody great pig, over a metre in length, snorting and snuffling, seemingly smiling at me, quite content that I was giving it attention. I called to Jeni to come see and give me the iPhone from her pocket to take some shots. This was difficult because it was well hidden in the bushes and I wasn't sure how I might be received.

'Maybe it belongs to Peter Barry,' said Jeni, 'I'll give him a ring.'

'Maybe it's one of his three little pigs, although I must say it's bloody large for a little pig. Here, take the phone.'

'No, not mine,' said Peter, 'try David Meanie, he has pigs.'

'Yes,' said David, 'he's been missing for a couple of days. I was wondering where he was. I'll finish what I'm doing and come over for him.'

Next morning in the vineyard David poked along in his ute and stopped for a chat.

'Drove all around on my quad last evening looking for him, but no luck. They're quite intelligent animals, you know. He'll probably find his own way back to the sty,' said David. 'On the other hand he's just as likely to be sleeping under a bush somewhere. He spends a lot of time sleeping.'

'Are you going to turn him into Christmas hams?' asked Jeni.

'Hell no, he's too old for eating. Peter gave him to me along with a sow and I was going to breed them, but the sow snuffed it and he's just been getting bigger and older ever since.'

It was a couple of days before Dave located him, down by the dam, sleeping in the shade. Dave, on his quad and with a prod, ushered the porker up The Hill and down the track for over a kilometre, to its sty.

Cherries go well with Christmas and ham. There are a number of cherry growers in The Valley but this year they were in trouble. Jon Cameron-Hill from Piambong Farm was talking to us on ABC Radio's early morning *Rural Report*, how the winter hadn't been cold enough to set the fruit. Flowering hadn't gone well as the bees from a number of hives especially brought in to help with pollination didn't want to work because of overcast weather and cold days, then hot winds followed to blow off a proportion of the remaining flowers, to be followed by the black frost which burnt off new shoots and fruit.

We buy many kilos of cherries each year from the Cameron-Hills and received an email to advise 'cherry time was a bit of a disappointment this year with yield down two thirds so there will be limitations on quantity available to each of our customers.'

Jon takes a somewhat idiosyncratic approach in marketing his cherries. He maintains a very strict control on the quality of cherries sold as fruit. Those that don't look so good end as pickles or preserves and some of the morello cherry discards end up being co-fermented with Sangiovese grapes to make an alternative table wine, Sancheri, and then some of this with further vinification is turned into a Port. There's innovation for you. And I think I heard him say on radio that some cherries would be used for brewing a beer!

~ * ~

Scarlattis was now an 'in' venue for weddings. Medium-size venues were scarce and we could hold eighty to a hundred comfortably for a sit-down meal, and up to 150 for a cocktail-style buffet. One bride-to-be called in; she would like a hen's pizza party for her twenty female friends. We negotiated a menu and a price. Five types of pizzas: traditional including chorizo, black olives and mozzarella; Middle Eastern with minced lamb, chickpeas and preserved lemon topped with fresh oregano and yoghurt; a pizzaladiere with caramelised onion, anchovies and black olives; and a vegetarian/vegan offering. All of these had an olive oil and tomato base of course. Fresh Greek salad along with our Viognier and Nebbiolo were served.

Then two sweet pizzas: simmered quince slices and ricotta cheese, and goat's curd, roasted almonds and drizzled Leatherwood honey, both matched with the 100 Blossoms wine. What a blow-out. They were delighted. One of the young ladies loved one of the paintings and just had to purchase it.

Sweet quince and ricotta cheese pizza

Topping ingredients for a 25-cm yeast dough base

2 medium quince

250 g caster sugar

500 mL water

2 tbs rosewater

1 tsp cinnamon

1 tbs vanilla essence

250 g ricotta cheese

olive oil

Peel and core the quince and cut into eighths.

Dissolve the sugar in the water over a low heat.

Into a baking dish place the quinces, sugar water, rosewater, cinnamon and vanilla, cover with alfoil and bake at 160°C for about 2 hours, or until soft and easy to mash. Remove the quinces from the syrup, drain and slightly mash the slices.

Lightly oil the pizza base and prick with a fork. Spread the quince on the base and top with the ricotta. Bake the pizza at 250°C for about 15 minutes or until the dough base is cooked.

Wine match: Gewürztraminer, Spanish Pedro Ximenez Sherry, Petit Manseng

Then another young enthusiast phoned to say she would like to organise a wine tasting for seventeen guests as part of her pre-wedding hen's do. As usual with a group tasting booking Jeni explained there would be a five dollar per person charge for the tasting with the five dollars refunded to each person who purchased a bottle. The bride-to-be replied she would think about it. We heard no more from her.

Every week we receive phone calls and emails from individuals and groups urging us to donate to an extraordinary range of happenings. These people don't come to the cellar door to engage with us personally; and if a donation is made forget to acknowledge our donation formally. There is no *quid pro quo* such as I'll bring ten of my mates and have lunch in Scarlattis, or coffee and homemade cake on the terrace.

We have learnt from these experiences. At one stage I toted up our wine give-aways for a year and was surprised to see a figure of twenty-five per cent of wine stock turnover. We now focus our donations to support local causes – the library (three cases to Friends of the Library to purchase a commercial-grade DVD cleaner), Rotary, Apex, Heartbeat, Writers' Week, Brooks Lookout, VAPAA, CFS and Clare Valley Racing Club to name a few. Then of course there are the many cases used for Scarlattis' exhibition openings and the annual tribute of four cases to the Clare Valley Winemakers Inc. for use in supporting its work. Many Australian wine regions facing a similar situation now charge for a tasting. Perhaps Clare will too one day.

We are happy for people to use the car park, particularly the countless photographers taking advantage of our hilltop location for panoramic shots, including bridal parties getting married and having their reception somewhere else.

One unusual request was from the family of an older man who all came for a tasting. He told me he was born in the cottage we could see down on the Main Road with three palm trees. Some months later two of his adult kids came for a chat saying their dad had died. After his visit to our cellar door and the look down to his first home, he thought he would prefer to have his ashes scattered on The Hill rather than interred in the rather wet, obscure site he had booked in the Clare cemetery. We agreed to the request but asked they did not broadcast the decision.

~ * ~

We know that our wines are good because they have been awarded many medals; that is, if you accept awards achieved at wine shows as a measure of quality. But how do we know about the quality of the art exhibitions we present? Do we base it on the number of pieces sold, or the overall monetary value of the pieces sold, or the reputation of the artist?

One artist, a Scot from one of the Outer Hebrides, was an unknown in the Mid North. His pieces were well priced because he was returning home and wanted to offload his artworks. Of the forty-seven paintings offered, we sold forty-two. These works told the story of the fishermen from his home island. These families rented a cottage and small plot but if the fisherman lost his job, or more often, his life at sea, there was no income for rent resulting in eviction of his wife and children. The ghoulish figures of the bereaved wives, tall, gaunt, dressed in long, dark garb, haunted the landscape looking for relief. It was a memorable exhibition.

Then there was Debra Zwar, her husband from a farm to our north, who paints abstracts with great flair and a certain kind of madness. She works at night, very quickly to loud music, until early the next morning. Her exhibition, *No Boundaries*, presented energetic, colourful and immediately appealing works, which sold well as decorative pieces. The professional artist Ditter Engler commented on Debra's 'audacious use of colour'. She is an emerging artist and will go a long way. It was interesting to compare her works with those of another abstract artist who professes psychology. These were very large works, deep, meaningful and profound, and difficult to interpret. We sold only one piece. The market is our only guide to public preference. We eschew judgement, leaving it to public choice.

The most famous artist to exhibit in Scarlattis is Jeff Mincham, one of Australia's top, if not *the* top, ceramists. Most of the pieces exhibited were large pots, waist high, the last of his big works, and wc sold many. Over many years of creating these superb large pieces Jeff's hips were rooted, requiring replacements, and his shoulders were unable to throw and work the significant weight of clay. His latest works are experiments with colour alignments on smaller pieces. These are exquisite.

~ * ~

Our beautiful kelpies were not getting any younger, like the rest of us, but somehow you don't expect dogs to grow old. On the way home from town I stopped at the gates to let them out for a run up The Hill. As usual Janette ambled along, stopping at every scent opportunity to examine it in detail, scratching at the fallen leaves and dampish earth to unlock smells surviving from previous winters and sun-dried summers and now mulching back to enrich tomorrow.

Jackie's wont was to run a few metres in front of the vehicle to bark it up The Hill, her tail in fast circular motion, protesting every metre of the way whilst I honked the horn, to her utter delight. Not today though. Jackie didn't want to leave the vehicle. I lifted her out and placed her on the ground but she just sat, her beautiful brown eyes imploring me not to make her run and holding up her paw for me to inspect. There was nothing wrong with it. I picked her up and placed her in the passenger seat, a special treat. She sat up straight, 'like Jacky,' as it were, but she didn't cover me in kisses, the usual reward for such a treat.

'I think there's something the matter with Jackie,' I said to Jeni when finally I arrived at the house. 'She didn't want to run up The Hill, so I put her in the passenger seat and she didn't give me a bark of thanks.'

'I've been wondering about her. She didn't want to get out of bed this morning and she didn't eat anything, which is most unusual.'

Jackie wouldn't eat or drink that night, and next morning wanted to stay on her bed. I put my fingers in the water and held them to her mouth for her to lick as she wouldn't take water from the bowl. We agreed she must go to the vet.

'See in this X-ray, this swelling around the heart. I'll give her medication to drain out that liquid. She'll have to stay overnight for observations and another X-ray in the morning.'

Jackie didn't like being left overnight at the vet's. No doubt she could smell the fear of the other animals and sense their illness. I felt I was abandoning her as I departed, leaving her with sickness all around.

Jackie had been home a few days and each morning I carried her outside to hold her standing while she emptied out. I was surprised at the amount of urine she produced given she was not drinking. This morning she slipped to the ground from my hold and, lying on her side, vomited and excreted, without a murmur of distress.

'Jeni,' I shouted, 'come here. It's Jackie!' Jeni rushed out to see our dear little Jackie lying there panting, surrounded by her vomit and faeces. 'Oh no! Dear little thing. I'll ring the vet.'

I found some cloths and wiped her mouth and backside. I wrapped her in a towel and placed her on Jeni's lap in the vehicle.

'She must be on the way out, Burtie. We'll probably have to have her put down. I don't want her to go but we can't have her in distress like this.'

The vet agreed. The needle worked very quickly. Little Jackie lay still and soft with her beautiful large, triangular ears erect, listening. We selected a site on the side of The Hill looking west, over the paddock where she and Janette as puppies had rounded up Hopkin's sheep. Despite recent rain the ground was rock solid requiring a pick and crowbar to get the hole deep enough. Before placing the body bag in the ground I opened it to reveal Jackie's head and a large, velvety, warm ear. Gently I kissed it whilst Jeni fondled her muzzle. Resealing the thick plastic bag I placed it in the hole and started to push soil on top. I drove the car to our 'formal garden' to collect large rocks then back to cover the grave with these and an area around it, to deter foxes from digging in.

Jeni brought a two-seater from the terrace and we sat, holding hands, watching the setting sun. High overhead, in graceful, soaring, silent flight, the pair of wedge-tailed eagles circled ever so slowly as they paid their tribute to a fellow hunter.

'Jeni, my love, she is the first of our little family to go. Listen! Did you feel that? I thought I felt The Hill shudder.'

Jeni was in deep contemplation, silent tears caressing her cheeks.

14

The origin of the name 'Mildura' is uncertain but probably could be traced back to the language of the local Latje Latje tribe. The first sheep station in the district was established in 1857, but it was the Chaffey brothers from Canada with their irrigation scheme that led to the town being settled about 1887 on the south bank of the Murray River in northern Victoria. The aim was to improve 'a barren and empty landscape by developing an irrigated oasis in the midst of an arid land'.

After overcoming the economic depression and rabbit plagues of the 1890s the fledgling town began to thrive as orchards and vineyards were planted, watered from the huge volume of water flowing down the Murray. The vigorous, hugely successful fruit growing industry attracted migrant workers whose Mediterranean influence began to influence the local cuisine and their grapes attracted the attention of the burgeoning Australian wine industry. The town celebrated its 125th year on 31 May 2012.

We were in Mildura for the Australian Alternative Varieties Wine Show (AAVWS). This annual November gathering of grape growers, winemakers, judges and food aficionados 'aims to provide an alternative to the mainstream wine shows, a dedicated forum for alternative or emerging wine grape varieties and to encourage alternative, more cutting edge judging procedures'. Its interest and relevance for us was obvious, to learn more about alternative varieties and, more importantly, how to market them. We had learnt about having a point of difference but nobody had gone on to say how to market alternative varieties about which Australian wine buyers knew very little, even though some of the old Victorian wineries had grown some for the past 100 years. AAVWS contributed much to overcoming this situation. We now regularly make the four-hour drive from our property to attend both the show and its excellent long lunch.

Mildura has a reputation for fine food and attractive, interesting restaurants. One of the most important contributions to its food pre-eminence has been made by local identity Stefano de Pieri. Born in the Veneto city of Treviso, he migrated to Australia in 1974 and settled in Mildura after his marriage to Donata Carrazza in 1991. His dynamic energy, enthusiasm, prodigious talents and growing love of the Sunraysia region made him one of Mildura's favourite sons. His restaurant in the Grand Hotel and associated ventures – including a micro-brewery and a providore store – brought Mildura national prominence. His autobiographical notebook on his culinary education in the Veneto guided by his mother, and his culinary exploits in Sunraysia, was published as *A Gondola on the Murray* and became a successful TV series under the same name. With his brother Sergio, an internationally famous classical organist, Stefano established a local arts festival, and the Grand Hotel became the venue for an equally prestigious annual writers' gathering.

So while AAVWS is our main target in Mildura, we also thoroughly enjoy the many other treats the town and the region offer. We stay in a small motel just five minutes' walk from the Grand Hotel and about ten minutes to the riverside where the paddle-steamer is berthed on which the show's degustation lunch will be presented by Stefano and his associates. The actual wine judging takes place a bit further away in a large building at the sports arena, where the wine show participants and public may taste the results of the judging. This is about a thirty-minute walk from our motel, but it's best not to drive if you're going to taste your way through the winning wines.

You may, of course, taste a few hundred wines, if you are so inclined. It's a great opportunity for those who want to know more about Australia's emerging alternative variety wines, to taste the winners of so many varieties, and to talk to the judges about why one wine receives a gold medal and another, made from the same grape variety, a low ranking. You can also meet and talk with the growers.

We have been awarded medals for our Mt Surmon Viognier, and Sparkling Pinot Gris made using the traditional method. In 2003 we were delighted to receive a bronze for our Sparkling Nebbiolo, also made traditionally, a silver for our Reserve Nebbiolo, and a gold for the Nebbiolo. The latter had been left on oak for twelve months and the Reserve for twenty-four.

The Chief Judge was Tim White, a Nebbiolo lover and wine writer for the *Australian Financial Review.* At the lunch he discussed the judging results and how popular many new varieties had become. As lunch proceeded Tim talked about the awards for the different varieties asking a spokesperson for each winning wine to say a few words. Tim was obviously impressed with the Mt Surmon Nebbiolo success, despite claiming he had never heard of our label. 'So where the fuck is Mt Surmon, and who is Mt Surmon?' he queried, to the amused bon vivants.

It was up to me to respond. With tongue firmly in cheek I said, 'Tim, I'm surprised that one as erudite as yourself, and with such a huge knowledge of Australian wine, doesn't know where to find Mt Surmon cellar door. So, I'll tell you where the fuck Mt Surmon is. It's on The Hill at the northern entrance to the Clare Valley overlooking the racecourse. I'd love you to come for a visit and I'll show you the block where the grapes for these wines are grown – along a rocky spur and alongside the old gums with which the vines compete.'

Tim came over to talk with Jeni and me after lunch and asked for some background on our property and vineyard so that he could fill out his article for the *Financial Review*. Published a few weeks later, his piece resulted in our selling out of these wines within the month.

Later we spoke to Stefano de Pieri who was also impressed with our success with the Nebbiolo grape. Stefano wanted to know the clone of the variety and when I told him it was 111, bred at University of California, he became quite passionate claiming that to breed out the viruses found in the original vines from the Piedmont was like getting rid of 'the soul of the grape' that gives greatness to the wine, even whilst admitting that the same viruses caused many difficulties in managing the vines. Clearly, Stefano had romance behind his creativity.

We had a number of long, leisurely talks with Stefano over drinks. He was fascinated to know why we planted this noble Italian grape and why we thought we had enjoyed such success with it.

'Love,' I said. 'It's to do with love. Love gives insight and reveals things, like why we bought The Hill and our life with our kelpies. As the song says, it's "the wind beneath your wings".'

During one of these talks we asked Stefano if he would consider coming to our gallery to present a degustation lunch featuring alternative wine varieties made in the Clare Valley. We had not planned to ask him to do this, it was simply made on the spur of the moment.

He said he would be delighted, he would be glad of a short break away from his everyday bustle, and he would bring Donata and their two kids. A consultation of our two diaries, especially Stefano's very busy one, led to our selecting a date in the following year.

~ * ~

The shine of our trip to Mildura that year was dulled on our return by the news of two major deaths. The first was that of revered winemaker Mr James Barry, the founder of the iconic Jim Barry Wines. We wended our way to St Aloysius at Sevenhill for the funeral. Jim had retired from active participation in the vineyards and winery a few years earlier, and we would have a chat and a beer with him some afternoons in the Taminga Hotel.

Jim's is a fascinating tale of someone who did so much to bring the Clare Valley wine region into the modern era. He was the seventeenth graduate in oenology from Roseworthy Agricultural College and the first qualified winemaker to practise his art in the Clare Valley, which he continued to do for fifty-seven years. He made an enormous contribution to bringing a scientific approach to vineyard management and winemaking in the region. He introduced the use of drip irrigation to The Valley thus fostering the importance of a minimum and controlled use of water to produce top-quality fruit for winemaking.

It was Jim who was largely responsible in Clare for predicting the move in the Australian wine market from predominantly fortified wines to table wines, and who fostered a wine and food club to popularise the matching of good wines with good foods. To reinforce the move to table wines he introduced Riesling, Cabernet Sauvignon and Merlot grapes to The Valley, making available to vineyard owners cuttings of these varieties free of charge, ensuring the further development of the wine industry in the region.

He undertook these innovations firstly as the manager of the Clare Vale Co-operative, then as winemaker at Taylors Wines, before founding his own winery. During this time he fostered the careers of many young winemakers, notably Brian Croser, Brother John May and Andrew Mitchell, and was the driving force in the founding of Clare Valley Winemakers Inc. to guide the development of the wine industry in this region.

His introduction of these three mainstream grape varieties to the Clare region really gave it the solid foundation on which it has built its reputation. Clare Valley's eminent position as Australia's leading region for the production of world-class Riesling stems from this initiative. Today, Clare Valley Winemakers Inc. justly claims the tag line, *The Heart of Australia's Riesling*.

A few months after Jim's funeral we suffered a further loss – that of our beloved Janette. We had watched as her eyesight and hearing and later other functions began to fade. The end came rather quickly when, early one morning, she, who never complained, woke us with a distressed call. She had defecated in her trampoline bed, unable to lift herself out of it or even to bark a warning. She was most embarrassed and distressed. We took her outside and cleaned her up. Over the next days, like Jackie, she refused food and water. It was obvious she was on the way out, dying rather quickly and without fuss. Loss of energy and mobility, vomiting and loss of bowel control, this noble dog, who had been so particular about her everyday cleanliness, could no longer tend to her own needs. Even so, we found the decision to take her to the vet a very difficult one to make; we both knew it would mean an injection to compassionately end her life.

Despite its name, The Hill isn't especially high, but it is enduring with its ironstone rock having withstood the battering of elements, responding to the extremes of heat and cold, deluge and drought, and only very gradually being broken down into soil that works its way down the slope. It was here, on the slope next to her sister Jackie, that we laid her out on that bleak morning.

Having interred her we sat again on the jarrah seat from Western Australia between the two graves, holding hands, reflecting, looking into the setting sun. 'Our proud, beautiful girls are no longer with us,' murmured Jeni. 'My mother always said the trouble with having dogs instead of children is that they die before you do.'

The peppery aroma of the artiplex and the sharp, blue savoury smell of rosemary gave us a fleeting something by which to remember this day. I thought I could feel The Hill breathing and sighing in the evening sun. From the ancient gum a crow squawked its dry, dead call to its mate, but Janette could no longer hear her to respond with a bark, nor hear the ewes in the paddock next door bemoaning the absence of their lambs.

I studied the canary yellow of the Trees for Life wattles and the greenish-yellow of the ripening canola fields enclosed by a myriad of blue-green gums. Jeni, remembering Janette's commitment and love, which had given meaning to our lives, silently shed tears.

~ * ~

We started the lead-up to Stefano's degustation lunch, the aim of which was to publicise The Valley's alternative varieties, of which there turned out to be a number. First we engaged Nick Stock, a fine South Australian wine writer, as MC for the lunch, to select the wines and liaise with Stefano on food and wine matching. This was an expensive exercise, but the *quid pro quo* was Nick's intention to publish an article about it in the *Adelaide Review*, the free Adelaide monthly. We thought this would give great publicity about alternatives in the Clare Valley, and our label in particular.

I then contacted the South Australian Phylloxera Board for access to their database to identify who was growing what, but the confidentiality clause in their data-gathering program did not allow the identification of grower name with variety grown. They were willing however to divulge varieties grown by area. It was a start. A couple of cellar doors were already offering them and by asking around in the pubs and cellar doors and talking to winemakers we were able to put variety to label, including locating a few small vineyards where the growers were making wines in their sheds, but whose labels weren't available at a cellar door.

We bought a few bottles each of these and dispatched them to Nick whose job was to pick through them and select the best to drink with Stefano's food. We also engaged a winemaker from McLaren Vale to talk to the lunch crowd about Nebbiolo, and another to support Nick in providing background on these emerging varieties.

Next we arranged for Louise Haines, the wonderful Clare caterer, to be our anchor in Clare, to respond to Stefano's countless questions about local foods – availability, cost, quantity, and so on. To provide kitchen-hands we engaged Graham and Kym from Hillsview Estate in Auburn, two talented men who had recently arrived in the The Valley looking to set up a field-catering business. Who better for them to meet for help and information than Louise Haines? She was such a generous mentor that at one of the kitchen sessions Louise told Kym and Graham that she was to retire from field catering and would give them her pre-booked clients to get them started, much to their delight.

Stefano brought along Luke as sous chef and Luke brought Lisa as his assistant. We were now able to get a picture of the overall costs for the lunch – accommodation for everyone from Mildura, travel costs here and back, speakers, food, wines, waiting and beverage staff, kitchen staff, publicity, printing – and so it went. Adding this up and putting in a bit for overheads and contingencies the sum was then divided by a hundred, the licensed number for our gallery, giving us $130 as the cost per person for the event.

As the bookings came in, our limit on numbers looked as though it would be breached. We discussed this with a couple of experienced tour operators whose firm advice was never to knock back anyone. But we had to stop at 130 simply because there was no space left for tables and chairs in the gallery. The extra numbers meant tables and chairs and napery for the occasion had to be hired and a temporary liquor licence obtained along with the requisite number of mobile dunnies.

Stefano and Nick came up with the following eight-stage menu with wine matches:

~ Freshly shucked oysters with asparagus and scrambled eggs served with gorgonzola frittata pieces

Mt Surmon Wines Sparkling Pinot Gris and Crabtree Zibibbo

~ Cured fish on baby rocket with olive oil

Tim Adams Pinot Gris and Pikes Viognier

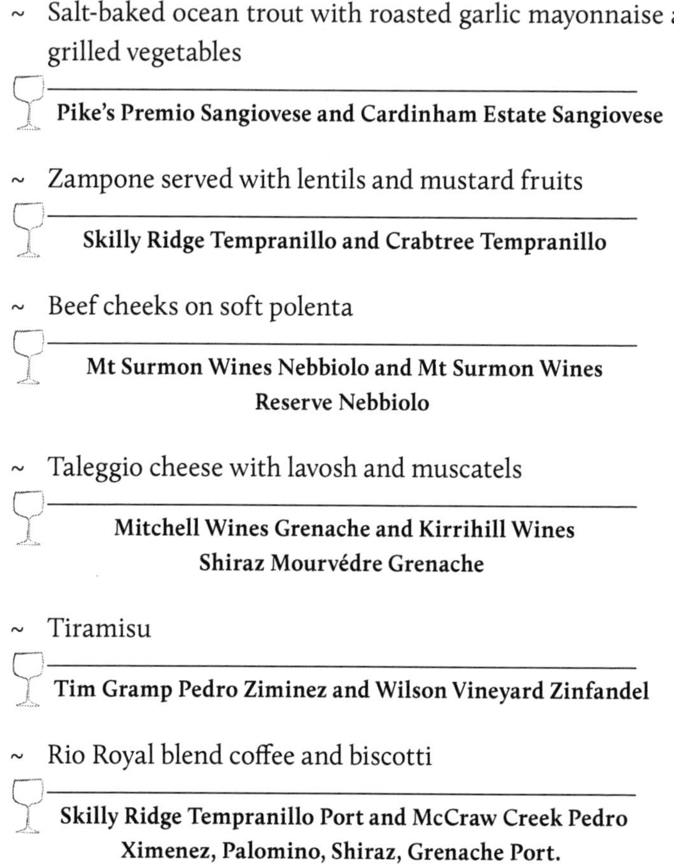

~ Salt-baked ocean trout with roasted garlic mayonnaise and grilled vegetables

Pike's Premio Sangiovese and Cardinham Estate Sangiovese

~ Zampone served with lentils and mustard fruits

Skilly Ridge Tempranillo and Crabtree Tempranillo

~ Beef cheeks on soft polenta

Mt Surmon Wines Nebbiolo and Mt Surmon Wines Reserve Nebbiolo

~ Taleggio cheese with lavosh and muscatels

Mitchell Wines Grenache and Kirrihill Wines Shiraz Mourvédre Grenache

~ Tiramisu

Tim Gramp Pedro Ziminez and Wilson Vineyard Zinfandel

~ Rio Royal blend coffee and biscotti

Skilly Ridge Tempranillo Port and McCraw Creek Pedro Ximenez, Palomino, Shiraz, Grenache Port.

There are a few interesting things about this menu. One is that Pinot Gris, Grenache and anything with a good percentage of Shiraz are no longer eligible for entry into the AAVWS. This is because many of the varieties originally on the acceptable list are now so popular they are considered to be mainstream. And, would you believe, the salt-baked ocean trout was cooked in a batter of salt and egg whites for which eighty dozen eggs were required. Despite this prodigality, the batter was stripped from the fish before serving and discarded. Finally, Stefano especially added the beef cheek dish to highlight our Regular and Reserve Nebbiolo wines.

Beef (calf) cheeks in red wine

Ingredients for 4 servings

4 beef cheeks
150 mL olive oil
1 x 400 g tin of tomatoes
2 tbs tomato paste
1 onion, chopped
1 red capsicum, chopped
2 sticks celery, chopped
5 cloves garlic, chopped
handful of parsley, chopped
2 springs of sage, chopped
2 sprigs of rosemary, chopped
4 sprigs of thyme, chopped
salt, pepper, grated nutmeg
250 mL beef stock
half a bottle of Nebbiolo

Wash the cheeks well. Put half of the oil into a large saucepan and sauté the cheeks until brown on both sides. Remove the cheeks.
Add the remaining oil, vegetables, tinned tomatoes and tomato paste to the pot, cook for a few minutes then add the garlic, spices and herbs, and cook for 10 minutes, stirring occasionally to stop from sticking, in which case add a little stock.
Now add the cheeks, stock and red wine. Reduce the heat, put the lid on and cook gently for 5 hours.

Remove the lid, increase the temperature a little and cook for another hour to reduce the liquid to a sauce consistency.

Remove the cheeks and slice into smaller pieces. Return to the pot to reheat for 10 minutes.

Put the cheeks into a warmed serving bowl, pour over the sauce and dress with parsley.

Wine match: aged Nebbiolo, Mataro/Mourvèdre, Durif

The lunch was a roaring success, according to the diners who greeted the chefs, kitchen hands, waiting and drinks staff with a ten-minute standing ovation. Stefano provided a resounding finale with his passionate thoughts on slow cooking and matching wines with food, concluding with an emotional observation that 'Food is the fuel of the soul', to resounding applause.

Of the 130 invited, 120 were paying guests, giving an income of $15,600 for the lunch. We nevertheless lost $1500 on the event. We received a full-page write-up in the local *Northern Argus*, which was great publicity, but the article in the *Adelaide Review* did not eventuate. Nick said the editor wasn't interested in a lunch that had already taken place. Young Luke and his partner were so taken by the Clare Valley and its cellar doors that they stayed on for a few days to recuperate and restock.

That justly famous and memorable lunch was held at a time when $130 was a furious price per head to pay for lunch, but it is small beer compared with New York's Del Posto Restaurant's price of $338 for a *glass* of Colle Brunello di Montalcino. Montalcino is a clone of Sangiovese, claimed by its growers to be superior, although Jancis Robinson, wine critic for the *Financial Times* and editor of the *Oxford Companion to Wine*, considers the micro climate at higher elevations is a more significant factor than specific clones in creating the characteristics of the wine.

I like the bit about higher elevations being important in improving fruit quality because that's where The Hill comes in, rising to 400 metres, catching every breeze and gust, cooling hot summer days and bringing nocturnal relief to the vines. I remember with affection what Vince said when showing us how to take soil samples when we first started to develop our vineyard. He summed up the process with the thought that what is in the soil is in the grape, what is in the grape is in the wine, and what is in the wine is close to our hearts.

The Hill has an easterly aspect so, on very hot summer afternoons, the sun's rays come in at an oblique angle, resulting in less heat stress compared with vines on the opposite side of the valley which receive the full blast of a scorcher. Vines close down when the heat rises above the high thirties. In the afternoon our vines are on the shady side of the valley and exposed to any passing breeze so I think they weather the heat better and go on ripening, resulting in an early harvest. They say early fruits are the best.

The ripening process in The Valley starts at the end of December or early January depending on the variety and location, when the very small, very hard, dark-green berries start to enlarge and change colour. This process, 'the grand period of growth', as the French call it, when the berries swell quickly and whites changing to a straw-green colour and the reds to a deep or purplish red (except for the Pinot Gris which, as the name suggests, turns to grey-white-pink) lasts six to eight weeks. Then the refractometer comes into play.

This meter measures the level of sugar in the grape either in Baumé, the French measure, or in Brix, the German measure. We walk the rows picking berries randomly throughout the block, squashing them to rub the pulp on the receiving glass of the refractometer, shutting the lid and looking into the eyepiece to see a shadow line alongside a numbered scale. Our meter measures in Brix, which may be converted to Baumé by halving the Brix number and adding one, as a rough approximation, so that 25° Brix becomes approximately 13.5° Baumé.

It's about time then to call in the winemaker to walk the rows tasting the berries looking for evidence of physiological ripeness – ripeness that displays full fruit characters. If the winemaker is too busy to inspect every block to be processed, the grower will take a sample bagful to the winery for assessment.

Once the harvest starts, we're all working at full stretch for the next few months. This is blood-pumping time for the pickers, and the people driving the harvesters, tractors and trucks, starting in the middle of the night and working throughout the day and, for those who are handpicking, in the searing heat.

In the wineries there is a palpable excitement as cellar rats, winemakers and laboratory staff work through the laborious tasks of processing the fruit from receival bin through pressings and into holding tanks and then, if changing from red grapes to white, having to wash everything down. It's usual for the whites to ripen first, but it is not unknown for reds to be ripening along with the whites, which is incredibly difficult for the winery workers, although it's a crazy three months anyway.

We receive many emails from young people in Europe, England, South America and the US asking for employment in the vineyard or winery over this period. But Mt Surmon Wines is not a processing winery. We forward the emails to the wineries processing our fruit. As a result, many of these young people come to work a vintage in the Clare Valley and have a great time doing it;

many of them come to our cellar door for a tasting. We love to hear their comments on our approach to winemaking. For instance, they had not come across a *méthode traditionelle* Sparkling Pinot Gris or Sparkling Nebbiolo before, and had not heard about a vintage-style Port, which seems to be an Australian phenomenon, let alone one made from fifty-five per cent Nebbiolo and forty-five per cent Shiraz with a good belt of brandy spirit. In Portugal a vintage Port is one declared when the vintage is considered to have been exceptional.

Our vintage Port was not well received by the AAVWS chief judge Max Allen the year we put it up. 'Why would you want to use Nebbiolo in a vintage Port?' he asked, rather derisively. 'To see what happened,' I said, somewhat naively.

'Well, now you know.' Bull's eye.

But we reckon Max was wrong. A vintage Port goes on maturing in the bottle and this wine, some years after Max's judgement, is drinking beautifully. We used the Nebbiolo fruit to capture the strawberry and dark berry fruit characters that give the palate a nice richness.

~ * ~

The local chapter of the University of the Third Age (U3A), among many other things, runs classes teaching watercolour art. We arranged with them to mount an exhibition of their best watercolours from the year's class and to enter the Every Generation Festival held in South Australia each year under the auspices of the Council on the Ageing SA. It was the only one entered for the Mid North.

We ran this for two years and both exhibitions were very successful, jolly affairs so far as the number of visitors at the official openings were concerned and the amount of free wine consumed. But the cost incurred for the wines, administration, publicity and so on, amounted to several hundreds dollars each time, even after U3A paid the festival entrance fee. Sales were minimal.

The quality of the works presented and their prices were reasonable and appropriate but, as one of the exhibitors said, 'The family members of the exhibitors will wait till Gran takes her work home and then ask for it as a gift.'

Breaking even would have been acceptable, but losses can't be sustained for long and we had to withdraw our support. This annual event is still running locally but in another venue.

Then there's the annual SALA, the South Australian Living Artists Festival. Scarlattis was the first gallery in the region to participate from the beginning, when the Adelaide sculptor Paul Greenaway launched this celebration. The festival is now statewide, with hundreds of artists and venues taking part. We show mainly local artists for SALA, including Julianne Pulford, young Joel Plevin, who is showing remarkable talent at just fifteen years of age, and metalworker Jayne Lane, a farmer from Lochiel.

This year we asked Peter Goers, the Adelaide ABC radio host and journalist, to open our SALA exhibition. Peter is a great raconteur and had the participants in stitches for half an hour with his cutting wit. A young mother was present with her four-year-old, who found it difficult being quiet during the speech. Peter stopped in full flight, paused for a few seconds to look at the child, and then said, 'Don't you just love children? I love them, but I couldn't eat a whole one by myself.' The tot was silenced by its mother.

The other exhibition we mount annually as a community service is to show the work of seniors in the photography stream at Clare High School, as a culmination of their end-of-year assessment. Although these works are of an extremely high standard and carry a very low price tag they do not sell well. No photography exhibition does as those viewing the works loftily proclaim they could do better with their iPhones.

We tried for years to get the art teachers at Balaklava and Clare high schools to show their best art students but without success until Matt Walker, who took over the photography stream, came along. He considered it a great way to tutor his students in the niceties of how to prepare themselves and their works for a public exhibition. We invited a professor from one of the red-brick universities to open the first of these and his discussion of the burgeoning talent of the young exhibitors was well received by the many parents present. Well past closing time people were still enjoying the wines and food. To encourage a finale to proceedings, I put on a DVD of the *pas de deux* from the Nutcracker Suite and turned the volume to fortissimo, much to the amusement of the sophisticated partner of the professor.

'Jesus, Burtie,' she burst out, 'only you would think you could get away with blasting out that old cliché, quadruple forte.'

'Go on,' I said, 'everybody loves a cliché, especially when it's so bloody romantic.'

Brother John May from the Sevenhill Seminary usually comes to these Sunday afternoon openings to consider the paintings and to taste our red wines. His favourite is our Nebbiolo; he buys a bottle to take back for dinner that evening with the Brothers. Whilst small galleries may come and go the overall trend for the art scene in Clare Valley is vibrant, going from strength to strength with its disparate offerings.

~ * ~

Peter Barry and Phil Lehmann arranged a get-together in Clare for the Barossa and Clare Valley winemakers. Phil's mob came over by the coachload and we assembled in the Stables at the Rising Sun Hotel in Auburn. This great hotel recently had been taken over by Ken Noak and his family.

Ken has his own vineyard and for many years also worked for Taylors Wines in their vineyard management section, including acting as Grower Liaison Officer. It was in this capacity that we worked with him when we were selling some of our fruit to Taylors. Today, Ken is a very busy man managing both vineyard and hotel.

The great thing about the hotel and its new owners is the high standard of cuisine. Ken's delightful daughter runs front of house and her partner runs the kitchen. His talents came up with the following menu for the get-together.

Canapés

- ~ Fresh Cowell Oysters – natural, Bloody Mary shooters, chilli, lime, honeydew, gin
- ~ Cider-pickled Japanese scallops
- ~ House-made duck liver pâté en croute with caramelised onion
- ~ House-smoked baby lamb cutlets with cherry tomato salsa

Antipasto platter

- ~ Charred vegetables, marinaded mushrooms, pickled cauliflower, olives, cured meats

BBQ Platters

- ~ Piri Piri BBQ spatchcock
- ~ House-smoked chorizo and king prawn skewers
- ~ Honey soy-soused belly of pork with bok choy and udon noodles
- ~ Merguez-spiced slow roasted shoulder of lamb with sautéed spinach

Sides

- ~ Rosemary and sea salt roasted potatoes
- ~ Hot smoked salmon with green bean and fried caper salad
- ~ Greek salad

Cheese

- ~ Camembert
- ~ Danish blue
- ~ Vintage cheddar
- ~ Relish and nuts

Fruit

- ~ Fresh and dried fruits

Each diner had to bring a bottle of young wine and a bottle of older wine resulting in a tremendous assortment for tasting and matching. The catch was that, after lunch, each diner had to weigh in. The weight was recorded, to be held until the weigh-in next year as evidence of indulgence, or healthy living.

As you can see the food scene in Clare Valley is indulgent, offering variety and quality and lots of fun.

Chorizo in brandy and red wine

Ingredients for 6 servings as hors d'oeuvre

2 chorizo sausages

200 mL red wine

2 tbs brandy

Prick the whole chorizo with a fork and simmer in the wine until most of the wine has reduced. Remove the sausages and allow to cool.

Thinly slice the sausages and place in a serving dish.

Heat the brandy, pour over the sausage slices and light the brandy. Serve immediately as an aperitive.

Wine match: Sangiovese, Nebbiolo, Barbera, Malbec

15

Boom and bust cycles are the norm for the marketing of agricultural products; the Australian wine industry is no exception. By about 2006 it had hit the worldwide competition wall. South American countries and South Africa were now producing commercial wines of reasonable quality at lower prices than their Australian competitors. The Australian dollar had appreciated making export prices much dearer and its large markets in the UK and US had become disaffected with the commercial-grade wines produced by the biggest Australian wineries.

The prices of imported wines into Australia were much lower because of the high value of the dollar, and not only were the large supermarkets importing bulk, commercial-grade wines they also bought vineyards and wineries in Australia and hundreds of hotels to flood the market with commercial-grade wines under their own numerous labels.

Vineyards producing D-grade fruit were being grubbed, smaller entities were being amalgamated into larger enterprises to gain efficiencies of scale, and so Clare Valley wineries and vineyards were fighting back successfully. Retailer wine clubs flourished and, to compete, wineries were supplementing their cellar door offerings with emarketing platforms, although one wonders about the seemingly mindless messaging via Facebook and Twitter to smart phones and iPads looking for the rare viral sellout.

Our family affair was minuscule, our costs high because of small production runs and our label virtually unknown. But we saw these variables as a source of marketing strength; we couldn't compete with the large firms but we could pitch to wine drinkers looking for a decent drop from a romantic unknown.

So the email which arrived from the University of Adelaide Business School was timely. It pointed in a new direction. We were asked to complete a questionnaire and invited to a seminar three months later to hear a discussion of the results. The expressed aim was 'understanding and leveraging marketing opportunities by engaging wine buyers through virtual communities and other e-based social channels'. The only way to find out what these words meant – obscure as they were to us at the time – was to get involved and try to understand the intricacies and subtleties of this new wine marketing thinking. Whatever the result, the seminar most likely would mean good finger food, conviviality and networking afterwards.

The questionnaire asked if we had a website for on-line wine sales and if we used Facebook, Twitter and iPhone apps to promote our brand. Our answer was both yes and no. Our website had been established to promote our wines, and to take sales payment on-line – one of the few in Australia at the time, we were to learn at the seminar. But we weren't Facebook and Twitter users. These social media didn't appeal to us as a way to sell our wines.

The survey feedback seminar was held at the National Wine Centre in Adelaide. The first speaker addressed the development of 'virtual communities', purchasers who develop loyalty to a brand and won't buy any other. The first example of this theory at work was Club Med, which over the years developed a cult following of young French people holidaying at the company's resorts. In due course many holiday companionships resulted in marriages and then children, with the families returning year after year to the Club Med resorts as loyal brand members. The point of this example was to show that organic, consumer-led growth in the sale of the Club's products was the glue that bound members to the brand. The members 'owned' the brand and cosseted its development to supply products to meet their needs. The 'clubby ownership' subsequently fell apart when the originator of the concept sold to commercial interests who tried to push new developments to meet the interests of the company rather than those of the members.

Jeni lent over to me halfway through this delivery and said, 'What *have* we let ourselves in for?'

'That's how it's supposed to work, but it's hard to see where it goes from here.' I tried to be reassuring.

The second speaker, reporting feedback from the questionnaire, said that of all Australian wineries (there are about 2500 listed in *James Halliday's Wine Companion*, published yearly) only 200 had websites, only a handful of which were set up for on-line sales, few of which were kept up-to-date and nearly all lacked professional presentation. As for social media, no Australian winery at that stage was selling wine on Facebook or Twitter.

'So,' said Jeni, 'we may be a small player but at least we're in the game.'

The third speaker was Dr Roberta Crouch who outlined the research she and her colleagues were to undertake for the Grape and Wine Research Development Corporation. Their task was to work out how to use the Club Med example to foster on-line brand loyalty.

Later, over canapés and wine, we thought what we had heard

was too specialised for our requirements and we doubted if we could apply it. Still, the refreshments were excellent, so we decided to attend the follow-up seminar to hear the report on progress and perhaps come to a better understanding of this new approach to marketing wine.

This time we were in the function room at Ayers House in Adelaide, another venerable monument, like the National Wine Centre, entrusted to the stewardship of the University of Adelaide. We learned that the first part of the project would be run in conjunction with the Adelaide Hills winemakers' group and would include live streaming of events featuring winemakers discussing how they made their wines, describing their attributes and qualities. What it meant was that Adelaide people didn't have to drive to the wineries. All they needed to buy wine was a well-functioning computer and fast and reliable internet.

At the end of the seminar, Dr Crouch introduced herself and asked us about our views on the research. I asked why the Adelaide Hills wine region had been selected for the study. The answer was because it was closest to the University.

She asked lots of questions about us and Clare and alternative varieties so I suggested she could include in her project something much different from the Adelaide Hills group, such as some small wineries in Clare, like ours, producing alternative variety wines. She agreed immediately. We were flabbergasted and offered to round up others in the Clare Valley who would be interested to participate in her project.

On the way back to the motel we walked past the Oyster Bar on East Terrace and feeling elated decided to celebrate with a couple of dozen oysters and a bottle of fizz as we contemplated the ramifications of our decision to participate.

Over the next week I made a number of phone calls and found seven Clare wineries interested in hearing more. A couple of days before Dr Crouch was due to visit I called them all again only to find that six had decided not to pursue it. We were left with a married couple with an obscure label as our sole audience. I rang Dr Crouch, thinking she would cancel, but she said two was fine. She asked me to call her Roberta and accepted our invitation to stay the night in The Retreat.

Roberta's laptop presentation was the same as the paper she had presented at the last seminar in Adelaide but something wasn't connecting between Roberta and the husband and wife team. The wife became progressively more pointed in her comments and after the presentation was completed the already tense atmosphere rapidly deteriorated, with dagger words from both sides. It seemed to me that I had let Roberta down after promising so much. Over drinks, after the others had gone, I apologised for the dismal showing, suggesting that there was no use pursuing it. But Roberta wasn't the least perturbed.

'I think we should run just with Mt Surmon Wines,' she said. 'Given your products and your location you've got a great story to tell, and the two of you are really funky, which all makes for a rich mix.'

We didn't know what 'really funky' meant but took it as a compliment, and so we were in – but in what? The answer proved to be a rigorous overhaul of the way our brand was presented – labels, flyers, website, and so on. Roberta invited us to a meeting with a couple of young blokes who ran *Voice Design*, their design agency in Adelaide. We discussed our labels and website and talked about our enterprise and our marketing plan. We invited them to come to Clare to see for themselves and to get the feel of The Hill, which they did. They said they were elated and were blown away by the image of the cellar door squatting on top of The Hill and peering into the vista.

The redesign process that went on over months was a shock. We had designed what we needed as we grew – the house, cellar door, the positioning of external art pieces, even the car park. We had landscaped the surrounds, designed internal and external lighting, colour schemes, labels and logo – the lot – with little outside help. These young blokes, however, concluded that our labels and logo, though passable, nevertheless were not contemporary enough to hold a strong place in the market. What we had, they all agreed, was full of potential.

They asked us to talk about how we got started, what drove us, what we were trying to create and were very interested in, even a little astonished by, our stories about the kelpies, the kangaroos, foxes, wedgetailed eagles, agave attenuate, the many sculptures, the food. All of these subsequently appeared in one form or another in label designs, website home page and banners.

At this stage at the end of winter there was an outbreak of golden orb spiders in the vineyard, which pleased us because they would keep unwanted bugs under control. A number of these large arachnids had also spun webs on the terrace and were a source of interest to cellar door visitors who watched and photographed them mating. Judging by her reactions, Roberta wasn't so keen, and, although golden orbs appeared in the first draft label designs, she later vetoed them. In my view with them in the label the place looked like a kind of sleepy hollow. We were assured it was important that we felt comfortable with the final designs – we had to live with them, after all – but there was little tolerance for our free-wheeling, maybe even funky, observations about the designs

which seemed to be taken as if we were criticising the opinion of a medical specialist.

Meanwhile, Roberta and her colleagues were running workshops at Adelaide University, probing consumer perceptions of label designs and the assumed cost and quality of the wines in the bottles they adorned. They rounded up students, academics, administrative staff and passers-by on North Terrace requesting their cooperation and offering two bottles of wine as recompense. We sold her thirty-five dozen of our wines at 'mate's rates' to cover the demand.

Roberta was pleased with the designs for our labels, logo and website home page so it was time to bring in another team to redesign the inner workings of our website to enable it to log the data she wanted to extract from our soon-to-begin streaming activities. While these developments were underway, she was off to conferences and teaching commitments in Paris and Helsinki – early October being the beginning of the European university year – and later to Beijing and Singapore. Our story featured in these academic activities and she told us the designs for our labels and logo were received with enthusiasm and applause.

On her return, Roberta was interacting with the Adelaide Hills winemakers and reported an anecdote from a winemaker in the Barossa who said he wasn't interested in e-marketing to virtual communities. Having decades of vintages under his belt, he said he tried to obtain the truest expression of the grapes each vintage, with minimal intervention in the winemaking process. 'This is my offering. Some people appreciate my efforts – others don't,' Roberta reported him as saying. She was horrified he wouldn't do everything possible to optimise sales by producing what his customers may want.

We identified with the traditional winemaking approach but at the same time we found ourselves trying to set up virtual communities to market our wines. We found it demanding but at the same time it was enjoyable and enlightening. Roberta asked us to draw up a twelve-month program of the work and changes in the vineyard, beginning in February, for inclusion in our program of fortnightly video streams to her computer room at the University.

We chose to demonstrate menus to match with each of our six wines; four recipes for each wine to cover the 48-week program. The idea was to film us in our kitchen explaining the preparation of the food and discussing our wine match. On our kitchen bench a laptop was hooked to two computer screens, linked to a small camera and microphone on a stand opposite where we stood. All of this was connected to a cable especially installed to take the signal to our radio satellite transmitter on the roof. This signal was then picked up by computers in the lab at Adelaide University where Roberta and her crew had assembled a group to follow us, by asking questions and making observations about our wines, which they were then tasting, and the recipes we were demonstrating.

Red capsicum with a dash

Ingredients for 2 servings as an entrée or side plate with a main

2 large red capsicums (bell peppers)

1 medium red onion, sliced

1 tsp Spanish capers

6 canned anchovies

freshly ground pepper, sea salt flakes

1 tbs olive oil

freshly grated nutmeg
a dash or 3 of Tabasco
crusty bread

Heat the oil in a pan.
Core and deseed the peppers and cut into long 10-mm-wide strips.
Sauté the onions until soft and then add the peppers and anchovies.
Cook until al dente, just as they start to change colour. Do not overcook.
Place in a shallow serving bowl. Dress with cracked pepper, salt, nutmeg, capers and add a dash more olive oil and the Tabasco.
Serve with crusty bread to mop up the oil.

Wine match: Grenache, Nebbiolo, Montepulciano, Barbera

That was the easy part. More challenging was Jeni's new role as technical officer as she wrestled with the complex technology of live streaming. Streaming was a unique experience without rehearsal or the possibility of retakes. We didn't know what might go wrong from one moment to the next. We felt confident about our cooking skills, but comments from the group about the recipes, the wines, The Retreat, our cellar door, art exhibitions and how we got into the wine industry were flowing in from the twelve to fifteen people and had to be dealt with as they appeared on our screens, despite the continued demands of stove, oven and recipe. The only time a mention was made specifically about our wines, where to buy them or their price, was in answer to questions. No hard sell, in fact no obvious sell at all.

At this time Roberta and her team were also interacting with winemakers in the Adelaide Hills and Barossa as collectives. Their

streaming events mainly concentrated on technical aspects of wine production and analysis of the results. By comparison our winery is very much an artisan's 'ma and pa' affair. Jeni and myself are highly congruent with our brand.

The year-long effort certainly led to the development of community engagement and brand attachment involving people who would not otherwise have known of our existence, as our wines are sold only through our cellar door and on line. We think resources invested in this project – finance, time, other jobs left undone – were well spent given the resulting development of a wider potential client base and, certainly, e-marketing by direct on-line streaming to a distant audience was a pioneering project for The Valley.

Another digital technique we adopted was to register a QR code – a small printed square of squiggles, dots and dashes. A QR code is accessible by downloading an 'app' into your smartphone. When the camera of your phone is held over the printed square, you are linked immediately to our website giving details of our wines and suggested food matches. We use the QR code on our labels, flyers and letterheads, and so on.

~ * ~

To add depth to their marketing initiatives, twelve winemaking families established Australia's First Families of Wine. Twelve family-owned wineries from sixteen regions across four states act as a collective to highlight the quality and diversity of Australian wine. Membership requires more than two generations over more than fifty years with 'landmark wines' in their portfolios. The aim of this initiative is to 'present a powerful showcase of terrific regional wines of great diversity'. Interestingly, five of these families

are from South Australia with two from Clare Valley – Jim Barry Wines and Taylors Wines.

Clare Valley wineries take very different approaches to selling their wines, developing brand loyalty and attracting publicity. Taylors Wines, for instance, have installed a giant outdoor screen near the cellar door for screening films during summer months. As a contribution to Australia Day celebrations, for instance, guests are invited at modest cost to a sunset screening, encouraged to bring their picnic hampers, with wines available for sale from cellar door.

In another vein, Sevenhill Cellars, producers of sacramental wines, now also caters to the laity with a strong marketing push towards Roman Catholics with labels such as Inigo, St Ignatius, St Aloysius and St Francis. It also pitches to a wider audience through its 'Shakespeare in the Vines' season with live performances of plays beautifully presented by Essential Theatre in February each year. Guests sit under olive trees with their picnic baskets, buy their choice of wine at the cellar door and participate like 'groundlings' in the Globe Theatre.

Another February attraction but considerably less sedate is 'Day on the Green' presented at Annie's Lane Winery at Quelltaler. Here the historic buildings, lawns and olive trees pulsate to a large, noisy, younger audience rocking to the beat of popular performers like Jimmy Barnes, Baby Animals, the Dead Daisies and, sensationally in 2013, Leonard Cohen. This is now a huge attraction bringing rock fans and other musicians, poets, songwriters and large, enthusiastic audiences to The Valley. The Retreat is booked immediately following announcement of the dates for these various events.

Then there is Greg Cooley Wines at the southern entrance

to Clare presenting tenor Danny di Vito and soprano Marsha Waddington, with more romantic offerings of classical music, and various combinations of singers and actors and their comedy skits.

The tourism industry, with accommodation and other services to support these thriving activities, makes different contributions with farmers' markets, art exhibitions and, of course, bicycle riding along the Riesling Trail. Snaking just up the ridge to the east of us for 33 kilometres along the former railway corridor from Auburn in the south to Barinia in the north, the Riesling Trail is said to have been the brain child of Tony Brady from Wendouree Cellars and his friend Evan Hiscock.

The trail is strategically and attractively signposted, directing walkers, cyclists, strollers, mothers with their babies in prams and carers pushing wheelchairs to wineries, vineyards, accommodation and assorted small restaurants or courtyard-style eateries. Some wineries have created diversionary loops from the main trail to their cellar doors.

Tourists interested in the history of farming in the Mid North should head to Bungaree Station just a ten-minute drive to the north of our cellar door, which both benefits from and contributes to Clare Valley's offerings as a wine region. Bungaree is presented as a living record of rural South Australia since 1841 when George Hawker and brothers James and Charles acquired a huge area of land to develop as a wool- and meat-producing venture. By 1880 the Station was running 100,000 head of sheep, with a self-contained community at its heart dominated by the grand sandstone homestead overlooking the woolshed, shearers' quarters, manager's house and staff quarters, store and church and, eventually, council chambers. For today's visitors restored agricultural machinery, artefacts and plant are on view.

This huge fiefdom was gradually whittled down by government decree to encourage closer settlement, but the Station still functions as a mixed farm under management of Victoria Hawker and partner Mark Stewart. The main buildings have been refurbished as tourist accommodation units with the old shearing shed now a function venue for conferences, weddings and school excursions. Self-guided walks and tours of the Station are available and we benefit on The Hill as Vicki and Mark direct many of their guests to our cellar door for food platters and wine on the terrace.

Another special historic property in The Valley is Martindale Hall, a Georgian mansion that was used in 1975 as the setting for the girls' school in the Australian film *Picnic at Hanging Rock*. Edmund Bowman moved from Tasmania to establish a merino stud near Mintaro. Being a keen sportsman, he arrived with his hunting horses and dogs and subsequently developed a cricket ground, polo field and horse track. In 1866 he drowned in the Wakefield River leaving his estate to his eldest son Edmund, who was eleven years of age at the time. On turning twenty-one Edmund was able to access his inheritance and used part of the large fortune to build Martindale Hall along with its impressive coach-house and stables which were completed in 1880. Situated on a rise overlooking the 450-hectare property the Georgian hall is now heritage listed. It functioned for many years as tourist accommodation and attracted daytrip sightseers who come to explore Clare Valley's wineries, ride the Riesling Trail and lunch in historic Mintaro.

A variation on the theme of how to sell grapes and wine appeared recently in the form of a small local vineyard-winery offering to process grapes for growers facing difficulties in selling their fruit because of the downturn in the wine market. Stone Bridge Wines on the Skilly Hill Road, just to the west of the caravan

park, offers growers the opportunity to value add by processing their fruit for sale on the bulk wine market rather than selling the grapes at prices below cost of production. The proposal is attractive, although the grower still has to find a buyer for the bulk wine willing to pay a price above the cost of producing the grapes, plus the cost of freight and processing the fruit, and a margin to make it all worthwhile. Nevertheless, if the fruit is of high quality, the risk may be worth taking.

Of all events aimed at wine tourism in the Clare Valley, however, the annual Gourmet Weekend is the grandest, biggest and most varied. This celebration offered by members of the Clare Valley Winemakers matches gourmet food with first-class Clare Valley wines. Held on the weekend in May after Mother's Day, it offers large retailers, bulk wine buyers and wine writers the opportunity to sample white wines from that year's harvest and gives the general public the opportunity to celebrate the just completed vintage.

Those who appreciate wines may visit cellar doors and vineyards and meet the winemakers for the opportunity to talk about the art, technology and romance of winemaking. The Clare Valley Gourmet Weekend was the first such event of its kind in Australia and in 2014 celebrated its thirtieth birthday. The original event had two objectives – to draw the attention of people to the idea of matching food with appropriate table wines, as against fortified wines, and to gain free advertising in papers and magazines and on radio. The concept rapidly spread to all Australian and New Zealand wine regions.

I came to the first Clare event, camped in the caravan park and visited stalls along Main Street in Clare, which had been closed to traffic, tasting wines and buying food for an unmatched al fresco

experience. From this beginning wineries now prefer guests to come to their cellar doors for a more personal encounter, thus spreading visitors around and easing congestion at favourite spots.

Many of the wineries partner with restaurants in Adelaide who bring their staff with them to offer special menus not always available in The Valley. In 2001, the first year we opened our cellar door, we joined in these festivities offering food we prepared ourselves in our kitchen – Scarlatti's Kitchen – to give it a more romantic ring.

With a couple of years' experience we came to realise people arriving in The Valley from the north arrived at our cellar door around morning coffee time and those coming from the south arrived around afternoon coffee time. Few visited for lunch. So we changed our plan, dropped the lunch offerings and concentrated on coffee, chocolate and wine – yes, chocolate. Many people, especially women apparently, find an affinity between red wine and chocolate, maybe because their sensitive palates pick up on the chocolate and mocha overtones in the wines coming from the oak in which the wine has aged.

We offer two unusual, couverture chocolate treats – one cake with a rich topping and the other a baked chocolate pudding, usually with almond meal instead of flour, with a liqueur cream and presented in large coffee cups. The favourite red selected by our customers to match these is our award-winning Nebbiolo with its intense aroma of dark berries. We base next year's planning on this year's sales plus ten per cent, but we often have to make more supplies on Saturday night for sale on Sunday, hoping all the while that we haven't over-catered. We advertise a peaceful location with conservative tastes so as not to attract coachloads of young and the ensuing need to hire security.

Malted chocolate pudding in a cup

Ingredients for 6 servings

185 g dark couverture chocolate, chopped

185 g butter

½ cup malted milk power

4 eggs, separated

½ cup sugar

½ cup almond meal (ground almonds)

⅓ cup plain flour

3 tbs sugar, extra

Preheat the oven to 160°C.

Place the chocolate, butter and malted milk powder in a saucepan over very low heat and stir until melted and smooth. Remove from the heat and set aside.

Place the egg yolks and sugar in a bowl and beat until light and creamy. Fold the chocolate mixture, the almonds and the flour through the egg yolks.

Place the egg whites in a bowl and beat until soft peaks form. While beating, gradually add the extra sugar until the mixture is glossy. Fold this egg white mixture through the chocolate mixture.

Pour the mixture into 6 greased 250-mL coffee cups. Place on a baking tray and pour enough hot water into the tray to come halfway up the sides of the cups. Bake for 25 minutes or until the edges are cooked but the centres are a little soft.

Serve with thick cream in coffee cup and saucer.

Wine match: Muscat, Madeira, liqueur Riesling; for those who like a red with their chocolate try Shiraz, Touriga, Nebbiolo

The large wineries cater for greater numbers, offering live music, inviting 'foodies to forage and feast'. Farmers' markets add to the offerings while Clare Valley Rotary Club stages its annual art exhibition in the Town Hall for aspiring and professional artists and serves wines donated by Clare Valley Winemakers. The umbrella group, Clare Valley Cuisine, sets up shop offering locally produced food and giving food preparation demonstrations. All of these activities offer a thank you to the end of a successful vintage. May, of course, is not only the end of the vineyard year, but also the beginning of the next. The celebration, then, is a fond farewell to the past vintage but also a welcome to the coming one.

I remember talking with Jim Barry in the Taminga pub when I was secretary of Fork and Cork, a bunch of likeminded bon vivants that meets throughout the year bringing in a noted chef to present his or her offerings matched with local and imported wines in an unusual venue, such as the Norman's shearing shed, or the old Soldiers Memorial Hall at Stanley Flat. I invited Jim to join our merry group, which he graciously declined but told me he had organised a similar group when first he and his wife Nancy arrived in The Valley in 1947. He made efforts to persuade local publicans to offer something different from the Sunday roast, and he would round up a group of friends and bring his wines to complement whatever food was offered. Perhaps this was the twinkle in the eye of the future Gourmet Weekend.

Whilst the Clare Valley winemakers were the first in Australia to establish gourmet weekends, matching great wines with appropriate foods, the local food scene has matured with the depth and quality of its offerings, in the many fine restaurants on the one hand, to its farmers' markets and quality artisan products from sausages to lamb, baked pastries, breads, pies and beyond.

~ * ~

Our friends Sue and Peter were coming for lunch, nothing too elaborate, just simple food matched with interesting wines. They were late of course and we had started on a bottle of Taylor's Pinot Chardonnay Brut, NV Bottle Fermented 12.5%, the label proudly claimed. The wine had spent time on the yeast lees in the bottle, which added complexity and subtle characters of toast and butter along with a fine acid palate. Jeni roasted almonds and added a few spices, which nicely complemented the fizz. Our guests arrived in time to help us to finish the bottle.

The entree consisted of steamed asparagus spears, al dente, on a croute of pidé bread sliced into squares and chasseured with a little olive oil, then spread with home-made mayonnaise. The spears were placed on this and then chopped pickled egg liberally sprinkled on top with a little more mayo added along with freshly cracked pepper and salt. Two contrasting wines were matched with this, our own young Mt Surmon Wines 2014 Viognier and a Jim Barry Wines Florita 2004 Cellar Door Release Riesling. The Viognier was drinking beautifully with a crisp acid palate and up-front fruit characters. The Riesling was eleven years old with its fruit derived from the Florita Vineyard first established by Leo Buring in Watervale in 1946. This was a great example of this style of wine with primary flavours of citrus and stone fruits over secondary characters of honey, spice and toast, and still with a long acid spine.

We were off to a nice start with Peter talking of his recent trip to his Asian buyers and Sue saying she was off with her girlfriends for a Mediterranean cruise before meeting up with Peter in Paris for a wine show in a few weeks, which sounded very romantic even if it also would have been quite hectic.

Mains consisted of chateaubriands seared and crisped on the hot coals of the barbie for a few minutes and then placed on crouton to sop up the juices. Jeni had created a béarnaise sauce to splash over the steaks, served with a dishful of roasted root vegetables – spuds, sweet potato, white turnip, carrot, pumpkin and beetroot – cut into small triangles for extra crispness, along with small brown onions and fresh herbs. A side dish consisted of fresh salad created with rocket leaves, chives, sliced red onion, pomegranate seeds – all home grown – and grated parmesan. The wine was a Kilikanoon Prodigal Grenache 2009. Grenache had made a welcome return from the varietal wilderness thanks in part to Kevin Mitchell at Kilikanoon with the fruit sourced from two small sixty-year-old vineyards of low yielding, dry grown vines and aged in small oak casks. This is an intensely flavoured and perfumed wine which blended beautifully with the vegetables and beef and especially with the English Stilton cheese that followed.

I mentioned to Peter that I was thinking of writing a book about the Clare Valley and our twenty years experience growing grapes and selling wines. To my surprise he quoted Socrates, that 'the unexamined life is not worth living'.

16

'Hello.'

'Hi, Jeni, it's Stan. We want to buy your vineyard.'

'What? Really! You're not playing around are you? Well anyway, I'm in Woollies right now.'

'When will you get home?'

'Oh, let's say half an hour.'

'OK, see you then.'

It was two days before Christmas. We had been down in the vineyard all morning cutting out *Eutypa lata* from the vine arms, otherwise known as dead arm.

Jen arrived home breathless to tell me the good news, as she put it. Two days before Christmas! What a time to drop such an alarming statement into the peace of The Hill.

Such startling news was too much to add to my aching back from the morning's work.

'Well, tell them to get fucked,' was my immediate response. 'Why would we want to sell halfway through the season? We've spent forty-odd thousand dollars so far on this vintage and I bet they'll want to take the fruit for nothing. Besides which, it's what we do. It's who we are. We created it. It's us. And what would we do to keep ourselves sane? We'd wither away.'

'Burtie, we *are* withering away. We're getting bloody old. Look at how much we do in the vineyard these days. Twenty years ago we were down there ten to twelve hours a day, just about every day. Now we do a few hours and we're rooted. I bet your back is aching as much as mine is right now.'

'Well, that's life. No, fuck 'em. It's our baby. We created it and we're doing pretty well. Over the last two years we've halved our debt, selling most of our wine in bulk instead of selling the grapes for a pittance. We're getting a really good per-litre price as well as the WET rebate. We could pay off our entire debt in a couple more years. KBO, as Churchill was wont to say.'

'What the hell does KBO mean and what's Churchill got to do with it?' Jeni spat out.

'I read the other day that when things were not going too well Churchill would murmur KBO to those present, being code for 'keep buggering on'.

'What bullshit, Burtie, we're more likely to drop dead if we continue on. We're getting old and decrepit and it's about time you realised it.'

'Certainly we're not getting any younger and I'm sorry to see that you didn't enjoy my attempt at humour to calm this emotional moment. Why don't we change the subject and open a bottle, it might help calm things a bit.'

'I'll have a red, and I think we should sleep on it rather than get all het up. Calm, cool, calculation is required to think it through.'

'That's right, KBO. But there you go.'

I agreed with her on the principle that it's better to move on whilst one's able to rather than because one has to. But this was a startling development to drop on me so suddenly. I couldn't, or maybe wouldn't, get my brain to think beyond memories that flooded in, such a rich vein to draw from.

Actually, a few years earlier we had put the whole shebang

on the market. Jeni by then had a yearning to join our friends in Auburn to live a 'dissipated lifestyle', as she would have it. Perhaps it was the price I wanted for the property that resulted in it not selling, but from the feedback received from the many interested parties who looked at our venture and our books we came to realise that what we were offering was too idiosyncratic, too complicated for others to get their thinking around what was required to manage the show. Managing a 20-hectare vineyard in itself was a complicated enough ask, demanding an understanding of the rhythm of grapevines over the year, and understanding weed control and pruning and the temperament of the bores, pumps and solenoids of the irrigation system, repairs and maintenance, harvesting and the intricacies of a depressed market.

And that's just the vineyard. What about managing the cellar door, to say nothing of the gallery and exotic artists and The Retreat? When I think about it like that I can see why a prospective buyer lacking experience would feel somewhat daunted. We had grown up with all of that and felt quite comfortable about running the show but, I had to admit, Jeni was right, we weren't getting any younger.

As a result of that experience we had gone to the council planner to discuss the possibility of using the former possessory title, which we now owned, to separate the main building and a curtilage onto a title separate from the vineyard. This was agreed to by the council officer, as was my idea of developing four cabins on the hillside just to the south of the main building to accommodate eight people; the council was keen to see more tourism units developed. Jeni wasn't enthusiastic about the thought of servicing four cabins in addition to The Retreat with all of the cleaning and linen washing that would entail, so this concept was put on hold.

We were now in a position to sell the vineyard as a separate entity. Realistically, I knew that at some stage in the future we would have to sell, not so much because of the physical strain, which was considerable (although there was always the contractor to call on) but mainly because of market trends. Things had become very difficult for small wineries and vineyards. Throughout Australia many small old vineyards were being grubbed and many small cellar doors, and some larger ones, were closing or going into receivership. And so, on the principle that it's best to move on whilst we are able to rather than because we have to, I agreed to put our beloved enterprise up for sale but I would ask a decent price because of the quality of our fruit and our unique hillside location.

We knew the quality of our grapes was excellent because the large winery we used to sell fruit to told us so. Each year in September the manager and head winemaker would invite us down to taste the wines made from our fruit from that year's harvest. We were told our Shiraz and Cabernet Sauvignon grapes were the best and the next best fruit from all of their other growers and even their own grapes. To which I would respond that the grapes then were worthy of a large bonus as they would be used for their top grade wines.

'Oh no,' said the manager, 'only our own estate-grown grapes go into our best labels.'

'Well,' I responded, stupidly, 'that really doesn't make sense, to use the best grapes, our grapes, for secondary labels.'

As a result we were no longer asked for an annual taste-off. So in the year when the contract with this winery was due to end I started to talk with a winemaker, well favoured by James Halliday and with whom we had become friends, about looking us over with a view to taking the grapes from the Red Kelpie Creek block.

‘What a lovely block,’ he exclaimed after an extensive wander through the vines, ‘wish it was mine. The grapes are excellent.’

He agreed to take all of the grapes from the eight-hectare block.

‘What about a contract then? I queried.

‘Isn’t word of mouth and a handshake good enough?’

I responded with a strong handshake.

This arrangement went on for a couple of years until our other blocks of Shiraz and Cab came out of contract and our winemaker friend agreed to take the lot. The winery he worked for was consolidating its affairs, selling its vineyards in other regions and looking to buy in The Valley. And so it came to pass that Jeni arrived home two days before Christmas and burst out with that amazing statement, and I flipped – at the idea of giving up what we had created, and going against my own thinking about moving whilst we are able to.

Besides, I reasoned with myself, we really were doing OK, even giving the drop in discretionary spending caused by the GFC. Our art sales had dropped but some artists understood the trend and dropped their prices as well as presenting somewhat smaller canvases. The ones who didn’t were emerging amateurs, on the whole, convinced that their works were worthy of every highly priced dollar they were asking, pointing to the costs of materials and framing and the long hours put into their creation. We would advise the artists about market trends and the move towards bold showy pieces, especially brightly coloured abstracts. Those who listened still sold well.

City people were no longer taking short country holidays and income from The Retreat had fallen off, although recently it had very much improved, for some unknown reason. The same with food sales. Nonetheless, the quality of our offerings – wine, food, art, accommodation and bulk wine sales – enabled us to pay down debt, which the bank manager told us was unusual in The Valley at that time. So, should we sell? And why had I flipped when Jeni burst forth with the news?

Certainly we were doing much better than our friends, professionals who had weekend getaways in The Valley, and who had invested in tax-planning schemes offering community title vineyard and winery developments. Yes, they could claim their share of development and management costs against their income but the schemes had never declared a profit payment; they received only invoices to cover their share of the never-reducing costs of running the enterprise.

The wine business scene in Australia toward the end of the first decade of the twenty-first century wasn't all that dissimilar to that of the Keating vine-pull days, with an oversupply of grapes and contracting wine markets. As Commonwealth Treasurer, Keating had financed the scheme to remove a wine surplus by removing vineyards growing inferior fruit – theoretically old vineyards requiring upgrading – but sales included old vines producing some of the best wine. Keating was blamed for this tragedy but really the blame lay just as much with the wine companies who wouldn't buy this fruit.

Booms and busts are a common feature in agricultural pursuits and once again it was the turn of the wine industry to have to nut out how to deal with another serious downturn. So, as Jeni pointed out, we had an unknown future; very true.

Grape-growing and winery organisations began to run workshops and conferences to try to get a grip on how to deal with the crisis. Cold region fruit growers blamed the warm region growers for producing crap fruit (that actually went into the low-priced wines so popular in the UK) while the warm region people blamed the lower level crap fruit coming from the cold regions – and all blamed the tax planning schemes that had contributed to such large and rapid vineyard development.

The industry had concluded that the way to overcome the problem was to remove the bottom twenty per cent of grapes – those that fell consistently into the D category grape classification. And who would admit to growing such inferior grapes? That was left to the wineries buying the fruit. I put a strong argument to Jeni that our fruit didn't fall into this category. But I could admit we weren't getting any younger, and working a 20-hectare vineyard is very hard yakka.

Having sorted a solution to the over-supply problem (vineyard owners would soon sort out if they were viable or not), the industry then started to worry about climate change and the cost of energy. Many issues were being considered, including the use of sheep as organic weed control to save on the costs of chemicals and fuel, would you believe? We too had considered these issues, using minimum water to irrigate, installing a 10Kw solar system on our roof, and using sheep for organic weed control, thus saving on greenhouse emissions resulting from fuel use, along with the cost of tractor use, manpower and chemicals. But who knew how the climate issue would play out, it was just something else for the vineyard owner to worry about. How specifically would the future climate impact on The Hill?

Given all of these considerations it was interesting to observe the dogged nature of vineyard and winery owners, a very large percentage of whom are not making a profit on their endeavours. They face all of these issues, while not making a profit, and climate change is starting to impact negatively on their efforts. Yet still they hang on. What about trading carbon, and what about turning their vineyards into solar farms? But we were making an annual profit. So, stuff 'em!

We had come to understand the dogged determination required to grow a vineyard in stages, in our case to 20 hectares, and the even higher level of chutzpah required to move into developing a cellar-door gallery with our very own wine label – and then accommodation, food, weddings, conferences and private lunches and dinners. Finding qualified staff to help with these events was not easy. But then my son who, with his Roseworthy College agricultural degree had moved to Clare to undertake vineyard work, told us about the Three Fillies with whom he was working, Filipino women well versed in the requirements of working a vineyard and cleaning houses. The Three Fillies, along with many others from their country, had settled in the region and our son had developed an ongoing relationship with one.

Here was doggedness; people who knew how to work and were willing to take on any task including waiting on tables and kitchen work. What a find! We ended introducing some of them to our friends in the trade looking for staff to take on odd jobs at a moment's notice. The fame of these very industrious and dedicated women spread. Their generosity and bonhomie is amazing and their cooking skills second to none.

Weddings especially had represented a great income source, but they meant hard work in the couple of weeks leading up to the event and in the following week with the clean-up required; eventually we let these drop away. Conferences were another great source of activity and Scarlattis with its amazing scenery became a popular venue, until the dreaded GFC started to bite. And so, quietly, over the years we dropped these activities to concentrate on growing grapes along with cellar door and gallery activities.

Estela's crème caramel

Ingredients for 8 servings

20-cm baking dish
20-cm leak-proof cake tin
6 large or 8 small egg yolks
1½ cans evaporated milk
¾ can condensed milk
3 tsp vanilla essence
3 tsp raw or brown sugar
lemon zest

Set the oven at 160°C.
Whisk the eggs for 150 beats(!). Add everything else (except the lemon zest) and combine.
Pour into the baking dish. Place the dish into a bain-marie or over a saucepan with water and steam cook for 30 minutes.
Pour this egg mixture into the cake tin and top with lemon zest.
Place into the oven and bake until the mixture is firm.
Remove the dish from the oven and let it cool.
Place a flat serving plate over the cake tin and turn over so that the crème caramel slips onto the plate.

Wine match: liqueur/late-picked Riesling, Gewürztraminer, Spanish Pedro Ximenez Sherry, Vermentino

~ * ~

Two mornings later, over our mugs of jasmine and lotus tea, I murmured to a bleary Jeni, 'It's not a bad offer really, is it?'

'It's a really good offer and I'm all for taking it,' came a remarkably awake response.

'I guess I overreacted, having the offer dumped in my lap without warning. Right, we'll take it then, but I'll try again for us to keep this year's fruit.'

~ * ~

'No!' Stan was adamant, 'we'll take this year's grapes.'

'Well, Stan, we've got the Pinot Gris contracted to another winery. We'll be in deep shit if we don't honour that.'

'All right, you keep the Pinot Gris, we don't have that in our portfolio. Same with the Viognier.'

'And what about the Nebbiolo? I think I have a buyer for that.'

'Done, let's shake on it.'

'What about settlement in four weeks?'

'OK, we'll try for that but the Christmas holidays might hold things up.'

He was right, settlement occurred on 31 January.

Unfortunately, someone at Stan's end must have been very pleased with the deal and placed an item in the last issue of the local paper before Christmas to advise of the sale of 'Mt Surmon Wines'. This precipitous event caused us much strife. The buyer of the Pinot Gris rang and barked down the line, 'What about my Pinot?' Cap in hand I was able to calm his fears. Graciously, he accepted my apologies conceding that crap does happen. I hastily rang our vineyard contractor to offer an explanation and apologies about the abrupt ending of our arrangements, worth between $80,000 and $100,000 to his company annually. Having such a significant work program suddenly disappear would leave a hole in the company's income.

Just as importantly I rang the buyer to ask for an explanation as to why he hadn't run the press release past us first, told him about the consternation it had caused, and asked him to place a correction in the next edition that Mt Surmon Wines, our registered business name, had not been bought, only a vineyard from Mt Surmon. This sort of flutter can make one look a bloody fool, and it was contrary to our careful management of our business and professional interactions.

Everybody knew of the sale. The mobile rang many times as our vineyard-owning friends offered their congratulations. 'Lucky buggers, wish it was us,' or 'Wish we had the same luck,' they said. Just shows you how much out of touch I was, pining for the loss of what we had created.

It was very pleasing however when we paid off all of our debts and asked the bank to hand back the title to the remaining property. That led to more congratulations being proffered. But of course Murphy is always lurking, is he not?

~ * ~

It was a Friday evening. I had finished hanging the next exhibition, which was to open that Sunday, when the power failed – lights, coolroom and freezer – the lot.

'Must be an outage,' I stated the obvious, 'looks like an early night.'

Next morning, still no power and no mention of it in the news from the battery-operated radio.

'That's odd,' mused Jeni, 'not to mention an outage on the news. Maybe I'd best call ETSA.'

'No,' came the response, 'nothing to report our end. I'll get our bloke to call and have a look.'

Mike, the local electrician, was the bloke who came to have a look, about lunchtime Saturday. 'No, nothing wrong from the incoming side. The problem has to be on your side of the fence.'

He and his offsider started the hunt but it was a couple of hours before they came up with an answer. 'There are white ants in the conduit carrying the cable from where it enters this property and up to this building.'

'Heavens,' said Jeni, 'I better call our pest man, we've had some problems with white ants recently.'

Peter arrived and, with his device, helped to trace the ants' track. The conduit ran underground from a Stobie pole at the edge of our boundary, then a couple of hundred metres underground up the hill to the main building where it ducked under the gallery to emerge at the back of the house. Yes, the cellar-door gallery had been built over the top of the buried cable. The electrician who fitted out the house twenty years earlier had not sealed off the conduit, allowing the ants to enter and over the years to work their way down its entire length. The solution? To dig up the conduit and replace the cable. Simple? First one bobcat arrived to start digging and then another and then a mobile coolroom to take care of the contents of ours.

By now it was after eight o'clock; Mike and his mate, who were rooted, decided to call it a day and promised to be back early next morning, Sunday. At seven we were blasted out of our jasmine and lotus tea reverie by the unmistakable sound of a jackhammer and the bobcats. Then Mike dropped in to say they were unable to dig up more piping because it disappeared under The Trees for Life shrubs and treelings we had had planted around the large car park. Apart from denuding the northern slope of the car park, to remove the vegetation would take far too long. They would need to dig a new trench all the way down to the Stobie. And, yes, he understood about the need to have an electricity supply for the exhibition opening on such a hot day.

The trench was dug, and conduit and new cable inserted (actually, double the cable because Mike considered a single one not to be adequate). The trench was filled in including the section through the steps leading from the terrace to The Retreat, and the new cable joined to that which ran under the gallery. Time to test.

'Good,' said Mike.

'No good at all,' said I. 'Each time the bobcat filling in the trench runs over the cable the phone doesn't work.' (The phone cable being in the same trench.)

'Right, dig it up again,' says Mike. So they did, trying various arrangements to find a solution. Which they did. Fill in the trench again, replace the steps. Test and retest.

'Bloody bewdy,' exclaimed Mike, 'we can all go home for Sunday lunch.' It was one o'clock and we expected the exhibition mob to start arriving at one thirty.

Yes, the exhibition opening was a success and, yes, Dan the landscaper did a wonderful job on the Monday morning making it all look serene again. The two half days of work with all of those blokes and machines and materials cost $10,000. Like I say, Murphy can always be called upon.

~ * ~

At last settlement day arrived, and title and money changed hands. We no longer had to front our beloved vines, no more dead arm to be cut out, no new weeds to bother about.

What should we do? 'Go to Europe for a month,' said the oracle over our jasmine and lotus tea. Which we did. Four weeks in Italy, travelling south from Naples around the ankle boot of southern Italy. Then back to The Hill. Wonderful. But we couldn't keep away from the vineyard, we were out early the next day for a morning walk. The excuse? To see what had happened over the previous months. Little things can sometimes seem so unbelievably important and precious.

A few deer were nibbling along the rows of vines in the northwest corner, a couple of rabbits darted about but our beloved kelpies were not here to give chase. And look, here was a caltrop plant, and there, two paddymelons. How many hours over the years had we spent, on hands and knees, digging up these weeds and small melons to put into bags and then using sponges to mop up the three-cornered jacks from the caltrop. Like the one that had worked its way into Janette's anal scent gland and which the young vet, after a digital examination, had told us was cancer, but subsequently put it into a solution in a small vial for me to keep, which I still have. But these weeds were far removed from where we had previously strived so hard to eliminate them. What were they doing here?

Light bulb! The weed seeds would have been spread by the sheep roving over the vineyard in winter months: our environmentally friendly weed-control system, which the grape-growing authorities were now considering using for the very reasons we had. Should I talk with them about our weed-seed-spreading experience?

'Get over it, Burtie, let yourself go, don't keep looking back. You know from experience that you should never revisit something that you have loved and lost.'

~ * ~

We used the Viognier grapes to make our last batch of wine. It's selling very well and was written up in the December 2014 issue of *Gourmet Traveller Wine*:

> This Viognier manages to achieve ripe flavour at a modest 12.5 per cent alcohol and successfully treads the fine line that makes Viognier so difficult. It has spicy varietal fruit aromas that are clean, fresh and vibrant. Flavours are generous and rich.
>
> * * * * 90 points

Asparagus spears en croute with pickled eggs

Ingredients for 2 people as an entrée

2 thick slices of ciabatta bread
2 pickled eggs
12 asparagus spears
whole egg mayonnaise (recipe below)
extra virgin olive oil
sea salt, black pepper

For pickled eggs you will need free-range eggs and white wine vinegar.
For mayonnaise you will need an egg yolk, extra-virgin olive oil and Dijon mustard.

For pickled eggs:
Cover eggs with cold water and bring to the boil then slowly simmer for 7 minutes. Allow to cool, then peel. Put in a jar and cover with

white wine vinegar. The eggs will be ready to eat within a day or two and will keep for up to 4 weeks.

To make mayonnaise:
Whisk an egg yolk until pale, add olive oil in a very slow drizzle whilst whisking continuously until desired thickness is reached. This could be done in a food processor. Stir in Dijon mustard. This will keep for a week or two.

Break off the hard bottom part of each asparagus spear. Bring a saucepan of salted water to the boil then simmer the asparagus spears for 2 minutes, remove and run under cold water to stop cooking process. Set aside.
Paint each side of the ciabatta bread with olive oil and brown in a chasseur or BBQ plate until golden striped on each side.

To assemble:
Put the eggs through an egg slice.
Spread the ciabatta with a generous amount of mayonnaise. Place the 6 asparagus spears on each slice then place the pickled egg slices across the spears. Top with sea salt and freshly ground black pepper. Drizzle more mayo over the top.

Wine match: Viognier, dry Riesling, Semillon, Chardonnay

Those vines have now been grubbed. Some winemakers say Viognier is difficult to sell because people don't know how to pronounce the name. What about Nebbiolo then? Who knows how to pronounce that? People who are looking for something different, that's who. We continue to sell both of these wines along with our award-winning Shiraz and our platters as we run down our stocks. Then what?

Well, over lunch in Auburn one of the guests came over for a chat about what we might be doing with our cellar-door gallery. She had the interesting idea that eco-camping was becoming all the rage for interesting get-aways. No, don't build log cabins for a rustic touch, use up-market tents supplied with all the necessities to make for up-market short-stay experiences. Nestle them in against the gums on the side of The Hill facing southeast; map out walking trails along the old government road provisions; talk to the bloke next door who runs tourist coaches and scenic flights to prepare exotic cellar door and famous chef food experiences – and who knows what else. Hot air balloon flights, anyone? The sky's the limit you might say.

'I've sold my business and have a lot of money to invest and I'm bored. I really need something to get my teeth into. What do you say?'

~ * ~

We sat by the winter fire with a glass of our Nebbiolo and a platter of pincho, musing over what we had achieved on The Hill, watching the evening mist moving like an opalescent sea in the valley below. The Hill seemingly floating in a sky of fresh, gelid air, utterly still and soundless, with the vast panorama to the north clearly etched above the fog.

'Well,' I murmured, 'at least we're still able to set off each morning for a walk along the back tracks. We may be struggling somewhat with the limits our ageing backs and limbs impose, but at least we know we're alive and still living our dream.'

'Do you think our friend from Auburn was fair dinkum, Burtie? Maybe she was a bit pissed, just being pleasant to see if we're still daring enough to get into something new.'

'Yes, maybe. We'll just have to wait and see. But, I guess

Pincho (Spanish savouries)

Ingredients for 6 servings

18 canned anchovy fillets

2 large soused herring fillets

18 green olives, pitted

5 medium pickled onions cut into quarters

18 smallish sweet and sour gherkins

1 small can of tuna in oil

54 toothpicks

chopped parsley

cheese biscuits

Wrap each anchovy fillet around a green olive and secure with a toothpick.

Slice the herring fillets into 18 long slices and wrap around a ¼ of a pickled onion and secure with a toothpick.

Nearly slice each of the gherkins through lengthwise, place a piece of tuna into the slice and secure with a toothpick.

Arrange the pieces and the biscuits on a serving plate and garnish with the parsley.

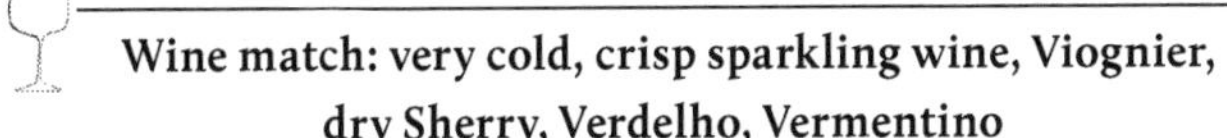

Wine match: very cold, crisp sparkling wine, Viognier, dry Sherry, Verdelho, Vermentino

eventually we'll sell. Someone will come along, appreciate the possibilities of what we have started and take it to the next level. Clare Valley is a well-loved tourist destination for its great wines and food offerings and there are all the other possibilities with art galleries, the Riesling Trail and its beautiful hills and valleys. It's such a romantic setting. What more could you want?'

‘Well,’ said Jeni, ‘I guess we’ll just have to poke along for a bit longer. It will take a couple more years to sell our wine stock and we can still run the art exhibitions.’

‘And for some reason,’ I responded, ‘bookings for The Retreat have really picked up since got back from Europe. We’ll just have to wait and see!’

The world of those dwelling along the bottom of the ridges was obscured by mist, leaving us to ourselves, in a world where time ceased to impinge.

‘You know, Jeni, in this light I can begin to understand what Lloyd Rees meant when he wrote “when a painting gets underway it takes on its own light and it’s got to move the way it wants to move. Nature provides this motivation”.’ I was nicely relaxed by the Nebbiolo.

‘Well, in this light, this clear, fresh air, Burtie, we can see a long, long way.’

‘On a Clare day, my love, we can see forever.’

Acknowledgements

I express my gratitude to Jeni for her suggestion that I write this book, her help with my minimal computer skills, her reading of a great many early drafts, and her fulsome ongoing support; to David Wright for commenting on an early draft; to Clare Valley Winemakers Inc. for allowing inclusion of their cellar door map; and to Brother John May SJ OA for agreeing to launch the book.

And an especially big thank you to Michael Bollen, Julia Beaven and the dedicated band of workers at Wakefield Press.

Recipe Index

Wakefield Press is an independent publishing and distribution company based in Adelaide, South Australia. We love good stories and publish beautiful books. To see our full range of books, please visit our website at www.wakefieldpress.com.au where all titles are available for purchase.

Find us!

Twitter: www.twitter.com/wakefieldpress
Facebook: www.facebook.com/wakefield.press
Instagram: instagram.com/wakefieldpress

Printed in Australia
AUOC01n0730210717
287768AU00001B/1/P

9 781743 054819